Drink Spiking and Prec

Pamela Donovan

Drink Spiking and Predatory Drugging

A Modern History

Pamela Donovan
Pennsylvania, USA

ISBN 978-1-349-93491-1   ISBN 978-1-137-57517-3 (eBook)
DOI 10.1057/978-1-137-57517-3

Library of Congress Control Number: 2016942670

© The Editor(s) (if applicable) and The Author(s) 2016
Softcover reprint of the hardcover 1st edition 2018 978-1-137-57516-6

This work is subject to copyright. All rights are solely and exclusively licensed by the Publisher, whether the whole or part of the material is concerned, specifically the rights of translation, reprinting, reuse of illustrations, recitation, broadcasting, reproduction on microfilms or in any other physical way, and transmission or information storage and retrieval, electronic adaptation, computer software, or by similar or dissimilar methodology now known or hereafter developed.
The use of general descriptive names, registered names, trademarks, service marks, etc. in this publication does not imply, even in the absence of a specific statement, that such names are exempt from the relevant protective laws and regulations and therefore free for general use.
The publisher, the authors and the editors are safe to assume that the advice and information in this book are believed to be true and accurate at the date of publication. Neither the publisher nor the authors or the editors give a warranty, express or implied, with respect to the material contained herein or for any errors or omissions that may have been made.

Cover image: © Doug Steley B / Alamy Stock Photo

Printed on acid-free paper

This Palgrave Macmillan imprint is published by Springer Nature
The registered company is Nature America Inc. New York

Acknowledgments

I would like to thank the many people who encouraged me in this project and who acted as faithful, careful readers of many proposals and chapter drafts, including Pamela Brunskill, Randal Doane, Claire Lawrence, and Janet Rosen. The germination of the project came in conversations, and later fruitful research collaboration, with Adam Burgess and Sarah E.H. Moore, and Véronique Campion-Vincent has been a great partner in dialogue about our overlapping interests. Rifat Anjum Salam gave me a good push in the right direction at the right time. I would also like to thank an anonymous reviewer for Palgrave Macmillan who provided very cogent feedback on the proposal. Thanks also to Gregory Raml at the American Museum of Natural History and Andrea Schwartz, Darla Bressler, and Linda Neyer at the Andruss Library at Bloomsburg University, who helped me obtain some fairly obscure materials.

Contents

1 Introduction ... 1

2 Chloral and Its Sisters: Synthetic Genesis and Parallel Demon ... 15

3 Good Girls, Hyenas, and Cheap Novel Fiends: The Scourge of Chloral at the Turn of the Twentieth Century ... 53

4 Baby, It's Cold War Outside: An Era of Pharma-Ubiquity ... 83

5 A "New" Problem Appears in the 1990s: The Birth of the Contemporary Date Rape Drugs Scare ... 123

6 Who and Where Are the Druggers? ... 173

7 What Do We Know (and Not Know) About Predatory Drugging? ... 215

| 8 | Drugs, Drinking, College, and Warding off Blame | 239 |
| 9 | Conclusion | 267 |

| **Suggested Reading** | 283 |
| **Index** | 285 |

1

Introduction

When I began this project I actually knew very little about the topic of drink spiking aside from stories I had heard along the way growing up. As a teenager I had heard rumors of malicious drink spiking, where the object was to give a peer mind-altering drugs they would never take themselves, or to wreak vengeance on someone by putting laxative chocolate in their drink. Older kids talked about spiking nonalcoholic punch with grain alcohol at parties, but these plans (often just wishful thinking) were thoroughly for their own consumption and enjoyment, and the joke was only on the adults. Unsuspecting ingesters were not intentional victims; they simply did not know, and did not think to ask.

Whether mild tampering or more dangerous drugs spiking is involved, law enforcement has tended to label such acts "malicious" when they are an end in themselves. It was only when I began to investigate the modern concern with so-called date rape drugs that I began to think of drink spiking as a criminally instrumental, rather than merely expressive, act. A large part of the time, drink spiking is actually an end in itself.

Not all surreptitious drugging—or fears and suspicion of such—involves drink spiking. Undesired drugs can come in food, can be inhaled, and can be substituted for other (desired) drugs. Our contemporary familiarity with the topic—from the current scare about so-called date rape drugs—tends to lead us to assume that only drugs that knock people out—central nervous system (CNS) depressants or CNS drugs—are used this way. In fact, there is a long history of stimulants working their way into the surreptitious drugging scenario. Aphrodisiacs, of course, can also be slipped to someone. In all cases, druggers may misunderstand the effects of a drug as much as those of us who simply read about it in the papers. Our misunderstandings are great in number: what druggers intend, how common surreptitious drugging is, how drugged people react, and whether advice about the problem is really useful?

My aim in this book is to look at the modern history of drugging, particularly drink spiking, starting with the dawn of the industrial era, at least in the USA, in the early to mid-1800s. At this time, cities grew large with new immigrants and in-migrants from rural areas for the promise of urban life and economic advancement. Both new social relationships and feelings of anonymity ensued, and the pace of life intensified. The time clock's reign and the speed of movement increased. At the same time, modern pharmaceuticals were born, and some were quickly pressed into service to quell the agitation that came from a world spinning faster. Medicine both promoted and resisted psychoactive answers to this problem, and often times, ordinary people figured out how to use substances old and new to self-medicate.

While certainly one can find occasional references to drink tampering and drugging in literature and history from earlier times, spiking and involuntary drugging did not become a consolidated concern until such time as there was a mass audience for newspapers to warn people of the threat posed by the new synthetic pharmaceuticals. It was also then that the view began to hold that spiking was nearly always a means to an end—robbery, involuntary conscription, mass manipulation, initiation into drug or alcohol dependency, and later, sexual assault.

Yet my early experience of the idea—which seems fairly common—also sensitized me to the need to understand such behavior as more than instrumental; broader than just criminal incapacitation. Much like the history of poisoning, spiking has a variety of motivations. Pranks and humiliations, involuntary magic dust ingestion that the purveyor thinks is benevolent, mixed and hesitant motivations for drugging—these are all found throughout the history of the problem. It may be inherently manipulative and dangerous to give someone something they did not ask for; however, there turn out to be a wide variety of reasons for it.

Much as malicious spiking is a kind of folk practice—whether merely mischievous or downright deadly—fear of it is also. Alongside the volume of cases found in each era is also a rich folklore that develops around the threat of drink spiking, and worries about the problem develop and innovate with much of the same dynamism with which new drugs arise, are prescribed, and come to be used recreationally or as drugs of addiction. Almost without exception, scares about drugging are preceded by an era of boundless and myopic optimism about new psychoactive drugs.

Fear of drugging is not constant—there are distinct times in the modern era where the fear "flares up"—often apropos of not very much, concretely speaking. Instead of genuinely increased incidences and risk, we often find at those times a host of existing cultural tensions that excess focus on drugging attempts to solve. The incidence of the problem is miniscule in relationship to the problems wrought by willing self-ingestion, but whatever small number of cases emerge during a particular scare provide a reservoir of meaning. Hearing from the authorities—in medicine or law enforcement—time after time that the fear of the problem is much greater than warranted appears to not be much of a damper. Fears are also sometimes enthusiasms, and drink spiking appears to have this quality.

It is easy to see how our magical views of medicine transferred over to our reaction to news that drugs could be used upon us without our knowledge. The first surge in drugging emerged with the rise of synthetic drugs in the mid-1800s, and probably the most widely procured—and feared—was chloral hydrate. Known as "knockout drops," mostly for self-administration for mood alterers and insomniacs alike, chloral, as it was commonly known, was a widely used synthetic opiate. Chloral hydrate (trichloroacetaldehyde monohydrate) was synthesized in 1832, but first used therapeutically in 1869. Its potential uses were thought to be broad, for a variety of nervous disorders, including alcohol withdrawal, manias, and insomnia. Enthusiasm for its use was vivid, because it was more stable and predictable than natural opiates, which were already widely accessible. Yet chloral hydrate was not without negative effects, which included all of the potential drawbacks of opiates—such as the risk of addiction or overdose—and then some new ones as well.

Like other CNS depressants, chloral and its inhaled cousin, chloroform, often produce a stage of excitability and disinhibition before they reduce consciousness. Chloral was in some sense a novel threat—a narcotic-like substance that dissolved effortlessly in alcohol and could easily sneak by the senses to depress the CNS—quickly, as it was meant to in anesthesia, and with no time in which a victim might sense that something had gone wrong with their drink. From early reports of drugging, we also learn about the social and psychological agonies of one of its key hallmarks—*anterograde amnesia*, or the complete inability to account for a period of time. Specifically, the brain's ability to form and store memories is impaired temporarily, which means that the subjective experience of the time in question is lost permanently. Thus, as with rapid and heavy alcohol consumption, one can experience a "blackout." This state of affairs is, of course, a real benefit in the legitimate medical use of these drugs. What patient would enjoy remembering a surgery? But in the context of unintentional use, the missing puzzle piece can be experienced as a double violation.

By the turn of the twentieth century, chloral hydrate had been implicated in robbery, burglary, rape, and involuntary conscription into the military or merchant marines. Then, as now, the problem of drink spiking had been interwoven with other broad social concerns. In the USA, in particular, the politics of Temperance and the saloon have played a central role. Here and in Britain, drink spiking has also been tied with cycles of hope and fear regarding technology—and pharmaceutical innovation—over the last two centuries. The rise of chloral hydrate also coincides with the rise of forensic science (then called "medical jurisprudence") and toxicology. Police departments and courts desired a new and scientific approach to evidence, but what could be known by carefully gathering evidence and what could be inferred from the emerging rudimentary techniques was limited. That did not stop anyone from declaring any certainties, however. Forensic science had made such a dramatic leap that it was tempting to rely upon new scientific techniques instead of circumstances and situations, unearthed by traditional investigation, which might have better explained the plight of victims.

The plain fact is that even setting aside the incapacitating qualities of alcohol—often cited in the current caution, "alcohol is the number one date rape drug"—the means, motive, and opportunity for drug-facilitated crime and just plain tampering has always been present. Contrary to current claims that there are distinct and new substances for nefarious purposes, drugging has always been a possibility, particularly since the rise of synthetic anesthetics in the mid-1800s. To simply dropping a powder or a pill in a drink, there have never been formidable barriers.

Nonetheless, there are certain consistencies in the drugging *fear* over time, too. Fear of drink spiking and drugging tends to attach to public places like saloons, bars, nightclubs, theaters, cafes, and parties rather than private settings. Documented cases, for reasons of physical and social logistics, are just as likely, if not more likely, to take case in private settings. Drugging is often thought of as purely a means to an end, rather than an end in itself, and this can often lead investigators and news reporters alike astray. Some spiking—like other forms of tampering and poisoning—is often an end in itself.

If we look at reactions to a relatively rare threat such as drink spiking—and a smaller subset of incidents—drink spiking to facilitate another crime, we find a whole other set of social, political, cultural, and psychological concerns. Among these are what psychologists call the inner versus outer locus of control, the distribution of responsibility among victim and predator, the nature of the will and its loss more generally when we consider intoxication, and our complex responses to antialcohol and antidrug crusades. These themes are as vivid when the victim is a male and the object robbery as it is when the topic is women and the object sexual assault.

In the contemporary age of what can be called "pharma-ubiquity," CNS depressants are readily available and plentiful. Communities struggle with misuse and addiction, and legitimate prescriptions still often leave us wondering whether we are taking the right path to manage pain, both physical and psychic. Drugs are everywhere, and not hard to come by.

With drink spiking, it is important to keep at least three different kinds of motivation in mind. The first is malicious or capricious, where altering someone else's consciousness is more or less both means and an end. Some of the evidence I look at in this book suggests that this motivation is far more common than we think. To cause a person to become intoxicated by drugs fulfills a desire of the perpetrator or perpetrators to watch what happens next to the victim. The goal, if it can be separated from the act, is perhaps to experience the thrill of chemical mastery over another, or to hope that drugs will cause them to embarrass themselves, or simply for revenge, or just to wreak havoc and produce collective fear.

The second, somewhat less well-defined motivation is what I would call coercive. Here, there is some long-range object in mind, such as fostering an addiction to the substance, or forcing a set of psychoactive consequences on the victim. In the latter case, the perpetrator might even tend to think of the end result as positive for the target rather than negative. This is the reason that I distinguish it from the former "malicious" category. Although the outcomes can be equally negative, the motivation is not quite the same, exploitative and dangerous though the act may be. Drugs (or extra alcohol) might loosen up a nervous friend, or introduce them to hallucinogenic insights, or help them cope with acute emotional distress. The former case—fostering addiction—is often associated in the public mind with drug dealers and a profit motive. The perpetrator now has a new customer who becomes hooked, but coercive drugging can also be relational in nature. By relational, I mean that the drugs are surreptitiously given to another to keep them close—as friends, as lovers, or as emotional dependents in some fashion. Serving up a double or triple shot to a friend who asked for "just a little" is hardly an innovation.

Fear of coercion into drugs in this way waxes and wanes at different times historically. For instance, as the Temperance movement gained strength in the USA approaching the twentieth century, coercive themes gained ground dramatically, and blame for alcoholism or drug dependence increasingly was directed at purveyors rather than consumers. At the turn of the century, when any number of strange and troubling incidents were linked in the media to knockout drops in people's drinks, the same papers were reporting on the exploits of the anti-saloon movement. The politics of alcohol itself and drink spiking have always been deeply intertwined. Then, as Prohibition lifted, the spiking fear seemed to drift away.

The third and final category is the predatory, where drink spiking or drugging is a means or method to another criminal end. Essentially, drugs substitute for physical force for a number of tactical reasons. Drugs may have the desired effect of neutralizing resistance to rape, robbery, or abduction; it may foster amnesia and therefore uncertainty on the part of the victim; or, particularly in some cases of rape, satisfy a paraphiliac's desire for an unresponsive sexual "partner" (sometimes referred to as *somnophilia*) or satisfy a predator's particular modus operandi needs—acting upon another person without them acting back—that would make them recoil from other forms of force.

In real cases, where predation is the motivation, because drugs are a substitute for physical force, people who have been so victimized often assume, probably erroneously, that had drugs not incapacitated them, they would have been able to fend off the subsequent crime. Particularly in the case of rape, we know that no special vulnerability is needed on the part of the victim. Social trust—not always deep trust, but merely the level of routine mutual assurance that allows any society to function—is essentially the primary vulnerability, though enhanced opportunity certainly can aid a perpetrator of any crime. In fact, most reported cases of modern spiking have this kind of context—the victim is already trusting of the predator, and is often already in a private location.

The modern date rape drugs scare was originally tied to the revival of what sociologists Karen Weiss and Corey Colyer call "the protected narrative" of drink spiking.[1] In other words, rather than being a full-range drug scourge episode, it is very particular in its logistics. The drugs that animated the onset of the current scare—what I like to call the Big Three—flunitrazepam ("roofies"), gamma hydroxybutyric acid (GHB), and ketamine—were, in the early 1990s, covered by the press in what had become a conventional manner: hey, there are some new drugs out there, people are using them to get high, here are some of their attractions, here are a bunch of negative outcomes—there may be an ominous threat to our youth on the horizon.

But then in 1996, a media niche emerged that emphasized a particular sequence of events: a woman goes to a bar, party, or nightclub, her drink is spiked, she leaves with or is cornered by her assailant, and sexually

---

[1] Karen G. Weiss and Corey J. Colyer, "Roofies, Mickies and Cautionary Tales: Examining the Persistence of the 'date-rape drug' Crime Narrative," *Deviant Behavior*, 31, 2010, 348–379.

assaulted. In fact, Florida prosecutors in the Mark Perez case were widely quoted nationwide as explicitly saying that this setup (which did characterize the Perez case) was typical.[2] But in the ensuing years even other notorious serial rape cases involving drugging (which, instead, typically took place in the assailant's home) did not break up this focus on public venue drink spiking. Despite how sensational elements of those cases were, the press by and large preferred *the protected narrative*. In many ways it is a revival of an earlier protected narrative—chloral hydrate spiking followed by abduction followed by forced prostitution: essentially what is known to historian as "white slavery" legends. This narrative emerged in the mid-1800s in Britain and in the late 1800s in the USA, and rapidly gained steam in both places with the rise of antiprostitution and other social purity movements. It died down by the 1920s and was revived briefly in the 1970s as "The Attempted Abduction"—a scenario implicating malls and fashion boutiques and injected drugs for the purpose of kidnapping young women and children into sex slavery.[3]

Can we really know the true balance of motivations for drink spiking behavior historically? Probably not. Record keeping on this matter is fraught with problems. The first problem concerns official investigation and confirmation. In the past, we know that police reports only sporadically reported the suspected presence of drugs associated with a crime, and for sexual assault in particular, reporting rates have been very low regardless of the circumstances. Forensic analysis and toxicology have been able to address suspicions of drugging only recently.[4] And in those few confirmed cases, we do not always know the motivation. In particular, we tend to ignore the possibility of simple malicious motivation, even though the evidence suggests otherwise. This is not very satisfying as an answer: we want to know why.

---

[2] Nichols quoted in: Jackie Hallifax, "Illegal Sedative Used on Rape Victims," *Los Angeles Times*, June 9, 1996. Accessed January 11, 2016. http://articles.latimes.com/1996-06-09/news/mn-13222_1_roofie.

[3] Edgar Morin, *Rumour in Orléans*, (New York: Pantheon), 1971; Jan Harold Brunvand, *The Mexican Pet: More "New" Urban Legends and Some Old Favorites*, (New York: Norton, 1986), 148–156, regarding the newer version involving minors.

[4] As improved as such sciences are, any extrapolation from them depends on our inferences about the representativeness of their samples. People who report suspicion that they were drugged are a subsample of something—but we are just not sure what.

The second problem concerns media coverage of drugging incidents. The fact that news outlets find drugging novel enough to report on individual cases still does not tell us much about the underlying unreported cases. They may be reported because they are interesting or because they are frightening. Suspected drugging is also not the same as confirmed drugging, and follow-up reports are rare.

Since drink spiking is both an actual practice and a socially shared fear, its presence may be suspected in cases where similar symptoms appear, or at times when victims of violence or exploitation—unfairly, in my view— feel the need to explain their vulnerability. Any number of substances— especially combined with physical states such as sleep deprivation, low blood sugar, or dehydration—can produce similar symptoms. These substances include: alcohol itself, either in high quantities or high proof; opiates and widely prescribed benzodiazepines that are self-ingested; and over-the-counter drugs like diphenhydramine. Alcohol mixed with these substances can produce a synergistic effect in some cases. In many toxicology studies, unreported illicit substances are found, including marijuana, cocaine, and methamphetamine. One of the things rarely found in toxicology tests: those drugs like Rohypnol labeled "date rape drugs."

The current preoccupation with so-called date rape drugs often mistakes the problem for something new. But since the dawn of modern anesthetics, this potential problem was known, and a number of show trials dramatized these sorts of criminal allegations as early as the 1860s. Criminal law has also recognized that drugs can be used to aid crime, whether the fraudulent conscription of merchant seamen on the bustling wharves of the industrializing coasts, for robbery or sexual assault, or to neutralize a troublesome drunk in a bar. State laws vary, but most have had criminal code violations for using "any stupefying substance" to commit a crime against someone for over 100 years. Poisoning laws can also be used. Furthermore, the early twentieth century is replete with a number of high-profile drugging rape cases that made national and sometimes international news. So not only did the law specify this sort of predation as criminal, but under the right circumstances (with all of the usual caveats), prosecutors were willing to take assailants on.

It is a bit strange, then, not only that many opinion leaders regard the problem as new, but also as one that the law has not recognized. That is not at all the problem—there are poisoning laws, tampering laws, special penalties for felonies upon the incapacitated. Criminal codes typically define force as including, not excluding, the induced incapacitation of victims.

If we think we are right-sizing or refocusing concern just by acknowledging that "alcohol is the number one date rape drug" we are bound to be disappointed. The problem now in seeking justice for sexual assault victims is both ideological and practical, not legal. Ideological, because victims often blame themselves, and because some criminal justice agencies are discouraging to victims. Practical, because much like the more ordinary circumstances of interpersonal violence, proof is difficult. In regards to acquaintance rape, assailants can always say the sex was consensual, and who is to know for sure otherwise? A prosecutor has to overcome this defense, and it often involves a level of courtroom heroics that may expose the victim to even more blame and scrutiny. In the 1970s and 1980s states began to drop their requirements that corroboration was required for rape charges, and while this removed a barrier to prosecution, conviction rates have increased very little. Victims also have to cope with unpredictable or even hostile responses from friends and family.

Synthetic drugs—which have been on the scene since the mid-1800s—may have made it easier to drug someone, but by no means have the physical and social obstacles to what people often think of as "the perfect crime" disappeared. The contemporary date rape drugs preoccupation also has given a set of drugs typically used illicitly but voluntarily a kind of erroneous master identity as "date rape drugs." This label is so pervasive that trafficking and mass seizures of these diverted substances is often misinterpreted by the press, and even some governing agencies, as being somehow informative about the incipient threat of sexual violence. Similarly, the mere presence of such substances often seems to imply predation. One reviewer of his autobiography was perplexed to learn that musician Ozzy Osbourne had "done just about every drug under the sun—including when he drugged himself with Rohypnol, the date-rape drug."[5] One can assume that Osbourne had no intention of raping himself

---

[5] Nikki Mascali, "Novel Approach: The Madman Writes," *The Weekender* (Wilkes-Barre, Pennsylvania), March 26, 2010; Ozzy Osbourne, *I am Ozzy*, (New York: Grand Central Publishing), 2009.

with the drug—though he did know about its predatory reputation in the press—which is in fact a sleep disorder drug that has an illicit, recreational audience. The date rape drugging concept, meanwhile, has become so compelling to modern scaremongering constituencies that they attempt to apply it to other substances as well.

Neither drugging victims nor sexual assault victims, I will argue, are particularly well-aided by exaggerations of the prevalence of the problem, or by outsized fears of spiked drinks. While a suspected spiked drink might be a preferred explanation for negative events, including violence, better explained by high blood alcohol levels, misdirection about the nature of this threat impedes our understanding of real cases as well as diverts attention, once again, from the opportunism exercised by violent actors such as rapists.

We do actually know something about the psychology of the type of offenders we are interested in here. Though they represent only the subset of offenders who have been caught, they remind us that no particular foolhardiness on the part of victims is needed to produce an incident of victimization. No matter what *we* do, they have *their* reasons—and their means. Repeat offending also offers a criminal skill boost, and contrary to the popular image of widespread predatory drugging, this sort of predation actually does require some criminal sophistication.

It is clear that drugging scares also track with cultural and social anxieties, particularly regarding change and the new worlds that each young generation confronts. Some of the most interesting aspects of drugging scares, particularly modern ones, are their peer-advice character. The strongest concerns come not from the abstemious, but the otherwise enthusiastic partakers of nightlife, drugs, and alcohol. This may stem from subcultural boundary policing, a fairly common feature of youth subcultures—about which more will be said in the book. Who is a good and smart consumer of mind-altering substances? Who does the nightclub "correctly?" Who doesn't? This pro-partier current cultural context makes it somewhat different from drugging scares of the past, though with less contrast than I might have guessed: the *smart* girl has replaced the *proper* girl.

Fears of drugging and drink spiking also have contributed to the clamor for, and success of, drug prohibitions over the decades. Drugging and drink spiking incidents are often used to enhance claims about the dangerousness of certain drugs; it is often the case that reformers feel they cannot make a strong enough case with just voluntary misuse—they need something more coercive, more furtive, and more ominous than just another "drug that can be abused."

Finally, drugging and the fear of it are linked to the increasing freedom of women in modern societies. Even the earliest newspaper accounts of drug rape cases often demonstrated broad sympathy for victims and nothing but contempt for the defendants, yet they also indicted the loss of protection that they believed traditional propriety—lacking, they thought, in many a "modern girl's" lifestyle—had afforded young women.

Somewhat obscured in the history of drink spiking is the prevalence of male victims, who were (and are, in many places in the world) the predominant target of drug-deploying robbers. The familiar term "shanghaied" refers to the practice of drugging young men in taverns and recruiting them to national or private naval forces. The problem was a high-profile one in the late 1800s—enough so that specific legislation was passed to outline bigger penalties for recruiters who resorted to these means.

One reasonable inference from this history is that, with a short lag time, drugging scares track the rise of "new" drugs. There is a fairly predictable trajectory from techno-utopianism to techno-horror, with both poles making generally unsustainable claims and hanging assessments on juicy anecdotes. There are some interesting exceptions—such as the rise of chloroform—that defy this pattern, and in looking at why it was such an exception, we can unearth a whole set of concerns about psychoactive drugs, even when prescribed medically. What is a drug's social identity? Who takes and favors it? Who denounces it? What kind of legitimate problem can a drug solve? Is it legitimate enough to accept its accompanying dangers?

I also believe a degree of uncomfortable subjectivity and judgment always remains unresolvable when social scientists say that worry about a particular threat is outsized compared to its actual likelihood, seriousness, or prevalence. After all, how much of a certain kind of danger need be present to justify vigilance against it, collective action against it, some level of specific precaution, or even just a fear of that thing which goes bump in the night? I do believe that there are ways of making oneself more precise about this matter—by engaging in useful comparisons, for instance, or by carefully looking at different types of data and identifying common findings. However, some judgment here is unavoidable. It might be quite rare, in fact, to succumb to a bolt of lightning; nonetheless, we observe all of those rules about avoiding bodies of water and trees during an electrical storm. We are not strict risk calculators. Danger weaves itself into both individual and social psyches in a variety of ways. Ultimately, it is as important to understand those weavings as it is to guard against all of the negative by-products of exaggerated threats, either for the individual or for societies. This is particularly true in an age when facts and dangers can be conjured up at whim, based on nothing at all, and gathering dangers can be willfully defined away altogether.

In the pages ahead, I have endeavored to look at real instances of modern drugging and drink spiking, alongside all of the mythologies, panics, and urban legends about such threats, which have always been legion, but have not always been the same. I will consider the ways in which certain dominant images of a drug at a given time—even what appear to be contrasting ones—can contribute to distortions in a drug's "master identity." In the process, we can learn a bit about the nature of some of our deepest fears regarding the power others might design to have over us through chemical mastery.

2

Chloral and Its Sisters: Synthetic Genesis and Parallel Demon

Before there was the roofie, before there was the Mickey, or the knockout drop, there was the poppy plant and its storied charms. Opium was identified as highly effective medicine—and yet a poison—well before it was thought of in a separate category of not-quite-fatal subduer. In Homer's *Odyssey*, it was likely opium or a similar narcotic plant that Helen used to drug Telemachus and all of the guests at a wedding party, in a desire to uplift them from their sorrows and futile journeys: "an herb that banishes all care, sorrow, and ill humour."[1] Telemachus and his men were grateful to Helen for this gifted deception. Opiates were widely available in both close to natural and pharmaceutical forms (such as laudanum, developed by Paracelsus in the 1500s by dissolving opium in wine) by the nineteenth century, dropping in price and generally regarded as legitimate. It was not until the last part of the century that scientific authorities were willing to reckon with its own addictive dangers in compounded pharmaceuticals. Since it had many legitimate uses in medicine, regret was slow, even with the warnings that came from women and men of letters in Britain, including Thomas De Quincey, and the families of Charlotte

---

[1] Samuel Butler, 1898 Translation of Homer's *Odyssey*. Gutenberg.org.

© The Editor(s) (if applicable) and The Author(s) 2016
P. Donovan, *Drink Spiking and Predatory Drugging*,
DOI 10.1057/978-1-137-57517-3_2

Bronte and Alfred Lord Tennyson, and even when coroners took note of the common role of opiate elixirs in infant death. [2]

But sensitivity to the problem of predatory drugging predates widespread recognition of the problem of addiction considerably. Consider the pivotal moment in Samuel Richardson's *Clarissa* (1748). In this eighteenth-century epistolary novel, the rake Lovelace steals the heroine's virtue by arranging her isolation and drugging her wine. Ultimately, the act destroys them both, and Richardson's depiction of the tragedy affords a glimpse into the most basic elements of the outrage of drugging and rape, both separately and together as forms of violation of the human will. Lovelace justifies his use of drugs to overcome Clarissa's resistance as a "generous design" which spares her the shame of relinquishing her virginity voluntarily. What he is not prepared for is her defiance; once "ruined" she decides to stay so rather than legitimating his "little innocent trick." Clarissa's self-punishment may be somewhat time-bound, but in a basic way, the reader can give at least grudging respect in refusing Lovelace's script for her present and future. Lovelace's pathologies also parallel what we know from modern studies of rapists' psychological mindsets; the victim's will is beside the point, and must be neutralized.

In London in the 1830s, laudanum was pressed into service to drug the drinks of fatal "burking" victims—who were targeted as potentially valuable corpses, to be sold to medical colleges. Scientific advancement coat-tailed along with it increasing criminal sophistication in alternative uses for drugs. Discussions of the potential weaponry of poisons in general trace back to the origin of the written word, but with the exception of a few metaphorical uses of the idea of induced stupor, drugging can be thought of, then, as a thoroughly modern, or only recently democratized, fear. Each time the idea of coerced intoxication develops a new permutation, the problem is understood as stemming from the ominous capacities of a new world. Morality is thought to have declined to a new low, in many accounts, to permit the desire to drug others. Society now

---

[2] T.E. Jordan, "The Keys of Paradise: Godfrey's cordial and children in Victorian Britain," *Journal of the Royal Society of Health*. vol. 107, no. 1, 1987, 19–22.

2 Chloral and Its Sisters: Synthetic Genesis and Parallel Demon   17

too anonymous, women or children too newly unsupervised, so as to permit it to occur.

From the beginning, dissatisfaction with the social costs of rapidly intensified commerce, and industrial capitalism's consolidation, manifested itself through a series of substance abuse scares. It would be an exaggeration to say that these served as a kind of diversion from the basic questions of power and powerlessness, because the social disorganization that accompanied rapid industrialization was real. Nonetheless, drug scares have a peculiar ability to draw energy from other kinds of social and political campaigns for change.

Opium, no newcomer to the demi-monde scene, nonetheless animated one of the first overt drugging scares in the USA in the 1870s: "In the 1870s a movement that raised the specter of Chinese men drugging white women into sexual slavery prompted California to pass the first law against opium smoking. The law was part of a campaign to enhance police and employer control over immigrant Chinese workers." [3] This scare eventually morphed into a general "white slavery" scare whereby prostitution of white girls and women itself was linked to a physical abduction, drugging, and turning out. The term also implied sex between white women and nonwhite, usually immigrant men, blamed for trafficking in girls and women. Certainly, prostitution as an underground industry developed a level of sophistication and organization as it matured, but as the idea of "white slave traffic" gained ground, it represented all prostitution as a coercive conspiracy. There was an underlying disbelief that prostitution—or drugs, for that matter, might hold their own allure. One had to be forced, or tricked—by shadowy others. This is necessary, in some sense, to falsely randomize the problem and thus implicate middle-class readers in the threat to their daughters.

Though the medical men who would develop synthetic opiates rarely had any comment on opium's social or illicit use, focused as they were on the practical problems of developing better (mainly more predictable) analgesics and anesthetics, an initial halo emerged around the new drugs. Not associated with the demi-monde and the medical protocols of the

---

[3] Harry Levine and Craig Reinarman, "What's Behind 'Jar Wars'?" *The Nation*, March 28, 1987. Retrieved January 16, 2016. http://www.thenation.com/article/whats-behind-jar-wars/.

classical ages, synthetics offered a promise of a new and orderly world. The techno-utopianism around new classes of drugs that appeared in the twentieth century really had its start with chloroform, ether, and chloral hydrate.

Approaching the mid-nineteenth century, scientific developments marked not only the rise of the pharmaceutical industry, but the ceding of expertise on sedation and mind alteration from folk practices to the new class of doctors—the research men. Shall we trust them and the innovations that they offer? In this chapter, I focus attention on the rise of chloral hydrate (later known as the "knockout drop") in its social context. By context, I mean two things. First, that the specific history of chloral hydrate is a concentrated version of the often-seen path from techno-utopianism to techno-terror that accompanies adjustment to new drugs—synthetic ones in particular—from chloral hydrate through lysergic acid diethylamide (LSD), through benzodiazepines, and on through synthetics of the 1990s like Ecstasy and GHB. Tales and frameworks of coercion—drugging, drink spiking, and forced intoxication—seem to accompany the point in the path where techno-wonder is supplanted by fear of misuse. Not surprisingly, this inflection point is often located with the spread of a drug's use, either via prescription or via underground markets. Second, in some cases, the larger set of social attitudes toward intoxication, excess, and addiction underscore the sense that malevolent forces primarily condition the attraction to drugs and drink. The Temperance movement, particularly the "late" American version of the late nineteenth and early twentieth century, heightened coercive themes about alcohol, which then reverberated with predatory drugging fears—although initially it competed with them.

Below I discuss the history of chloral hydrate. In its well-known role as knockout drops and later the "Mickey Finn," it has a contribution of its own to the contentiousness surrounding saloons and alcohol consumption at the time, a kind of multivalent, mischievous legacy of Temperance campaigns specifically and social purity campaigns more generally. But chloral, and the related anesthetic, chloroform, also brought along a "drugging fear" separate from that of the drugged drink per se.

The Evolution of Temperance as a Context for Drugging

Though there were stirrings of antialcohol advocacy in the USA as early as the 1770s, the first organized mass movement for Temperance (on both sides of the Atlantic) began in the early 1800s. Individual religious and civic organizations forbade alcohol use among their members before that, but prohibition with the aim of general social as well as physical salvation coincided with the Second Great Awakening religious revival. As a part of rapid conversion to evangelical and fundamentalist Protestant groups led by passionate, often itinerant preachers, the newly religious swore off alcohol as a general means of battling against the temptations of sin. That said, early Temperance had a greater focus on self-help and self-improvement.

The growth of support for alcohol abstinence was the growing involvement of physicians, such as Benjamin Rush, who in 1805 self-published an essay, "The Effects of Ardent Spirits Upon Man." Though partially devoted to his ideas about the deleterious effects of alcohol upon physical health, quite a bit of the essay addresses the psychosocial harms of drink. Owing to his general interest in social reform, he approached the problem of alcohol addiction as a medical problem more than a moral failing.[4] He even suggested that alcoholics be brought clean humanely with a mixture of opium and wine, especially to help them avoid *delirium tremens*.[5] Yet since alcohol had scant reputation in healing aside from what was then considered by professionalizing doctors as mere folk medicine or last-resort surgical pain reducer, Temperance as a health-and-wellness regime held more of an appeal.

The appearance of scientific backing for the Temperance cause allowed the movement to gain strength outside the confines of religious concerns, and among the more moneyed classes. Early Temperance advocates like Rush also differentiated between spirits and fermented drinks like beer

---

[4] Rush, already known and widely respected as a Philadelphia doctor, developed more than a few controversial views about bloodletting (he was an enthusiast), calomel mercury treatments, and why "negros" were darker in skin color than whites, attributing "negroidism" to a disease process. Nonetheless, he held a keen interest in humanitarian issues and was an early abolitionist.

[5] E. Behr, *Prohibition: Thirteen Years that Changed America*. (New York: Arcade Publishing, 1996).

and wine, finding the latter less objectionable and in moderation even healthful. When physicians wrote about drink and its bad effects, they typically did so without direct reference to Biblical injunctions or sin in the narrow sense. Instead, they referred to the readily observed effects of excessive alcohol consumption for the individual and society—amassing these concerns to underscore the need to abstain from and prohibit *any* alcohol consumption. As Temperance gained ground, full abstention views triumphed, tied to a general paternalistic view that the availability of spirits would hold back social development.

Was Temperance a "symbolic crusade" as Joseph Gusfield suggests, aimed at preserving bourgeois native Protestant values against the rise of new immigrant waves?[6] Certainly, in part. Other histories suggest that this view may be overstated. Perhaps it should be balanced with a recognition of the real growth in popular access to rum, gin, whisky, and other forms of what we now call hard alcohol.[7] In other words, Temperance movements, which changed dramatically between their inception and 1920s Volstead Act in the USA, were doing more than responding to anxieties about loss of social privilege and developing innovative forms of control over labor. They were also responding to real increases in social disorganization, rapid population growth, and urban poverty which were synergistic to excess alcohol consumption, in a parallel to drug epidemics of the twentieth century. This partly explains why the late Temperance movement in particular appealed to women, and to abolitionists and activists like Frederick Douglass, but also to evangelized white working-class men like John Gough, probably the best known and most widely lampooned of "Temperance rant" men.[8]

Though it does not seem reasonable to dismiss the notion that Temperance was aimed at increasing the means of social control by elites, it was by no means exclusively this alone. Nor it is enough to see popular interest in antialcohol movements, particularly in the USA, as a kind of

---

[6] Joseph Gusfield, *Symbolic Crusade: Status Politics and the American Temperance Movement*, (Urbana: University of Illinois Press), 1986.

[7] Ruth Bordin, *Woman and Temperance: the Quest for Power and Liberty*, 1873–1900. (Philadelphia: Temple University Press), 1981. Jordin, 1987.

[8] Anonymous, *Goffiana: A Review of the Life and Writings of John B. Gough*, (Boston: Ruggles and Company), 1845.

duping by strategic elites. Prohibition movements can also be peer-oriented, populist, and even responsive to real problems—and still ultimately be wrong-headed and corrosive.

Temperance in its various forms was fairly adept at responding sternly to pleas for moderation or half-measures. Early Temperance activists were willing to forgo condemning wine and beer and focus on abstaining from spirits. But going soft on fermented drinks by no means addressed the problem of excess and the reaction that such excess caused, and thus the underlying concerns were not addressed, in part because access to spirits went more or less unabated, and also in part because beer and wine were quite plainly capable of enabling misuse as well. But because drink was still widely embraced and the demands of Temperance activists resented, policy and legislative success in the nineteenth century was halting, sporadic (such as the dry town or county), and limited.

Adulteration of Alcohol

Yet the difference between fermented and distilled drinks was not the only counterargument made by advocates of the light or social drink to the Temperance movement's increasing stringency. In the 1800s, the scientific Temperance movement found itself fending off the idea that drugs or adulterants could be as present a danger to human health as alcohol. These physicians were skeptical of the popular claim that adulterants to alcohol explained some of the negative effects.[9] This stance resulted from a popular counterclaim that impurities and adulterations of alcohol were really to blame for the identified ills. "Adulteration, no doubt, is very extensively practiced;" noted Dr. F.S. Lees, in *Textbook of Temperance,* "but so far as Temperance is concerned, it may be stated as a rule that no other drug is worse than alcohol."[10]

This was a relatively new and bold assertion; for centuries, the beer-drinking countries of Europe had designated officers to inspect brews and brewers for impurities and adulterants, reflective of a culture that

---

[9] W.W. Spooner, *Cyclopaedia of Temperance and Prohibition,* (New York: Funk and Wagnalls), 1891.
[10] Dr. F.R. Lees, *Textbook of Temperance,* (New York: Stearns), 1869. Available at https://archive.org/details/permanenttemper00socigoog.

took its beer seriously.[11] Physicians active in the Temperance movement sometimes argued that even the small amount of alcohol ingested during treatment with a medicinal tincture was to be avoided. Narcotics, in the form of laudanum or morphia, even, would be preferred, though they were to be avoided as drugs of intoxication.[12]

The kinds of adulterants common at the manufacture level were numerous. They included other plants with intoxicant properties, common chemicals, narcotics, and known poisons. The practice was widespread. The purpose of such adulteration was typically to either mask inferior products or process, or enhance the intoxicating quality of the beverage with a smaller true-product amount. Lead oxide, or litharge, was used by unscrupulous vintners to resweeten turned or vinegarized wine. These episodes would sometimes cause severe illness, but more often chronic symptoms.[13] These were the primary sorts of contamination or adulteration that most concerned people who had a tradition of drinking wines, beers, or ciders.[14] On the one hand, ordinary drinkers mainly ingested whatever came their way without complaint, much as they did adulterated foods, teas, and coffees. Pubs had reputations to preserve, but flavor and strength variations owing to adulterants were not always suspicious.

Temperance changed the balance of worries. Once the "rum-sellers" themselves came under increasing legal pressure, particularly in civil courts, to be liable for the exploits of the intemperate, general scrutiny and suspicion of their motives followed, encouraged by the evolving and more aggressive Temperance movement that favored restrictive and strongly enforced measures against alcohol.

---

[11] Garrett Oliver, "Adulteration," *The Oxford Companion to Beer*, (New York: Oxford University Press), 14–16.

[12] American Temperance Society, *Permanent Temperance Documents of the American Temperance Society*, (Boston: Seth Bliss), 1835. Available at https://archive.org/details/permanenttemper00socigoog.

[13] Bee Wilson, *Swindled: the Dark History of Food Fraud, from Poisoned Candy to Counterfeit Coffee*, (Princeton: Princeton University Press), 2008, 36–39, 47–60.

[14] The laws in Europe against adulteration were aimed at manufacturers, and sometimes at importers who were questioned as to whether some plant species had a legitimate use. The Levant nut, for instance (*Cocculus indicus*), was imported into Britain in the 1870s in enough quantities to raise eyebrows. This fruit of the *Anamirta cocculus* plant was used to strengthen beer.

Broadened Temperance, Purity Campaigns, and the Emergence of the Drugging Fear

As Temperance in the USA gained a broader following, it eventually made more productive use of what might be called the *drugging narrative of ruin*. These narratives were lifted more or less verbatim from British sensations such as W.T. Stead's *Maiden Tribute to Modern Babylon* published in 1885 in the *Pall Mall Gazette*. The *Maiden Tribute*, which was an exposé on adolescent prostitution in London, shocked middle- and upper-class Victorians, who read it in serial form.[15] Riveting "real life" melodrama had already been the stuff of "penny dreadful" publications (equivalent to today's tabloids) aimed at working-class audiences, but the *Gazette* was a respectable broadsheet. The *Maiden Tribute* both transformed the ethos of respectable journalism, and decisively shaped the way prostitution would come to be understood by reformers in the late nineteenth century.[16] Stead maintained his focus on children, but his narrative engulfed the issue of prostitution as a whole.

Both progressive-minded and evangelical Christian reformers would tend to conflate the allure and seduction of the sex trade to girls and women with bounded economic and social choices with the specter of kidnapped, tricked, and violated girls. Stead posed as a girl buyer and potential seller. It was so widely read and embraced that it reenergized support for parliamentary action to raise the age of sexual consent from 13 to 16.

Stead also linked prostitution with class power and conflict, albeit in a direct rather than structural way. The *Maiden Tribute* was fundamentally a protest against the "continued immolation of the daughters of the people as a sacrifice to the vices of the rich." Did the *Pall Mall Gazette*'s readers need to believe that the poor and working-class girls were directly coerced (drugged, held captive, raped) in order to afford them any sympathy? Or did the sensational, *in extremis* elements appeal more directly to an audience normally caught up in dry parliamentary proposals?

---

[15] Now available online at: http://www.attackingthedevil.co.uk/pmg/tribute/mt1.php. Retrieved January 15, 2016.

[16] See Victor Pierce Jones, *Saint or Sensationalist: The Story of W. T. Stead*, (Chichester: Gooday), 1988.

This confusion over the nature of the lure into prostitution was reinforced by the tabloid journalism that came after it, as well, which was much less engaged in social reform and more interested in sensation. And the drugging-and-debauching-of-virgins threat, on its own, would become generalized to young women as a whole, even though it was part and parcel of emerging "white slavery" tales. It was a formulation that constantly tested that categorical boundary of potential victims, and location and setting that later became important to American Temperance: that was the key link to alcohol—the wretched, lurid saloon.

Yet when speaking of involuntary drugging in this era, it would be a mistake to project backward its current association with "date rape drugs" and think of the entire threat as one aimed at neutralizing women's resistance to violence and exploitation. From the onset of rapid pharmaceutical and anesthetic advancement, there were homemade, prior drink spiking narratives with a somewhat different understanding of what tamperers were up to. In these drugging narratives, the aim is embarrassment, seduction into addiction, labor exploitation, or criminal predation. Antialcohol movements of the time, however, refined the rhetoric of conspiracy and coercion even when drugs, per se, were absent.

An apt example is discussed in the work of historian Elaine Frantz Parsons on drunkards' narratives.[17] John B. Gough, one of the most famous redeemed drunkards of the century, slipped off the wagon a few times after his rise to fame—or was he pushed? He published his testimony in 1845, the same year he experienced a spectacular episode of insobriety. He said that someone had drugged his soda water and arranged for him to be found looking drunk to discredit him as a prominent man of Temperance. Blame was laid at the hands of conspiring spirits merchants threatened by the strength of activists such as him. Parsons notes that this is consistent with a very conspiratorial view of the liquor industry held by other Temperance followers. Coercion into drink for the otherwise temptation-resisting man, notes Parsons, plays a prominent role in these narratives, where the drunkard seeking sobriety tells a well-worn tale of literally being held down the first time, and alcohol poured down his throat.

---

[17] Elaine Frantz Parsons, *Manhood Lost: Fallen Drunkards and Redeeming Women in the Nineteenth Century United States*. (Baltimore: Johns Hopkins University Press), 2009.

2 Chloral and Its Sisters: Synthetic Genesis and Parallel Demon

Saloonkeepers in these narratives are charged with putting alcohol in nonalcoholic beverages, or putting drugs in them. In 1851 the *New York Times* editorialized that the licensure system for retail spirits were much too loose, as evidenced by a recent Grand Jury inquest relating to unregistered "grog sellers." These men of no account could be seen anywhere on the streets, "dealing out drugged brandy, and other poisoned compounds for alcoholic drinks, to men and women, whom it is certain to injure, and whom they have every reason to believe it will impoverish and destroy."[18] (*New York Times*, 1851) The tendency to conflate the problems of weak regulation, contamination, and facilitated alcoholism is hardly unique. Into a specific claim several others are injected, and this tendency became a pattern in later claims about drugging. Although from an argumentation standpoint this would seem risky—hanging a set of broad concerns about alcohol and society on specific reports and dubious motives for adulteration—it is far from uncommon, perhaps since adulteration could draw in concerned readers otherwise unmoved by the more mundane social and public health problems presented by excess drink. The only specific incident mentioned in the *Times* story is one in which a grog seller sells drink knowing it would subsequently be "forced down the throat of a child only six years old." Coercive and surreptitious themes surround reform talk about alcohol, and these kinds of claims seem necessary to establishing the menace of alcohol itself.

Temperance activists assumed that for the most part women were managers, and victims, of the drink habits of men, and not social drinkers themselves. So interpreters of women's drinking often searched for a reason. Who had led her to do so? What were their intentions? Explanations were rarely benign. Parsons notes that the drunkard's narrative bears similarity to narratives of sexual seduction of young women and even gang rape. The thematic blurring of sexual and intoxicated surrender would increase in such narratives and the notion that young women were being "plied" with drink when they chose to drink gained a permanent foothold. But plying is, and has always been, an unstable idea. Most women know they are drinking, and intend to consume alcohol when they do so. Like men, of course, they may dangerously underestimate

---

[18] *New York Times*, "The License Systems," April 28, 1851, 2. Via *New York Times* Archives.

their consumption levels, and be thus less able to detect and fend off menacing and aggressive behavior. The increasing availability of innovative pharmaceutical preparations that could be used in a criminally predatory manner made for one sort of alternative explanation of incapacitation, and from time to time, predators did design to neutralize victims this way. But the real consolidation of *the drugging narrative of ruin* would owe much to the rise of synthetic narcotics.

The Dawn of Synthetics

The rise in demand for chloral hydrate, and its widespread use in easy-to-obtain anodyne products, doesn't have a singular cause. It was certainly easier to use than ether or chloroform, and surpassed in predictability preparations made from natural opium. But other analgesics and anethetics were developed alongside chloral and gained acceptance – bromides and early barbiturates, for example. But the specter of abuse, in chloral's case, emerged quickly.

The matter is not entirely that of scientific advantage; culture and politics play a remarkable role. Snelders et al.'s model of psychotropic development suggests that the history of chloral hydrate parallels that of other drugs in fitting into a "Seige cycle" where acceptance, use, and proper fit between the two is not linear but cyclical, and interacts with all sorts of nontherapeutic considerations—the potential for illicit misuse, side effects, and negative social effects, either perceived or real.[19] But as chloral was a synthetic and thus a "discovery," it was assumed to be perfectible in therapeutic use, in contrast to naturally derived substances such as alcohol, cannabinoids, and opiates. It did not have all of the baggage of the others, notes Snelders, of hailing from a pre-science era and "the Orient" and already having pleasure-seeking enthusiasts in the West.

Proponents of therapeutic chloral, like the doctors that respected the properties of opium, at first denied any widespread adverse effects.

---

[19] Stephen Snelders, Charles Kaplan, and Toine Pieters, "On Cannabis, Chloral Hydrate, and Career Cycles of Psychotropic Drugs in Medicine," *Bulletin of the History of Medicine* 80: 1, 2006, 95–114. The cycle model is named for Max Seige, who first observed the cycle in 1912, at the height of psychotropic innovation.

2 Chloral and Its Sisters: Synthetic Genesis and Parallel Demon 27

Benjamin Ward Richardson, a British Temperance supporter who did some of the first researches on chloral, initially claimed that it harbored no danger of habituation as compared with opiates and alcohol.[20] As for adverse effects, including fatalities, they are attributed to early impure and substandard preparations.[21] The same dubious claims would later be made about chloroform deaths.

Yet one of the peculiarities of chloral is its noticeable stimulating phase in some takers before a phase of sedation. Dr. Gordon Stables, author of "The Confessions of an English Chloral-Eater" (1875), distinguishes between the feeling that opiates give—dreamlike, unreal—and those fostered by chloral, which feel like embellishments on the real. "Yes, chloral is, as it were, a new Juggernaut set moving in society, and thousands annually fall beneath its wheels."[22] He describes its functional quality: as a doctor, he had trusted the journals that praised it as a reliable sleep aid without a hangover, and it had helped him keep up with too many working hours when he was apprenticed. At first, he saw himself as rested and lucid in his work, then, abruptly became aware of the near-fatal mistakes he was making in compounding medicines for his patients. Further, a tenacious addiction followed, bringing ruin to his body and mind, and only the intervention of another doctor saved his life and helped him recover. Notable figures not just in medicine, but also the arts, succumbed to raging chloral addictions, including Dante Gabriel Rossetti and probably Friedrich Nietzsche.

The medical critics seemed to be saying that opiates brought on a set of expected effects; essentially, they had been a known quantity for centuries; since the third century BCE, as the poppy plant's analgesic effects were discovered by the Egyptians and Sumerians. Users had few illusions about opium. Morphine, isolated in 1804, was stronger yet still had a well-accumulated knowledge base behind it. But in the later case of chloral, the sensation of narcotizing seemed to still be accompanied by a sense

---

[20] Benjamin Ward Richardson, *Medical Times and Gazette*, February 1871. Cited by Louis Lewin, in *The untoward effects of drugs: a pharmacological and clinical manual*, 2nd ed., (Detroit: George S. Davis), 1883.

[21] Lewin, 1883.

[22] Gordon Stables, "The Confessions of an English Chloral-Eater" *Belgravia*, June, 1875, 179–190.

of vivid reality. It was illusory, rather than daydreamy. At first thought to be a feature, it was quickly recognized as a bug. With a synthetic high, it seemed, things still seemed real—things like the seasoned Dr. Stables' rote medical competence—but they were not. The sense of the unique dangers of chloral, even when it was being used legitimately, increased.

Chloroform: The Inhaled Joy

Chloroform, a natural substance and chemical cousin to chloral, was identified in the early 1800s and so named in 1834. It was first applied as an anesthetic in the 1840s, where it quickly supplanted the more unpredictable ether in some places, while competing with it in others. It is important to realize what a revelation it was to surgeons who performed both major and minor operations with it—it essentially replaced tying the patient down or giving them alcohol and hoping for speed, skill, and accuracy. Histories of anesthesia seem to agree that while the ancients made reference to stupefying substances in aid of surgery, this appears to have fallen out of favor by the European Middle Ages, and that *no anesthetic at all* was the most common regime.[23] Both ether and chloroform were used therapeutically in medical settings in the 1800s before they were used as anesthetics, and also by medical students recreationally, particularly in Scotland, where the embrace of the substances was the most enthusiastic and the doubts raised by adverse events most readily dismissed.

But not long after its introduction in 1847 in surgery, specifically by Edinburgh's James Simpson, it became a feared substance of misuse and suspected foul play. By 1855, the *New York Times* could declare, in an article on an alleged robbery of $1400 facilitated by chloroform in a crooked barber's hands, that "robberies by the aid of chloroform are becoming of almost daily occurrence," though the paper reported allegations from all over the USA and Europe, which suggests not quite enough local material to warrant this kind of hyperbole.[24] But chloroform plays

---

[23] Linda Stratmann, *Chloroform: the Quest for Oblivion*, (Gloucestershire, UK: Sutton), 2003.
[24] *New York Daily Times*, "Robberies by Chloroform," May 15, 1855, 4. Via *New York Times* Archive.

2 Chloral and Its Sisters: Synthetic Genesis and Parallel Demon

an interesting case, in that the advocates of its expanded use win for several decades—and chloroform is not so much regulated out of use as it is simply technologically supplanted by the 1920s.

This fear of predatory chloroform seemed to be wholly limited to the popular press and its readers—medical men were in fact extremely defensive about even the possibility that this prized breakthrough in medicine could be misused this way. Medical literature of the time seems even more defensive about chloroform being misused than about chloral hydrate being misused. Yet in the popular imagination, it has figured perhaps even more prominently than chloral hydrate, quickly labeled *knockout drops*, as a feared medical weapon. Unlike chloral, which must be ingested, and therefore implies that predation must first be preceded by some level of false convivial trust, chloroform's appeal in this respect may be related to its inhaled route of administration. Press and popular fiction saw chloroform as easily administered and effective in producing instant unconsciousness. Thus, in the imagined scenario, chloroform could be wafted into a room, could be breezed under a person's nose like smelling salts, could be briefly covered over a person's nose and mouth, and thus the victim would be gently put to sleep, to be kidnapped, robbed, or raped. As such, it often seems to take the place of brute force in many fictional depictions. The mechanism appears to render the victim insensible and unknowledgeable about what had transpired. In fictional accounts, which are numerous, it also seems to be used to tell us something subtle about the villain in question: sophisticated, perhaps playing a long game by having his prey out and disoriented for a while, even gentlemanly.

In some sense, the medical men were right to be skeptical as such claims began to appear in newspapers and police blotters and in melodramatic fiction. They harshly noted, generally accurately, that it does not really work that way. In putting people under in a medical or dentistry setting at the time, they discovered, it was necessary to carefully mix air and chloroform breaths, that the substance was caustic and blistering if it touched skin, and had to be carefully readministered every few minutes if the patient was to stay under. Too far from the face or too quickly put near the nose and withdrawn, and chloroform has no effect at all; too close, and it burns, and too much, as it was unfortunately discovered by trial and error, and the patient dies of cardiac arrest. Chloroform is indeed a poor choice for a predator unless the object is murder, because since the effect is not immediate, the victim will struggle and resist, at some point completely obviating the need for chloroform, since they will need to be physically subdued anyway.

That said, the defensiveness demonstrated by the medical journals and the physicians who were the innovators in the field of anesthesia went well beyond a healthy skepticism—they tended to use words like "impossible"—ignoring the cases where frail victims were targeted.[25] Further, the hold that chloroform had on the popular mind through the news stories and allegations of its use included potential predators, who themselves often bought into the "put them to sleep" image of the drug and therefore *did* try to use it, for a period of time after its rise, to subdue victims. This almost pleasant view of chloroform was itself somewhat exaggerated by these same medical men in places like *The Lancet*. The first doctor to use it in midwifery in 1847, James Simpson, described its effects as "far more agreeable and pleasant than those of ether" and that it "possesses an agreeable, fragrant, fruit-like odour, and a saccharine pleasant taste."[26] Lurking on the sidelines were also the difficult allegations of sexual assault by dentists and doctors using chloroform or ether on female patients, in some cases without witnesses present, a problem to which I will return.

The speed with which the public became alarmed at the perceived criminal capabilities of chloroform is evidenced by it being addressed in British law as early as 1851. In that year's version of the Prevention of Offences Act, the possible role of the newer stupefying agents in the aid of criminal predation were first clearly marked for an enhanced penalty in legislation first introduced by Lord Campbell. In the event that "any person shall unlawfully apply administer or attempt to apply or administer to any other any chloroform, laudanum or other stupifying or drug matter or thing with intent thereby to enable such or any other person to commit or with intent to assist such or other person in committing any felony," the convict is subject to an additional penalty of up to seven years or transport

---

[25] John Snow, "A Letter to the Right Honourable Lord Campbell, Lord Chief Justice of the Court of Queen's Bench, on the Clause Respecting Chloroform in the Proposed Prevention of Offences Bill," (London: John Churchill), 1851, 9–13.

[26] James Y. Simpson, *Notice of a new anaesthetic agent, as a substitute for sulphuric ether in surgery and midwifery*, (Edinburgh: Sutherland and Knox), 1847.

2 Chloral and Its Sisters: Synthetic Genesis and Parallel Demon

to Australia.[27] Though technically speaking, the medical advocates of chloroform had nothing to do with the criminal code, they actively sought to defend the drug's reputation and opposed the legislation. The famed John Snow claimed that it was impossible to drug an adult with it against their will, reiterating that it was hard enough to get it right with a willing one seeking anesthesia. While he does debunk a few suspicious claims of chloroform robbery, he also ignores the potential weaker victim or more than one assailant.[28] Still, it probably remains fair to say that the legislation owed more to fear than to a significant public threat.

Scientific writings of the present day seem in agreement that while it is theoretically possible to subdue someone with chloroform, it requires considerable physical force and still requires readministration every few minutes, generally making it a poor weapon unless the object is murder.[29] But it also seems obvious from the scattered case history of its criminal use that perpetrators are liable to fall for the easy-sleepy-cloth-over-the-nose mythology, as well. The overarching defensiveness from chloroform's medical advocates came from their *generally* defensive stance about it. They were resistant to medical claims from abroad that it caused unexpected death in healthy patients; too many to continue the new practice with unabated enthusiasm. They had to battle recalcitrant physicians who philosophically disagreed with surgical and obstetric pain relief, for either religious reasons or medical ones. As such, they saw themselves as noble modernizers who at every corner had to face all sorts of retrograde obstacles. As historian Linda Stratmann put it,

> The advantages of chloroform … were so self-evident that anyone who opposed its use was either hidebound by old dogmas or a fool. Nothing was to be permitted to stand in the way of the universal acceptance of this great boon to mankind.[30]

---

[27] Charles Sprengler Greaves, *Lord Campbell's Acts for the Further Improving of the Administration of Criminal Justice and the Better Prevention of Offences*, (London: Benning and Company), 1851, 39.

[28] Snow, 1851.

[29] John W.R. McIntyre, "The Criminal Use of Chloroform Administered by Inhalation," *Medicine and Law*, no. 7, 1988, 195–202; J. P. Payne, "The criminal use of chloroform," *Anaesthesia*, 1998, no. 53, 685–690.

[30] Stratmann, 41.

Stratmann suggests that Simpson and other advocates exaggerated religious objection to ward off other kinds of doubts within medicine, and to counterpose themselves to the Calvinists and traditionalists.

Dr. Simpson, in his initial article in *The Lancet* (1847), described also its obstetric use:

> I have never had the pleasure of watching over a series of better and more rapid recoveries, nor once witnessed any disagreeable result follow to either mother or child, whilst I have now seen an immense amount of maternal pain and agony saved by its employment ...[31]

The revolution in synthetic anesthesia was troubled especially by the question of its use during childbirth. Mary Poovey shows how debates emerged in the obstetrics literature about the best substance and manner to provide pain relief during childbirth—but without stimulating apparent sexual "passions" and movements during labor.[32] In fact, like other CNS depressants, chloral and chloroform often produce a stage of excitability and disinhibition before they reduce consciousness. This can manifest sometimes in sexual disinhibition. Fairly soon after Simpson's chloroform fanfare, correspondence in the medical journals began to appear, describing female patients whose "virtue" unraveled under the sweet fumes. Thus, any pain relief during childbirth was an occasion for worry about the propriety of contact between the doctor and his patient, who might, in the process of being relieved of labor pains, provide a kind of temptation and moral threat to herself and her doctor—now himself in danger of seduction. As such, drugged women by this time are seen not just as potential victims of sex without consent but—in almost siren–robot fashion—all powerful in their ability to draw men into transgression with them.

Doctors writing in textbooks and in *The Lancet*—once again, with overreaching defensiveness—linked these episodes either to "improper" use of ether or chloroform as an anesthetic or, in some cases, to doctors' own misinterpretations of involuntary spasms and utterances at the onset of

---

[31] James Y. Simpson, "Discovery of A New Anaesthetic Agent More Efficient Than Sulphuric Ether," *Lancet*, 2, 1847, 549.

[32] Mary Poovey, "'Scenes of an Indelicate Character': Medical 'Treatment' of Victorian Women," *Representations*, 14, Spring, 1986, 137–168.

2 Chloral and Its Sisters: Synthetic Genesis and Parallel Demon

anesthetic efficacy.[33] Some doctors suggested that since sexual utterances and sexual dreaming had been observed among women given chloroform in labor, the practice should be abandoned so as not to compromise the woman's propriety. Others, proponents of chloroform, counterclaimed that the whole matter existed only as an improper fantasy on the part of the doctors themselves; or, at most, merely a disinhibition-related characteristic of women already compromised in their virtue. This concerned a certain segment of physicians much more than it did the general public, who were by and large eager to have it in many situations. And it did not hurt that in 1853, Queen Victoria elected to have the royal obstetrician, the well-known Dr. John Snow, apply chloroform to her for the birth of Prince Leopold, and not long after, the daughter of the archbishop of Canterbury requested the same.

Patients far and wide shared the doctors' enthusiasm and requested it in dentistry, surgery, and childbirth quite commonly up through the early decades of the twentieth century. Chloroform can be self-administered for recreational and self-medicating purposes; it is moderately addictive, as is ether, and it had figured in a few sensational murders, yet it kept its halo. The genie was out of the bottle, both on the streets and in the operating theater. People used it on their own, they partied with it, some fatally overdosed on it, while others could apparently inhale it without a problem. They used it for asthma, insomnia, and a host of other everyday ills. So it was readily available to people if they wanted to misuse it. As much as the public embraced its anesthetic and therapeutic uses, they also read with great enthusiasm about allegations of its use in robbery and burglary.

I examined every article in the *New York Times* referring to chloroform between 1851 and 1870. I found a total of 146 articles; 25 referred to crime allegations across the USA and Europe involving chloroform. The most common type reported—about which we hear little now—was the high-stakes burglary, or what might be thought of as a soporific home invasion. The other common type was the railcar, ship, or street robbery allegation. Finally, there were the more difficult cases of alleged sexual exploitation of patients during anesthetic use. Neither the

---

[33] Poovey, 1986.

sexual dreaming problem, nor the opportunity afforded to the trusted exploiter by more effective anesthetics, was limited to the sensitivities of the birthing room. One of the most widely watched cases—by newsreaders and clinicians alike—was that of the arrest and trial of prominent Philadelphia dentist Stephen T. Beale, who administered ether to a patient who accused him of sexual assault while she was under. In 1854, a young married woman went to Beale, who had treated her and her family before, for an extraction. Seemingly unresponsive to initial doses and still in pain, she asked for a second dose of ether. After it was administered, she described a feeling of paralysis, during which the sexual assault takes place. After recovering from the anesthetic and the pain, she left the office for an ordinary round of activities. Troubled, nonetheless, by her recollection, she made an official complaint three days later.[34]

Beale's counsel mounted a vigorous and multifaceted defense. Aside from character witnesses, the physical circumstances of the alleged incident were described by various witnesses, including other patients and workmen being present, as unconducive to privacy. Doctors testified about the sexual dreaming problem already described in journals. The prosecution relied only on the accuser's testimony, expert testimony about the possibility of conscious paralysis under anesthesia, and an opinion of her physician, who did not perform an examination. Nonetheless, Beale was convicted and sentenced to more than four years, although a higher court pardoned him on the strength of scientific correspondence about the sexual dreaming problem and the view that no corroboration was made.[35] One of the most curious stages of the case, however, was at the point of conviction. T.K. Collins, a Philadelphia contemporary who gathered many documents relevant to the case in hope of publicizing the doctor's plight, took note of the jury's odd conclusion: guilty, but with a recommendation to mercy. As a matter of process, it came to light that the verdict reflected a split jury and its attempt to compromise. Another natural irony of the era was that in

---

[34] R.A. Strickland and J.F. Butterworth, "Sexual Dreaming during Anesthesia: Early Case Histories (1849–1888) of the Phenomenon," *Anesthesia*, no. 106, 2007, 1232–1236.
[35] PA Criminal Code 3121. Corroboration was, at the time, required under many states' sexual assault laws, including Pennsylvania. The corroboration requirement did not see widespread repeal until the 1970s; Pennsylvania removed its in 1976. See Cassia Spohn and Julie Horney, *Rape law reform: a grassroots revolution and its impact*, (New York: Springer), 1992, 74.

2 Chloral and Its Sisters: Synthetic Genesis and Parallel Demon

considering the fate of Beale, a man of Temperance, the jury had partaken of much brandy during the deliberations. The verdict pleased no one. As Beale's ardent defender, Collins notes:

> There is nothing to excuse, nothing to palliate guilt. If Dr. Beale was guilty at all; he was all guilty; guilty of a predetermined crime of calculating perfidy, that scarcely has an equal in the annals of sin. [36]

By the time of the Beale allegations, the emergence of the "problem" of sexualization during the initial phases of anesthetic use was known to medical journal subscribers for a few years. I use the term "sexualization" as an intentionally overbroad term—since the boundaries between hallucination, fantasy, allegation, perception, physical arousal, and actual exploitation or rape were not well established at this point among doctors considering the matter. Doctors defending Beale in his appeal suggest, in a noxious overreach, that if a drugged patient like Beale's accuser failed to resist an outrage, this would suggest that it had not occurred at all.[37]

Many reports of sexual ideation during anesthesia over the years—from chloroform in the late nineteenth century to benzodiazepines in the late twentieth century—have accumulated, and this concern is the source of the current advice that anesthesia should never be administered without third parties present as witnesses. Strickland and Butterworth's review of literature notes that studies consistently find that a fair portion—up to 1 in 5—people report sexual impressions or hallucinations accompanying anesthesia. Other kinds of illusions, some terrifying, are also reported.[38]

And so the problems of false charges of drugging and assault emerge relatively early in the history of modern anesthesia. Yet the problem raises two problems rather than one. The written record on the matter of sexual hallucination during sedation, not surprisingly, reflects the primary

---

[36] T.K. Collins, JR., ed. (1855) *Trial and Conviction or Dr. Stephen T. Beale with the letters of Chief Justice Lewis, and Judges Black and Woodward, on his case. Interesting ether cases, and letters of Prof. Gibson … &c.* (Philadelphia: T.K. Collins), 1855, 6. https://archive.org/details/55220150R.nlm.nih.gov. Retrieved January 16, 2016.

[37] Collins, 13.

[38] Anthony S. Wohl, *Endangered Lives: Public Health in Victorian Britain*, London: Methuen, 1984, 13.

concern of clinicians, which is to avoid false accusation. Hidden beneath this legitimate concern is the unwritten corollary of the lessons taken from the Beale case: had he in fact done it, it would have been the perfect crime, as any violation reported by a patient could be attributed to a drug illusion. In other words, the weapon itself, in its generation of vivid unreality, erased the basis for justice. In the Beale case, of course, there were other circumstances making the patient's claims dubious. But one of the pillars of complaint about the Beale verdict was the patient's lack of legitimacy, in critics view, as a claimant precisely because she was drugged: "she was not in a condition to know positively to the facts to which she swears."[39]

Insensibility then puts any real victim in a special kind of exile. This theme of double cruelty—an assault first on memory, on the continuity of time, on one's presumption to be telling the truth, and at the same time the physical violation of rape—stays with the fear of drugging through the present day. And in any case—early or modern—when drugs are involved and suspicion of rape is raised, regardless of any formal accusation or its absence (which we must always remember is the norm, not the exception), what of the sincere belief of violation in the absence of evidence, or even in the absence of certainty?

Much of this ambiguity would never be resolved and it kind of echoed the uncertainty about medical uses of chloroform; some adopters were very timid with its use and others were likely to attribute adverse effects to other causes and used it widely. The fact that chloroform withstood such difficulties is a testament to the significance of the problem that it solved, which cannot perhaps be said for other substances that fell first under scrutiny and later prohibition. The medical societies eventually did sour on chloroform, but not because of criminal diversion or predation. Probably because it was more than just tonic for the nerves, although inhalants can be used this way, sometimes addictively, as well. If chloral hydrate was singular in any way when it appeared, its effect was to democratize this uncertainty, exacerbating the psychic pain of crime victims under the influence and widening the playing field for the drug-nimble thug.

---

[39] Collins, 13.

2 Chloral and Its Sisters: Synthetic Genesis and Parallel Demon

The Popularization of the Remedy

The term "knockout drops" first appeared in Victorian England, and as slang, it appears to have dual meanings. It refers both to the predatory use of opiates or chloral and to their attraction as sleep aids—to self-administer or to dose wakeful children. The temporary unconsciousness implied by a "knockout" perhaps made such dosing decisions seem more benign than was wise. It must also be remembered that both opiates and synthetic narcotics like chloral routinely appeared in patent medicines for children from the mid-nineteenth through early twentieth centuries, and their marketing unabashedly appealed to the desire to quiet down the children. Wohl argues that declining usage stemmed less from regulations, which were often weak because they were opposed by the pharmaceutical interests, but rather because the conditions of working-class life improved incrementally enough to reduce demand for drugs that would restrain children's demands.

Chloral's rise no doubt accelerated both the fear of and, probably, the incidence of drugging. Chloral was in some sense a novel threat—a narcotic-like substance that dissolved effortlessly in alcohol and could easily sneak by the senses to depress the CNS—quickly, as it was meant to in anesthesia, and with no time in which a victim might sense that something had gone wrong with their drink. As such, the modern history of drink spiking begins with chloral hydrate—synthetic, medically trusted, with multiple uses, readily available, and more reliable than opiates.

When chloral hydrate was first introduced as a new anesthetic for surgery in 1869, its speed of effect and its predictability were regarded as truly revolutionary. It seemed not to have the volatility of ether or chloroform, which were in wide use. Yet a scant ten years after his research, Richardson saw mostly bad impacts of the discovery, "I almost feel a regret," he wrote in the *Contemporary Review*, "that I took any part whatever in the introduction of the agent into the practice of healing and the art of medicine."[40] Attraction to a sleep agent begins the habit he terms "chloralism" and notes that it has become widespread, but not yet among

---

[40] Benjamin Ward Richardson, "Chloral and other narcotics," *Littell's Living Age*, v142, #1835, 1879, 425–438. (Reprinted from the *Contemporary Review*.)

women or the poor, instead luring "middle-class men" in the trades, business, medicine, and academe. Advances in surgical anesthesia he does not consider worth the price if it "ministers to some luxurious desire or morbid inclination of mankind." As early as 1874, the *Sanitary Record* of London claimed that chloral simply was more evil in its effects, producing permanent nerve damage and "brain bloodlessness"—worse than anything the opiates could have wrought. In all likelihood, its accessibility and ease of use relative to chloroform made it a widespread menace in the making.

But alongside patent medicines, chloral became just one of many that fostered addictive behavior in some takers. By the turn of the century, no special concern surrounded it—except as the key ingredient in the much feared knockout drops.

Male Victims of Drugging

Men actually faced the specter of drugging first. In the 1800s, with the rapid intensification of industrialism, international trade, and resource extraction, working-class and poor men's gendered identity as hand-to-mouth breadwinners and laboring dogsbodies was what made them potentially vulnerable as drugging victims. It was men, after all, who had free reign to drink after work without approbation, and who could enter and leave a tavern of his peers without a pitying glance. Women were somewhat shielded by the gendered restrictions on their movements and the expectation that any drinking a woman did would be in small amounts, accompanied by others. Broadly, it was more men that people were worried about as potential inebriates than women; all manner of social ills were attributed to the drunk man's inability to provide resources, security, and leadership for his family.

The additional fear of having drugs put in your drink played an ambiguous role in antialcohol movements. Ideologically, Temperance indicted the normal course of drink and drinking, not the deviant case of a tampered drink. But the anti-saloon movement, focused as it was on the physical places people gathered to drink and socialize, tended to

2 Chloral and Its Sisters: Synthetic Genesis and Parallel Demon

champion any threat that might be present at such a venue. The places themselves were irredeemable. And it seems that some venues actually were. But at the turn of the twentieth century, everyone knew that men could be drugged, mostly for profiteering purposes: to extract their money or their labor, in some cases facilitating their enslavement, or to simply have over on them, for prank or for vengeance. Even the sly use of drugs by bartenders and bouncers, as neutralizers of a troublesome drunk, had the bottom line in mind.

Male victims of drugging have lent the world all manner of colorful slang phrases: after being *burked*, or turned into a convenient and profitable corpse, there was being *hocussed* or *shanghaied* (drugged and pressed into the military, ships' service, or servitude), or being the target of a Mickey Finn, after which you were removed from the premises or robbed blind, by either some good-time bar fellows feigning friendship or a friendly lady offering companionship. Typically, this involved drink spiking with a dose of knockout drops, in most cases, probably chloral hydrate.

Most of the drinking venues where such practices were suspected were ambiguous in their atmosphere: the regulars were bread and butter, the wealthier patrons desired, but the two did not always mix, even if the latter sought out a bit of edginess provided by the former. In order for the latter to come back again and spend money in your establishment, the former required, on occasion, some restraint. A third constituency had closer identification with the regulars, but more to gain from the wealthier patrons: those who drugged bar patrons to rob them. If that was going to work, roaring drunks on the barroom floor needed to go.

No warnings about predatory use of chloral appear in any US medical journal until 1895, when the *Journal of the American Medical Association* introduces the topic in "The Criminal Use of Choral." It is reported that police in New York's Tenderloin district were investigating the use of knockout drops to facilitate robbery of bar patrons. Yet as a tool to subdue robbery and rape victims, chloral already held a popular reputation, and sporadic news accounts were present at least 20 years earlier. In 1879, the *New York Times* reported that Frederick Ferguson, a jeweler who had entered a downtown pub, "spent his money liberally for liquor" and awoke to find himself on a bench near the river, relieved of his watch and wallet. Though he staggered to a police station, he fainted there again and suspicion was raised that his beer had been drugged. The saloon owner denied robbing him but produced the missing items, claiming he had given them to her for safekeeping. She was arrested. Other substances already had a reputation as an intoxicant aid to theft: the *British Medical Journal* reported in 1880 on the use of *Cocculus indicus* by thieves but without much supporting detail; the article was mainly about its therapeutic potential and its shady use by brewers in strengthening beer.[41] But it was assumed, perhaps correctly, that chloral might be easier to come by as it was largely unregulated at the time and popular as a sleep aid and analgesic.

Some of the earliest reports of predatory drugging concerned sailors "shanghaied" into ship service under influence of drugged drinks. In November 1852, the *New York Times* reprinted a New Orleans report on two English men who had taken drink at a sailor's boarding house and were "bundled" off onto a ship and into service. Found dead along with three other men in port, drugging and an accidental overdose were suspected, but no specific drug was mentioned. Intermediaries called *crimps* used a variety of methods to deliver unwitting men to the ships. Alcohol alone, in high enough quantities, was often enough.

On the West Coast, chloral in tavern drinks was reported to facilitate the shanghai of young men for merchant ships, who awoke at sea having no recollection of their voluntary conscription. The fear soon spread to being drugged into regular state or federal armed services. It was enough of a concern in New York that the state legislature added the shanghai to its criminal offenses:

> … whoever shall knowingly and willfully use or administer to any person any drug or stupefying substance, with intent, while such person is under the influence thereof, to induce such person to enter the military or naval

---

[41] *British Medical Journal*, "Recent Studies on Therapeutics. I. Picrotoxine and its Properties," January 18, 1880, 17, 96–97; allegations against brewers: H.B. Cornwall, "Adulteration of Beers," *Public Health Papers and Reports*, Volume 10. American Public Health Association, 1884.

service of the United States, or of this State, or of any other State, is also guilty of a felony.[42]

Much like the fear of knockout drops, the concern about the shanghai rested both on real cases and on cautionary folklore. Drugging clearly began to serve as a sort of "account" or preferred explanation for missing time and amnesia, or as a justification for mob violence. Military men at leisure, who drank at local establishments, enacted bar raids upon rumor or suspicion of drugging. In a report developed by the American Public Health Association in 1901, the committee described the problem as stemming in part from Congress' "sentimental" abolition of the authorized and regulated military canteen, kowtowing to the influence of the Temperance activists. In San Francisco that year, several reports of soldiers raiding Presidio saloons upon "real and imaginary grievances" of being drugged were reported. San Francisco's "Barbary Coast" had been ground zero for the crimpers in the decades before, and legend, rumor, and false accusations grew on the place's titillating reputation.

The Shanghai: Dogsbodies for the Ships' Service

It is not as if the life of a merchant marine was ever easy. But for one particular period in the mid-1800s, the conditions and pay for such work were so unattractive to all but a dedicated few that even down and out men avoided it. Shipping interests simply decided that this unorganized

---

[42] NY 4 Laws 1884, ch. 391, 889. Curiously, the offense was downgraded to a misdemeanor by 1909. *The Penal Code of the State of New York: In Force December 1, 1882, as Amended by Laws of 1882, 1883, 1884, 1885, with Notes of Decisions and a Full Index*, 1885. (NY Article 142, § 1482, in 1894 it was § 447). Appears to have been repealed as redundant or obsolete pursuant to chapter 5 of the Laws of 1889, those relevant laws now embodied in Penal Code or Code of Criminal Procedure. *Documents of the Assembly of the State of New York*, Volume 13, 1890. Refers to the original law as Military chapter 391, Laws of 1864, felony. "D*rugging person for enlistment*. A person who administers any drug or stupefying substance to another, with the intent, while such person ie under the influence thereof, to induce such person to enter the military or naval service of the United States, of this state, or any other state, country or government, is guilty of a misdemeanor. NY *Penal Code, J 447.*" The auxiliary businesses like boarding houses and bars that catered to sailors and wharfmen, who were often the conduits for the crimps, did constitute a fairly strong lobby. Nonetheless, by 1915, Federal law set minimum standards for the contracts, wages, and circumstances of merchant marine labor.

labor dissent would not be countenanced: they simply abducted men and put them on ships. Drugs and drink were quite helpful here: a bit of chloral in your beer at a wharfside bar meant that you could be "halfway to Shanghai" on the boat before you knew what had happened. And what had happened was: apparently some time after you had that fateful drink, you also signed a contract for merchant marine labor. While alcohol blackouts might facilitate the same outcome with less risk, and many shanghaied men did get captured this way, chloral was much more predictable.

Shipping interests, of course, did not do the dirty work themselves. They hired *crimpers*—agents who worked the bars, whose official charge was to "recruit" men onto ships. The crimpers would get a finders' fee per new marine. Good crimpers knew how to work all the target-rich places: dive bars, boarding houses, brothels, and betting parlors. Proprietors and managers got their own little quiet kickbacks. Often times, the men targeted were actually sailors of one sort or another but forced into service at poor terms in a place and time not of their choosing. Yet at the same time, there were sailors who agreed to poor terms (improper equipment, inherent danger, holding back of wages) simply to get on board or get back to some place that they wanted or needed to be.[43] While it can seem that the severe labor shortage in the industry drove the crimpers, and that it took a long time for that shortage to actually benefit the sailors, this alone would not explain why some men would accede to terrible conditions and pay, while others literally had to be forced into it.

What crimpers really did was deftly work the origin versus destination imbalances in the desirability of port towns at particular times. The legendary Barbary Coast port in San Francisco had always been known for its sailor's good times—seafaring men always desired to go there, and sometimes they did not want to leave. Famously, for instance, the same 1849 Gold Rush that brought more ships to California also meant that sailors abandoned the ships in droves, seeking their own fortune in the area. It would take more than standard conditions to lure the men back on board. Of the Barbary, then, it was said that every sailor wanted to go at least once, "though the crimps spoiled the fun somewhat."[44]

---

[43] Ronald Hope, *Poor Jack: the perilous history of the merchant seaman*, London: Chatham, 2001, 249–254

[44] Stan Hugill, *Sailortown*, London: Routledge and Kegan Paul, 1967; quoted in Hope, 2001, 252.

2 Chloral and Its Sisters: Synthetic Genesis and Parallel Demon

The same method appears to have been pressed into service to capture men for enslavement. Solomon Northup's 1853 memoir, *Twelve Years a Slave*, describes the similar use of shady intermediaries.[45] Northup was born and raised in the Northern USA and lived as a "free black" at the time of slavery in the South. His father had been emancipated by the man who "owned" him and relocated to New York State. Northup was lured to Washington, DC in the promise of work as a musician and was waylaid and sold into slavery in Louisiana; his captors probably used a narcotic in his drink. Again, acute, sporadic labor shortages may have created a niche for traders who specialized in capturing free black men into slavery.

The Generalized Threat of the Mickey

Despite the knowledge that certain circumstances could indeed foster drink spiking, a considerable amount of skepticism about bar-drugging tales emerged in the medical journals; again, while there were good reasons for skepticism in some cases, the vehemence shown by medical writers slips into overreaching claims of their own. In the Philadelphia *Medical and Surgical Reporter* (1884), the editors enjoin their readers not to believe tales of girls lured into bars and then fed drugged soda water. "[A]ny such story as this is rank nonsense. There is no drug known to medicine which will have any such effect."[46] The alleged victims, in their view, were rank liars and perhaps criminally inclined themselves. The Philadelphia journal was not an exception but rather a reiteration of a popular view among medical men. In 1876, the *Louisville Medical News* insisted that reports of "respectable" persons being drugged on ships, in hotels, and in elite resorts were to be taken with heavy skepticism:

> But we need not worry ourselves in this regard. No "drug" or agent exists capable of accomplishing such horrible ends under usual conditions, and

---

[45] Solomon Northup, *Twelve Years a Slave: Narrative of Solomon Northup*, (Auburn, NY: Derby and Miller), 1853. http://docsouth.unc.edu/fpn/northup/menu.html. Retrieved January 16, 2016.
[46] H.H. Kynett, D.G. Brinton, S. W. Butler, eds. *Philadelphia Medical and Surgical Reporter*, Volume 50, Number 115, January–July 1884, 596–597.

we think chemistry is incompetent to ever supply such an agent. We do not believe that any respectable, sober man or woman was ever "drugged," so as to pass into the power of another, against his or her will, under any ordinary conditions, whether awake or asleep, at home or abroad.[47]

The article laid the problem on the doorsteps of excess alcohol, implying that the alleged victims were mistaking the effects of excess alcohol for that of predatory drugging. Clearly, a new subterranean conflict was taking shape. Much like the overreaching skepticism of the Beale case, scattered reports of drugging that probably did often merit doubt caused the journals to take an absurdly defensive posture and define even the *possibility* of predatory drugging out of existence. So extreme in its claims, this kind of professional skepticism was easy, then, to simply dismiss via increasing anecdote. In a form of what I have previously called "scorched earth skepticism," the seemingly obvious obligation of the profession to clarify the scope and seriousness of the problems of chloral for an increasingly fearful public was evaded altogether.[48] Considering that doctors were using chloral, laudanum, and other small-dose anesthetics to treat men of means for neurasthenia, they surely knew that the drug could be powerful.

Knockout drops as an explanation for dissolution and periodic absence was an easy one to access—there was much fear and titillation in news accounts of the thieving gangs and partnerships who mostly victimized men to rob them. One of the more fascinating aspects of such mythologizing of sin is that these narratives held as much sway among those who were more openly fascinated by it as among the disdainful. Romantic accounts of the rough and tumble city, such as that of Herbert Asbury's *The Gangs of New York*, and *Gem of the Prairie*, about Chicago, mingle together well-documented accounts of the urban underworld with clearly folkloric ones. A combination of dread and desire always seems to follow the image of new underworlds; reformers who look on in horror and smitten chroniclers often reinforce each other's exaggerations, each for their own ends.

---

[47] *Louisville Medical News*, "Cases of Alleged Drugging," Vols. I and II, 1876, 228.
[48] Pamela Donovan, *No Way of Knowing: Crime, Urban Legends, and the Internet*, (New York: Routledge), 2004, 141–142.

2 Chloral and Its Sisters: Synthetic Genesis and Parallel Demon

This is as specifically true of Asbury's accounts of drink spiking and white slavery as historians have noted is generally true of his depictions of impoverishment and criminality in the burgeoning nineteenth-century American city. Such popular histories have shaped our views of the problem of drugging in public places. In *The Gangs of New York*, the "slipping of a Mickey" is associated with the rough New York Bowery taverns as early as 1866 (using snuff[49] or laudanum, then later chloral hydrate), and in *Gem of the Prairie*, it is in the saloons operated by a South Loop proprietor nicknamed Mickey Finn.[50] In both cases, the primary emphasis is on rolling drinkers for their valuables and cash, and on using some combination of chloral hydrate and a strong purgative to neutralize problem drinkers in the bar. "Since Prohibition," Asbury suggests, without considering the implications for his nineteenth-century-origin stories, "bootleg liquor has generally been found to be sufficiently efficacious."[51] Cecil Adams, in his newspaper column The Straight Dope (1991), aptly referred to his works as "colorful if not necessarily reliable" on the matter of the knockout drops or Mickey Finn origins, and James Inciardi raises serious questions about popular claims, that the Mickey Finn originated in either the West Coast shanghai or the doping out-of-saloon patrons in Chicago, suggesting instead that itinerant men had used the term "Mickey" to simply mean strong spirits well before the turn of the century.[52] That the famous bar owner might well have capitalized on this notoriety is far more in evidence.

Along with a series of egregiously inflated crime statistics, Asbury tends also to propagate the white slavery legends whereby skilled procurers and madams work together to drug hapless immigrant or prairie girls and lock them into brothels. Like his more reform-minded and less dazzled counterparts, Asbury tends to discard the inherent attractions

---

[49] "Snuff" in most cases refers to pulverized tobacco with fragrance. Of course, nicotine is a stimulant, so alone it would be a poor choice for predatory use. The term "snuff" also sometimes refers to any finely powdered substance.
[50] Herbert Asbury, *Gem of the Prairie*, (New York: Alfred A. Knopf), 1940.
[51] Herbert Asbury, *The Gangs of New York*, (New York: Alfred A. Knopf), 1927.
[52] Cecil Adams, "The Straight Dope: What's in a Mickey Finn?" *Chicago Reader*, January 18, 1991; James A. Inciardi, "The Changing Life of Mickey Finn: Some Notes On Chloral Hydrate Down Through the Ages," *Journal of Popular Culture*, vol. 11, no. 3, 1977, 591–596.

of voluntary drug and alcohol consumption among women who were neither virginal nor fallen. Even among the fallen, he assumed that when prostitutes were arrested with chloral, its presence was mainly predatory. It was certainly a useful tool in neutralizing a mark for robbery, or even a troublesome customer, but chloral held its own charms, as did alcohol.

It was not so much that street chroniclers, journalists, and police investigators did not know about the self-administration of chloral—news accounts provided plenty of evidence alongside health and medical publications about the matter. It is that—much like the popular understanding of GHB and flunitrazepam today—chloral developed a "master identity" as the knockout drug that belied its plentiful other uses.[53] In fact, chloral's attractions were more openly discussed in the nineteenth century, since there were few prohibitions to its use. The predatory use of chloral eventually obscured the recreational and medical self-help use of it, and the addictive use problem as well.

Chloral in Service of Robbery

Men in the late 1800s were also particular targets for drugging thieves in and around drinking establishments, and they still are. Like prank spiking, drugging-robbery requires very little scheming: spike the drink, wait for the mark to pass out, take his stuff. A drowsy looking or unconscious male at a tavern simply does not trigger the same alarm and intervention as a suddenly unconscious female. And certainly many more men are rolled when simply drunk, and in some cases, it is unclear whether drink alone or drugging explains the means of incapacitation.

Incidents that made the paper were typically of wealthier men as victims. In January 1901, the *New York Times* also reported on the apparent chloral drugging and robbery of Dr. J.B. Elster in a Newark tavern. He sat down to talk with John Meklin about a mutual friend, ordered a beer, and awoke several hours later to find Meklin gone, as well as $20 and a stud worth $175. When police sought out the suspect, he attempted to toss a vial of chloral upon arrest. Sort of a chemical variation on the old "we know people

---

[53] "Master identity" is a term used by sociologists, and others, usually to describe elements of a person's social identity that are dominant; it is here used to describe how a drug can have many uses but nonetheless have a singular identity.

in common" confidence game, the setup simply speeded up the robbery by slowing down Elster. Of course, once arrested, Meklin was now, in the eyes of the law, a thief *and* a poisoner. So much for the perfect crime.

It should be remembered, though, that just because drugs turn out to be not so superior as criminal facilitators does not mean that offenders know that. There will always be the one-off attempt to do things the easy way that actually turns out to be the hard way.

Chemical Destruction of Her Virtue

Although later, disputed drugging stories would be associated with young women of few means who found themselves in infamous situations, early reports came from the leisure class. This is hardly surprising, since this is where initial access to chloral, and later reports of addiction, came from. The medical journals and newspapers alike framed chloral mishaps—real and perceived—as a problem among the privileged. The *Galveston Daily News* in 1871 saw itself defending the honor of elite women who used chloral. Denouncing claims that addiction and chloral-induced "drunkenness" was spreading, the paper opined that the class of women who had access to chloral surely would not abuse it. "We may not desire to see ladies vote, but we have altogether too much respect for the sex for one moment to believe that habitual drunkenness, and drunkenness of so mean a kind, is one of its accustomed vices." Delicacy seemed to enhance the desire to simply paper over the emerging problem. Addiction and negative events coinciding with inebriation was a topic whose object was rightly the downtrodden classes, not one's peers.

But it did not take long for the chloral "account"– where a bad event or series of events is attributed to predatory drugging—to become democratized. Young middle- and working-class women saw its appeal immediately. Kunzel's study of homes for unmarried pregnant women in the early twentieth century shows that knockout drops were a popular explanation given to social workers who saw them as victims of male lust and seduction.[54] Unlike their evangelical predecessors, who were

---

[54] Regina Kunzel, *Fallen Women, Problem Girls: Unmarried Women and the Professionalization of Social Work, 1890–1945*, (New Haven: Yale University Press), 1993.

preoccupied by the girls' sin and eventual redemption through the virtues of motherhood, social workers, increasingly professionalized, saw them as "problem girls" who were the progeny of an increasingly corrupt society with ineffectual supervision of the young. Knockout drops helped these young women connect with both kinds of helpers by shifting the focus onto pregnancy as a result of drugging victimization rather than desire or premarital relationships. [55] Those who worked with unmarried pregnant girls, Kunzel notes, tended to be preoccupied with how they got that way. Both evangelical and social work–oriented supervisors saw themselves as frustrated in the search for the truth about the matter, and in return, girls revised and elaborated their stories until they made sense to the adults. Knockout drops were useful as they "kept sex unspeakable," which often owed more to the interpretive needs of the helpers than the girls themselves. "Many women were no doubt actually plied with alcohol," Kunzel writes, "but their loss of consciousness created literal black-outs in their stories that made their experience inaccessible to evangelical women and social workers."[56]

But as the white slavery panic around prostitution expanded, procurers and scoundrels were assumed to be bent on despoiling otherwise "respectable" girls.

One explanation of spiking intent that grew quite popular was the alleged systemic alliance between pub owners, bartenders, and procurers who used drugs to subdue their victims and later turn them out into prostitution. Temperance men of the late nineteenth century were particularly effective in supplying such cautionary tales, which were singularly focused on public drinking places. One reformed drinker told Charlton Edholm, who was a well-known Temperance activist and pamphleteer, that as a drunk he assisted procurers:

---

[55] Or, in some cases, being "merely" physically dominated during rape. The law at that time required women to fight an attacker "to the utmost" and, in some states, show visible signs of physical struggle or produce independent corroboration. It was an extremely high burden that discouraged sexual assault reporting well into the late twentieth century. See Susan Estrich, *Real Rape: How the Legal System Victimizes Women Who Say No*, (Cambridge MA: Harvard University Press), 1988. It may have shaped the way in which women interpreted rape victimization in relationship to legal recourse as well.

[56] Kunzel, 104–105.

2 Chloral and Its Sisters: Synthetic Genesis and Parallel Demon 49

> I would drop a little drug into whatever that girl had to eat or drink, and in a few moments she would be unconscious and that fellow would have a carriage drive to the door, that girl would be placed in it and driven right straight to a haunt of shame.[57]

In this way, Edholm and other women reformers of the time sought sympathy rather than condemnation of young women in prostitution, underscoring the accelerating preoccupation with "white-slave traffickers." White slavery as a concept drew on fears (and in many cases, by misrepresenting the nature of a myriad of real miseries) in order to advance a simpler, more conspiratorial view of the growth of prostitution and other vices like drug use. It could not, in the reformers' view, be populated without sudden, predatory, absconding violence. Whole legends of trickery and drugging surrounded some of the famous madams and gangsters of the time, with rural and middle-class girls as targets.

The possibility that the sex trade, drink, and drugs held their own attractions *sui generis*, to a generation of young men and women, could not be countenanced. The possibility of entering these worlds of vice voluntarily, or with a degree of curiosity or desire, seemed as impossible to middle-class reformers as the idea that young women might become pregnant as the result of voluntarily sleeping with men to whom they were attracted.

However, for Temperance women, the specter of drugs always necessarily led back to the evils produced by alcohol and the saloon. "The saloon and the brothel," Edholm wrote, "are twin barbarities." In the context of talking about her rescue mission work, she mentions one case in which she "buys" a girl out of such a place, but her claims about what would have happened had she chosen another route to help is, by its nature, ambiguous:

> Then we rescue workers did not dare to leave that child long enough to go for a policeman for we knew the moment our backs were turned a glass of whisky would be forced down her throat and when we would return with our police officer the cruel alcohol would have done its work and she would have forgotten about mother and about Jesus and would not want to go and you cannot force any one even out of a place like that. So we went

---

[57] Charlton Edholm, *Traffic in Girls and Work of Rescue Missions*. Chicago: The Temple, 1899.

down into our own pockets and handed the six dollars to that slave keeper and took that little girl with us to the Rescue Mission and there through the blood of the Lord Jesus Christ that cleansed you and cleansed me she was cleansed and today she is a happy wife and mother.[58]

In many ways, alcohol "acts" like drugs in these narratives about saloons. Drink must be forced down the girl's throat in order for her to remain. A shot of whisky is powerful—and multifaceted—enough for the girl to forgo her opportunity to leave. A few minutes delay to fetch a policeman is too much of a delay to save her.[59]

Loss of virtue (or sexual purity) is often conflated with prostitution in reform literature in much the way that it was among the medical defenders of chloroform. Kathy Peiss, in her study of working-class women's sexuality at the turn of the twentieth century through the lens of the records of vice commissions, suggests that many girls worried less about strict standards of virtue than their own ability to enjoy the meager fruits of their wage labor during their leisure time. "Charity girls" often engaged in sexual activity with men who were willing to treat them to nights out and the amusements that the cities had to offer. Other girls simply enjoyed sexual contact with these male companions and appeared to worry little that such activity would ruin them for life.[60] Either way, whether an expectation of sexual bartering was present or not, many young women desired access to a world of leisure and fun that men could provide for them, and there was little way for them to gain it otherwise—particularly if they were living at home and contributing to their parents' household, where domestic chores also added to their obligations. Reformers simply could not understand why girls would give up their most valuable asset. Though "social evil" abolitionists accused panderers of commodifying virginity, they clearly shared that same commercial view: once gone, ever

---

[58] Edholm, 16.

[59] An explanation of why the police were not fetched to the scene of alleged captivity often fails to accompany such rescue claims. It perhaps preserves the aura of powerful conspiracy and mystery; it obfuscates the push and pull of the girl's involvement, while simultaneously restraining from accusing the police of complicity.

[60] Kathy Peiss, "'Charity Girls' and City Pleasures: Historical Notes on Working-Class Sexuality, 1880–1920.," In J. Scanlon, ed., *The Gender and Consumer Culture Reader*, (New York: New York University Press), 2000.

scarred and unsalable as anything other than a fallen woman. Often times, reformers never bothered to speculate about girls' agency and motivation; if men had ill intent, that was all the explanation needed.

To Edholm and other reformers, though, all unchaperoned leisure leads to ruin, even if it steered clear of drug and drink. In this way, many such reformers signaled their discomfort with the pleasures enjoyed by the modern girl of the new twentieth century, including dancing. Edholm's widely circulated tract indicts waltz dancing in the same terms as other suspect experimentation, as it enlivens the sexual interest of young women.

Feminist historians have also reexamined assumptions about the sex trade made by the antiwhite slavery activist movements of the USA (in the 1900s and 1910s) and Great Britain (in the 1880s and 1890s).[61] Concern about the sex trade was animated not only by real increases in prostitution, but also by increased female participation in the workforce, particularly for poor and working-class women, which challenged Victorian norms. Reading backward, it seems apparent that the shift from "antialcohol" to "anti-saloon" activism in Late Temperance enhanced the Mickey Finn tales, aided by sordid testimonials and blind spots in the analysis of antivice reformers.

Enter the Saloon Villain

The active resistance the Temperance movement showed to indicting drugs tampering as a cause of intoxicated episodes was slipping away. In its place, we begin to see the rise of popular and reformer testimonies that indict (or romanticize) the saloon culture as a whole—with alcohol surely at the center, but the specter of criminal and predatory drink spiking, and gender and social class mixing creating the view of a debauched "third place" in American society.[62] But the transition from condemning drink

---

[61] Rosen, Ruth, *The Lost Sisterhood: Prostitution in America, 1900–1918*, Baltimore: Johns Hopkins University Press, 1982; Walkowitz, Judith R., *City of Dreadful Delight: Narratives of Sexual Danger in Late-Victorian London*, (Chicago: University of Chicago Press), 1992.
[62] "Third place" is a term coined by Ray Oldenburg (1989) in *The Great Good Place*. It means neither home nor work but third places to socialize, which Oldenburg sees in decline.

to focusing on the saloon and the public house begins earlier; again, this reflects Temperance's nimble response to critics who were increasingly successful at painting the movement as meddling in private affairs and choices, even threatening religious ritual involving drink.

Looking briefly into the lives of three women who were really were drugged and raped at the turn of the century, we can see not just how myth operates in cautionary tales and urban legends, but even as it attaches to, and shapes, real cases of violent victimization.

3

Good Girls, Hyenas, and Cheap Novel Fiends: The Scourge of Chloral at the Turn of the Twentieth Century

Introduction

Resonating as it did with our modern concern with date rape drugs, the *New York Daily News* ran on its historical pages in 2008 the story of one of the earliest sensational murder cases in the New York City region. The case, from the year 1900, involved four men charged in the murder of Jennie Bosschieter in Paterson, New Jersey, a rising industrial town. They had drugged the young woman's drink with chloral hydrate, raped her, and dumped her at an embankment near the Wagaraw Bridge. She was found the next morning, with an empty bottle of chloral nearby. The 2008 retrospective account began like this:

> On a mild October evening in 1900, a pretty teenager named Jennie Bosschieter walked to a drugstore from her home in Paterson, N.J., to fetch baby powder for an infant niece. She never returned. At next daybreak, a milkman found her body near the Passaic River. The "comely mill girl," as the 17-year-old came to be known in the newspapers, had been raped, then dumped beside the road like human trash.[1]

---

[1] David J. Kracijek, "Attacked by the Gang," *New York Daily News*, October 25, 2008. http://www.nydailynews.com/news/crime/attacked-gang-article-1.305483. Retrieved January 17, 2016.

© The Editor(s) (if applicable) and The Author(s) 2016
P. Donovan, *Drink Spiking and Predatory Drugging*,
DOI 10.1057/978-1-137-57517-3_3

This was a telling summary in that it reveals a continuing need for a script that barely resembles how it really came to be that Jennie was waylaid, brutalized, and left for dead. Similar transformations were made, at the time, of drugging victims Mabel Scofield in 1899 and Mary Paige in 1901 in the media's ongoing quest for the "perfect" victim. Working-class status, in the case of Jennie and Mary, and upper-middle-class status, in the case of Mabel, seem to figure decisively in how their stories are written and rewritten by news accounts, and perhaps by witnesses, in the days and weeks after their victimizations. In each case, parties sympathetic to the defendants were at work maligning the victims, but much of the newspaper coverage was sympathetic. Sympathy is arrived at, however, not by means of simple human pathos or solidarity, but in two other ways: an emphasis on the presence of chloral hydrate, and the transformation of these girls' activities—and thus the facts of the event—until they are what they need to be in order to elide blame and disparagement. The 2008 iteration in the *Daily News* suggests such a need to sanitize still exists.

Jennie's story, in particular, seems to have served as an origin story for the cautionary tales about drink spiking and drugging to follow in decades to come—up through the present day's outsize preoccupation with date rape drugs. Indeed, judgments about unchaperoned girls and girls drinking in public places are tied in directly to these cases. Implicit also is a suspicion of public sociability for women, even in sympathetic accounts.

Three Case Studies of Chloral as a Predatory Drug Against Women

A great deal can be learned about chloral hydrate ("chloral" in the truncated, widely used term of the day) and the drugging threat by looking at highly publicized real cases. Suspected drugging cases were unique enough to be reported in daily urban newspapers, and reasonably well-confirmed ones were an occasion for extensive publicity. Even speculation that a drugging accounted for a person's absence or amnesia was commonly reported, even when that explanation was later discarded and corrected. It is remarkable how much "drugging folklore" attaches even to real cases. No story, it turns out, speaks for itself; though it might be said that when chloral was present, it spoke louder than every other relevant circumstance.

Particularly when drugging and fatalities went together, major coverage ensued. Part of this fascination had to do with Americans' increasing concern about poison murders at the turn of the twentieth century. The entire field of forensic toxicology gained first its notoriety, and then its impeccable reputation, through news coverage of expert testimony in poison cases. "Medical jurisprudence, one of the liveliest areas of American medicine at this time," notes Mark Essig, "devoted more attention to poisoning than to any other topic but insanity."[2] Increasing popular concern about poisoning was fed by the ubiquitous news coverage of such cases:

> Every poison murder case that made it to trial raised the fear that scores more had gone undetected. This fear of undiscovered crime lay at the heart of the nineteenth-century obsession with poison murder. Poisoning involved a double secrecy. It was carried out secretly, within the home, behind closed doors, and usually by a person on intimate terms with the victim. This quality, though, was shared with other sorts of murder—one could, after all, bludgeon and shoot and stab in private. But there was another aspect to the secretness of poison: unlike other weapons, poison did its work on the interior of the body, leaving no visible signs of violence. Because the symptoms of some poisons resembled those of disease, it was often difficult to tell whether a person had died from poison or from natural causes.[3]

With poisons, as with both fatal and nonfatal drugging, uncertainty reigned. And because toxicology was still building a reputation for itself, uncertainty was a productive medium for both prosecutors and defense attorneys. What was, in fact, still unknowable yielded to certainty and exhortation in the courtroom and the press. Distinguished scientists often squared off on the expert witness circuit, each side maligning the other with implications of rushes-to-judgment, overconfidence, and fame-seeking. Dramatic courtroom demonstrations, involving everything from test tubes to sacrificing

---

[2] Mark Essig, "Poison Murder and Expert Testimony: Doubting the Physician in Late Nineteenth-Century America," *Yale Journal of Law & the Humanities*, Winter 2002, v14 n177.
[3] Essig, 2002.

cats to self-ingestion, in front of gasping juries, were the order of the day. Because often in these drugging cases, both the victims and the accused were young, the risk of error brought with it protective public sentiment and the moral risk of long-term miscarriages of justice.

Publicity in the papers had its own role to play; the tabloid-like standards of the day often meant that no rumor or claim, whether from an official source, a friend of a friend, a hanger-on, or someone interviewed on the street, was excluded from reporting on the cases. Wildly contradictory claims about the villains and the victims would often run on the same day. I noticed that in all three of the cases I am examining next, setting a pattern for drugging coverage to come, drugs trump everything else, and they shield the victim from otherwise harsh scrutiny as time wore on.

Below I examine three highly publicized chloral drugging cases, which alongside the general specter of knockout drops, provided a view of the problem for newspaper readers and reformers alike. Each of the female victims engaged in behavior that was normal and sociable from a modern viewpoint, but turn-of-the-century standards deviated from middle-class standards of behavior, a fact that prurient onlookers and detractors were only too eager to make mileage of. All three of the stories received national, rather than just regional, attention.

The Death of Mabel Scofield in Des Moines, 1899

Though the case of Jennie Bosschieter was more widely noted, it was a case the year earlier in Des Moines, Iowa that led to the development of several, overlapping popular accounts of drugging, and influenced the courts to examine exactly what *kind* of criminal intent and harm was embodied in dosing someone with chloral hydrate. The matter would not be settled in law immediately.

On October 22, 1899, the body of 21-year-old Mabel Scofield was pulled from the Des Moines River. She was fully dressed; in the same clothing she had worn the day before to see her visiting mother off to the train station. Mabel's body was notably unmarked; without signs of violence. Had she jumped into the river herself, in a fit of despondency, as some suggested? If she had been put in, who did it and why?

Interestingly, drugging with chloral was long suspected even before tests would, three years later, confirm its presence in her body. The local newspapers bandied about a number of engaging guesses, ranging from hypnosis by a "Svengali in disguise" to a sudden fit of suicidal despair over her foundering ambitions. Though elaborate speculation began in the papers immediately, the lapse of time between when Mabel died and her killer was arrested in 1902 meant that a variety of favored stories had time to flourish. Details of her death would be countenanced, then contradicted. The Scofield case became a major Midwestern preoccupation. Like other drugging victims who made the news, Mabel's case did not neatly fit into the symbolic needs of the press, and a considerable period of uncertainty enabled Mabel's brief life and tragic death to be rewritten again and again. These themes seemed almost a mirror image of the rewriting that went on of Jennie Bosschieter and Mary Paige as victims, and this appears to have some relationship to Mabel's distinct class origins.

Most speculations about Mabel's death favored the involvement of drugs somehow. By November 1, coverage was thick and wide ranging— including summaries of facts known to date, exhortations from various officials that the future of Des Moines hinged on the ability of the police to secure the safety of young women in the city, and reviews of theories of Mabel's death. Her death galvanized a whole set of social concerns about the growing city—and Des Moines opinion-makers hoped to save its reputation with a quick arrest. "Des Moines," wrote the city's *Daily News*, "owes that much to itself."[4] But this was not to be. Instead, a drama of innocent prairie girl destroyed by urban danger developed—up to a point.

Des Moines was founded in the 1850s at the nexus of the Des Moines and Raccoon Rivers. It became Iowa's largest city and industrial center. People flocked in from rural areas and other countries to work there. Boarding house life grew. For many young people like Mabel, it was a place desired for its opportunity—she aimed to become a dressmaker, and wanted experience in the dressmaking shops. Mabel hailed from the prairie town of Macksburg. Her father was a prominent physician, and he and her mother encouraged her artistic interests. Though they anticipated

---

[4] *Des Moines Daily News*, "Des Moines Duty," November 1, 1899, 2.

sending her to college, it was with their blessing that she went to Des Moines to learn the dressmaking trade. Yet she wrote to a friend not long after arriving in September that "working in the shops was not altogether a butterfly life."[5] Despite being unemployed when her mother came to visit in October, she planned to stay on to learn more.

There was never any suspicion of Mabel being "of unchaste character" before her death—a topic that would inevitably come up in later cases involving working-class girls. But the newspapers nonetheless seemed to have a need to see Mabel as a walking target for a variety of predatory forces in the big city. The facts of the case were faithfully reported, though often ignored as this theme developed. Eventually held in her murder was Charles Thomas, a relative of the boarding house keeper who had come under wide suspicion earlier despite an apparent alibi. He was charged several times, and freed, without trial until finally indicted and convicted in 1906. Notwithstanding the urban predation theme that emerged in the papers, Thomas' family came from Macksburg as well. Eventually police discovered that he had obtained chloral hydrate from a pharmacist on two different occasions, under false pretenses, and prosecutors charged that he administered it to Mabel at the boarding house. When she died, they said he enlisted friends to take her in a carriage to the river, leaving tire tracks on the banks that would eventually add to the substantial circumstantial evidence against him.

Thomas was convicted of murder in the first degree, sentenced, and imprisoned, but the case would go on in appeals courts for years. While a number of appeals were made about the quality of the evidence against him, the most consistent issue was the question not yet settled by law: clearly the predatory use of chloral was a form of criminal harm, but what kind was it? Akin to assault? Poisoning? Reckless behavior? If it could not be proved that the accused aimed at murder by administering knockout drops, should murder in the first degree apply? And was this a matter for a jury to sort out, or did the law on poisons cover it clearly enough? Criminal statutes in most states were ambiguous on the matter; they were really designed to address "poison" as a clear indication of premeditation to murder. Felony murder laws in the USA, on the other hand, in which

---

[5] *Daily Iowa Capital,* "Believe She Was Murdered," November 1, 1899, 2.

intent is "transferable" from another crime to first- or second-degree murder, if a death should occur, regardless of whether intent to kill can be established, have always varied from state to state. They have evolved based upon significant cases; not all *actus reus* (specific intended actions, usually physical, of the accused) establishing another felony crime will qualify as consequential if a death occurs. Poison had been specified as such an establishing act in its own right in most places, including Iowa, at the turn of the twentieth century, but chloral hydrate and opiates were not then considered poisons per se. They were medicines, and even when obtained with ill intent, often came in pharmaceutical form. In the Scofield case, speculation aired that, suffering from chronic headaches and having access to her father's pharmaceutical chest, Mabel might have taken the chloral herself. Evidence gathered at the time could not establish whether Mabel had died from ingesting chloral hydrate, or inhaling chloroform, or both.

Further complicating matters, the reluctance of male physicians to vigorously seek out evidence of sexual assault of female homicide victims, in deference to their families' sensitivities, often made the presumption of sexual assault weak once the prosecution arrived at the courtroom, even if that intent hewed to a fairly common-sense interpretation of the circumstances. In the Scofield case, the medical examiners had admitted that they spared Mabel's father the pain of knowing whether his daughter had been violated.[6] In this case and in others, the question was often in the hands of the jury without any forensic evidence.

Delays in the Scofield case were numerous. Thomas was not tried until 1905, as the police sought accomplices that they hoped to indict. The case remained a sensation, however. A $2500 reward leading to conviction apparently muddied the water a bit. The trial was held at the downtown Young Men's Christian Association (YMCA) due to overflow crowds.[7] The crowds seemed to see it as a group crime by its nature, though it was never really established that Thomas involved others beyond disposing of the body at nightfall.[8] Thomas' appeal raised a number of objections; only

---

[6] *Des Moines Daily News*, "Arrested for the Killing of Mabel Scofield," January 12, 1902, 1–2.
[7] *Duluth News Tribune*, "Will Attempt to Prove an Alibi," February 19, 1905, 9.
[8] *Des Moines Daily News*, "Arrested …" 1902.

a few are of interest here.[9] Thomas' counsel tried to raise the question of whether unintentional death through the administration of chloral could not really constitute manslaughter rather than murder and argued that lesser charges should have been offered to the jury. Iowa's death by poison statute, Code 4278, was seen by the higher court to be unambiguous, though it did not define poison nor specifically address drugging. Drugs as a means of harm were addressed separately, and that count against Thomas was eventually dropped—leaving only an allegation of "poison." The prosecutors had avoided the felony murder confusion by simply omitting rape charges—thus turning a lack of evidence gathered in their favor—and seeking to prove death by poison directly. Although Thomas' appeal on this matter was denied, the court turned to previous cases, small in number and just emerging in the first decade of the twentieth century, to address the issue of malice aforethought in drugging and poisoning.[10] Yet the point had been made—Iowa, like many other states, had not well established a logical chain of events in defining predatory drugging deaths under the "poison" rubric, and once chosen, the label "poison" posed its own questions rather than providing a clear typology of harm.

Paracelsus may have famously reminded healers and scientists that everything and nothing is a poison; that poisoning is a matter of dosage. But the status of chloral hydrate at the turn of the century was in flux; even its detractors would not have automatically equated its use and intent to poison—and there was no separate set of laws that covered involuntary intoxication, except as a criminal *defense* of limited scope.[11]

---

[9] The Supreme Court of Iowa ruled to affirm Thomas' conviction on November 21, 1906. *State v. Thomas*, in *Northwestern Reporter*, Vol. 109, 900; W.W. Cornwall (1908) *Reports of Cases at Law and in Equity Determined by the Supreme Court of the State of Iowa, May and September Terms, 1907*. Vol. XVIII. Chicago: T.H. Flood Publishers, 719–733.

[10] The irony was that when appealing the jury charge of murder alone and omitting manslaughter as an option, Thomas' counsel was the one who had to imply, though not specify, a motivation distinct from murder in the administration of "poison" (Supreme Court of Iowa, 1907). Thomas' counsel continued to argue that the alibi evidence had not been given its due, but it also argued that if Thomas had, as one witness testified, said that he'd accidentally killed Mabel with chloral, it was not because he was attempting to subdue or poison her but rather to administer a widely used narcotic pain reliever. The felony-to-murder transferability issue was not as easily settled without either sexual assault or poison murder as a primary intent.

[11] For a history of the involuntary intoxication defense, see S.M. Boyne and G.C. Mitchell, "Death in the Desert: A New Look at the Involuntary Intoxication Defense in New Mexico," *New Mexico Law Review*, Vol. 32, Spring 2002, 243–275.

A Date with Death: The Bosschieter Case

The murder of Jennie Bosschieter in Paterson confounded ideas of criminal harm as well. But the facts of her death were known within days, at least by looking at the clearest inferences from even the contradictory evidence given by the accused at the time. Jennie, aged 17 and working at a ribbon factory, was found dead on October 19, 1900. The previous evening, according to the testimony of her sister and mother, Jennie went out for the evening.[12] When her mother asked if she would pick up some baby powder for a niece, she replied that she might not return home that evening. Her mother testified that she believed Jennie might stay with a candy shop owner, Mrs. Klatte, as she had before when out later downtown.

The evening was warm and breezy, and a campaign parade went through downtown; many witnesses were about and saw Jennie out on the street. Meeting up with William Death, a former suitor, and Andrew Campbell, she chatted with them, greeted a neighbor passing by who perhaps heard her demurring either politely or sharply ("No, no") on Campbell's offer of a drink. Nonetheless, only a few minutes later, she was seen walking with two men into Saal's saloon. She sat with four men in a back parlor. These men were George Kerr, Walter McAlister, Andrew Campbell, and William Death, who would be charged with her murder. She had previously dated Death (actually pronounced "deeth"), but he married another young woman about a month earlier. Teasing him by stealing his tie pin, she may have demanded an explanation for the marriage at the saloon. She had several drinks, according to the bar owner, including an absinthe frappe, and the state charged—based on confessions of the others—that McAlister put chloral hydrate in her drink. Jennie had worked at McAlister's factory; in the wake of Jennie's murder, Walter's father, James, shut down the ribbon mill, which he had let Walter run for six years.[13]

---

[12] In using the term "testify," I refer to the published court record of the trial of Walter McAlister and accomplices and not newspaper summaries of the trial except where noted. Passaic County Oyer And Terminer, State Of New Jersey, Trial of Walter C. McAlister, Andrew J. Campbell, and William A. Death for the Murder of Jennie Bosschieter, 1901, Paterson: Paterson Publishing Co.

[13] *Fibre And Fabric*, November 10, 1900, vol. 32, no. 819, 148.

She went out in a carriage hired by Kerr—limp and unconscious, through a side door, according to the carriage hack's testimony, or upright but woozy, according to other witnesses—with them. The hack, August Sculthorpe, also testified that they raped her in a field while she was unconscious, then loaded her back in the carriage and tried to revive her, unsuccessfully. When a small-hours visit to a doctor brought the news she was dead, the men paid off the hack to let them dump her body near the Wagaraw Bridge.

Naturally, the men had a different story, though their cases were hobbled by two of them confessing during initial interrogation, in hopes that they would be spared the death penalty. The defense argued that not only had no one dosed Jennie's drink, the men had not raped her, either, and were guilty only of poor judgment under influence of panic when Jennie died. They claimed that Jennie seemed "dopey" at the tavern and that they hired a hack to take her out for some fresh air. They pulled her out of the hack onto a field, they said, in order to facilitate her vomiting, and did not assault her. It was true that initially the hack had said it was too dark to see anything when he returned from turning his rig around, and only later claimed that he had seen the men assaulting her. The defense found it fairly easy to impeach the integrity of this sole eyewitness—who changed his story and initially agreed to silence on the matter for the price of ten dollars that McAlister offered him. Of course, this same observation about Sculthorpe as an unreliable witness underscored the apparently guilty conscience of the defendants in offering the bribe in the first place. On the other hand, it meant the prosecution's star witness was a man who failed to protest a gang rape and body dump, and whose silence was easily bought. Sculthorpe (and the prosecution who used him as their star witness) faced rough music from those who were outraged by the murder, for standing by during the crime, and yet again from his fellow hackmen, for squealing on a customer.[14] Sculthorpe had his disadvantages as a star witness, not the least of which is that he stood idly by. (At one point, he told the *Herald* that McAlister and Kerr had threatened him at gunpoint, but this claim did not emerge in court.)[15]

---

[14] Nelson, S. G., "Bosschieter Verdict Approved in Paterson," *Brooklyn Daily Eagle*, January 19, 1901, 6.

[15] *New York Herald*, "Fear of Lynching in Paterson Murder," October 25, 1900, 7.

Were it not for the presence of chloral hydrate, the defense might have prevailed on the numerous uncertainties in the case. Malice aforethought was clearly what the prosecution hoped to prove by bringing in a widely renowned toxicologist, Dr. Rudolph Witthaus of Columbia University, who testified that his lab examination revealed about 5 grains of chloral in Jennie's stomach. (Conveniently, Sculthorpe, on a visit several days later to the body-dumping site with the police, located a small vial that turned out to have chloral in it, about 80–100 yards away from where the body was found.) The police initially made much of finding out that the chloral came from the same drug store—Kent's—where Jennie was seen on the street, and alleging that McAlister had improperly obtained it there. Nonetheless, nothing more about the bottle—other than its distance from the body—was actually presented at trial, despite reports in the paper that police had suspected at least one clerk of illegal, unregistered chloral sales.[16]

Witthaus used the Pellagri test and other similar tests as his testimony centered on producing a color match with chloral. The defense attorney instead tried to blame Jennie's death on the absinthe and the rapid ingestion of several servings of alcohol, producing their own toxicologist, a Dr. Horace Vandenberg, who clashed with Witthaus more than once in this era of courtroom parlor tricks. Vandenberg muddied the waters with the testimony that he produced "the same effect" in the laboratory with absinthe, whisky, champagne—which he purchased from the same saloon owner, Christopher Saal, and the same embalming fluid used to embalm Jennie's body before any examination had taken place. This claim was authoritative sounding but vague for the jury, as Vandenberg was never asked to explain what he meant by "the same effect" by either the prosecution or the defense. Vandenburg surmised how powerful the alcohol and absinthe might have been, and indirectly raised suspicion about the embalming process.

But testing for poisons and drugs was not entirely a settled matter of science, and skepticism about such tests was warranted. In fact, Witthaus

---

[16] *New York World*. "May Escape through Power of Wealth," October 25, 1900, 2. Ultimately, it does not appear that the specific bottle or any specific drug store sale was linked by the prosecutor to Jennie's death.

had squared off with other skeptics of the Pellagri test, in previous trials.[17] But given that toxicology was a rudimentary science at the time, it seems that neither side in the Bosschieter case dared explore the matter more. Indeed, the prosecutor Emley's approach to cross-examining Vandenberg was to briefly attack his credentials,[18] and then abandon the cross at the defense's first objection, simply hoping that Witthaus was more compelling, and that the Kent's bottle would create the proper inference. The relatively small dose that Witthaus estimated Jennie had been given was not remarked upon either.[19] Two other expert witnesses agreed that such a dose could have killed her.

Witthaus was not called in merely on his reputation, however. His portfolio on the forensic detection of chloral hydrate misuse specifically was significant. One key element of understanding chloral fatalities is that the drug can in some cases kill even at below therapeutic doses, and in other cases, can be ingested at high levels without causing death.[20] This variability was not always well understood by the public at large, nor was

---

[17] Dr. Victor Vaughan had challenged the accuracy of the Pellagri test in earlier trials where Witthaus had been a prosecution witness, such as the trial of Robert Buchanan in New York in 1893 for the killing of his wife by morphine overdose. In Vaughan's memoir, he noted that the Pellagri was considered unreliable by European courts, but that he knew New York courts use it widely and Witthaus had confidence in it. In the case of Buchanan, prosecution witnesses could not pick out the morphine sample from others based on color reaction, and Vaughan notes that visual differentiation was not easy. See Victor C. Vaughan, *A Doctor's Memories*, (Minneapolis, MN: Bobbs-Merrill), 1926. Buchanan, like the men who attacked Jennie Bosschieter, was convicted for other reasons. The dispute about the role of impure lab solvents throwing these tests off continued for years. The technique for conducting such tests can be found in Rudolph Witthaus' own *The Medical Student's Manual of Chemistry* (New York: William Wood and Company), 1906, and his own concerns about its limitations in the postmortem setting with suspected drugging are noted in his 1894 textbook, *Medical Jurisprudence, Forensic Medicine and Toxicology, Vol. 4* at page 132. I refer here, however, to the 1896 version (New York: William Wood, Publisher).

[18] Emley couldn't be too aggressive, however, since Vandenburg had been an instructor at New York City's Loomis Lab, which Witthaus had run the previous decade. Vandenburg's inference that embalming fluid can muddy postmortem toxicological results comes directly from concerns raised in Witthaus' own texts. The problem remained a lively one in scientific discussion and several scientists' work on the matter, including Witthaus', are reviewed in John James Reese and Henry Leffmann's 1903 *Text-book of Medical Jurisprudence and Toxicology* (Philadelphia: P. Blakiston's Son).

[19] Witthaus found 5 grains in her stomach, and estimated that she took a 10 grain dose. On the stand, Witthaus described 20 grains as potentially fatal. Using modern conversions, the 10 estimated grains would amount to 0.65 g. None was found in the embalming fluid. Medscape (reference.medscape.com) describes a typical therapeutic dose as 0.5–1.0 g.

[20] Witthaus, 1896.

the recognition that narcotics and alcohol potentially produced a synergistic effect. Although the physician first consulted by Police Chief Graul to examine Jennie's body said he considered the combination of alcohol and chloral potentially lethal, skepticism about alcohol's role abounded.[21] Under cross, in fact, Witthaus argued that he did not think that "a person could drink enough Manhattan cocktails to kill him."[22]

Unremarked at the time, though, was the curious conjunction of Witthaus' testimony in the Bosschieter case with soon-to-be-publicized court proceedings in Westchester County, New York. The former Mrs. Witthaus, as part of a continuing divorce proceeding against the professor, claimed that the doctor had, starting early in their marriage, prescribed her poisons of various sorts to treat her ailments. Appearing in court in "stylish" attire, Bly asked that her previous divorce settlement of 1897 be vacated, and averred that when she took ill in 1883, Witthaus "used his skill as a chemist to administer poisons to her to deprive her of her reason." An expert in Witthaus' defense claimed the chemicals—among them cocaine and arsenic in small amounts—were harmless in the recommended doses, and Witthaus counterclaimed that the former Mrs. Witthaus simply wanted more of the doctor's wealth.[23] Bly Witthaus' allegations, after years of bitter divorce proceedings, were first reported on in the *New York Times* in 1898.[24] Bly lost her suit in 1901.

Witthaus had developed a degree of prominence in the emerging area of poison and toxicology in part because of his 1894 textbook, *Medical Jurisprudence, Forensic Medicine and Toxicology*. Though making no specific note of chloral hydrate, he noted in it that "maniacal excitement" and "stuperous insanity" not uncommonly followed the administration of ether or chloroform.[25] A few decades of experimentation with anesthetic innovations had made doctors widely aware of this common paradoxical effect of otherwise narcotic-like drugs, in some cases, especially in the first few minutes after administration. Debate about the nature of

---

[21] Passaic County Oyer and Terminer, 1901.
[22] *New York Times*, "Jennie Bosschieter Killed by Chloral" January 15, 1901.
[23] *New York Times*, "Mrs. Witthaus Wants Her Divorce Vacated," March 3, 1901, 12.
[24] *New York Times*, "Mrs. Witthaus Charges," January 25, 1898. Via *New York Times* Archive.
[25] Witthaus, 1896.

this observation had gone on for decades. Would people truly act against character under the influence of a heavy drug? If so, where did responsibility lie if crime or violence, or allegations of it, emerged?

As to the allegation of rape—crucial in establishing the felony murder sequence and thus murder in the first degree—the prosecution could only hope to infer it from Sculthorpe's testimony and the initial confessions that Campbell and Death later recanted. The coroner's physicians had autopsied Jennie and found nothing remarkable in their pelvic dissection. Worse yet, Jennie's several petticoats and undergarments were intact and without stains. The prosecution averred that one of many undergarments was missing, with the implication that the men had taken it away to hide the assault, but it had never been established that she had been wearing it in the first place. As much as possible, the prosecution avoided the problem of physical evidence by trying to build a rather elaborate—and ultimately rickety—scenario of conspiracy and premeditation to lure Jennie into the country and rape her. While it was reported in the papers that McAlister had tried to drug another girl a few weeks earlier, this did not come up at trial. At one point, Judge Dixon himself ordered an investigation into these claims of Elizabeth Schaub, having read about it in the papers.

But in the Bosschieter case, inference as to the most likely case from circumstantial evidence won the day, though the jury hedged its bets with the finding of murder in the second degree rather than the first. Though to modern eyes, the absence of forensic evidence beyond that of the chloral in Jennie's stomach looks like intentional ellipsis, it must be remembered that toxicology was in its infancy, as were fingerprinting and blood typing. Only forensic dissection at autopsy was well established, and even then, doctors who performed them preferred description and left judgments to the coroner. Nonetheless, the callousness of the panicked body dump left a lasting impression, and McAlister's machinations afterward—bribing not only Sculthorpe but intending to buy off Christopher Saal—tipped his hand toward showing a conscience of guilt.

The men were convicted at trial and served a range of sentences, up to 15 years, though they were sentenced to 30. Had they been convicted of first-degree murder, they could have faced the death penalty. The judge was angered that the jury only saw fit to convict on murder in the second degree, which usually applies to unplanned fatal violence. Yet the law with regard to murder by poison at the time (New Jersey, 1895, statute 271) circumvented the interim possibility of assault with it—sexually motivated or otherwise. Poison was described as a means to murder, and whether it could be means to something else absent the intent to murder was simply not addressed. Essentially, it became a question for the jury to decide what kind of criminal harm had actually taken place.

The defense attorney had hooked onto a popular concern when he tried to shift blame onto Jennie's voluntary consumption of absinthe. The USA eventually banned the spirit in 1912, and it had a reputation as being more than the sum of its parts; the "green fairy" for its tinted color and was thought to be chemically more potent than other spirits.[26] "Are you not astounded," said the defense attorney in summation in the Bosschieter case, "by the fact that this girl … not quite 18 years of age, yet drinking poison in this manner?"[27] So far as the testimony went, it was a glass with some, or a pony glass full, or perhaps a frappe—a great deal, in any case. A defense witness, New York physician Charles Laffin, was brought in to emphasize the dangers of absinthe. On an empty stomach, he said, it would produce excitation and then "complete collapse." On cross-examination, he averred that chloral and absinthe would be "double poison." Though absinthe was regarded as a special kind of scourge, production continued to increase through the late 1800s and early 1900s. In truth, given its licorice-like flavor, it is simply easier to overconsume than other high-proof spirits. Jennie also drank whisky and champagne that night.

But chloral trumped absinthe in the public mind. Though many thought the latter dangerous, news coverage of its scourge status in Europe made it seem perilous in a sort of humorous mayhem way. Not so with chloral. Chloral was seen as a medical wonder, but a serious sedative

---

[26] "Absinthe was banned in America in 1912 because of health concerns fanned by some of the same anti-alcohol forces who would later push through Prohibition. Due to a reorganization of the government's food-safety bureaucracy, the ban was effectively lifted before World War II, although it took decades before anybody realized it." The first new approvals for sale in the USA were in 2007. Pete Wells, "Liquor of Legend Makes a Comeback," *New York Times*, December 5, 2007. http://www.nytimes.com/2007/12/05/dining/05absi.html?_r=0. Retrieved January 17, 2016.

[27] Passaic County Oyer and Terminer, 1901.

as well. In the defense's summary statement, counsel Scott let the jury know—accurately—that other courts had not yet settled the matter in cases where there was any indication that a fatal poison dose was not the criminal intent. Indeed, the men claimed they thought she had passed out from the drink and hoped a carriage ride would revive her.

Further complicating matters was the difference in class status between Bosschieter and the four men that did her in. They were middle-class young men, two were married, and each had connections with Paterson's government and merchant class. Jennie, a Dutch immigrant, worked in a ribbon factory. Quickly, partisans of victim and accused presented competing images of the girl: was she the innocent led astray on a baby powder errand? Or was she a drunk and freely affectionate girl who was poisoned by alcohol too rapidly consumed, accompanied by young men who took only what she happily offered, and were guilty only of panicking when she died? The *New York Times* truncated mother Dina Bosschieter's testimony to highlight the errand and downplayed Jennie's intention to be out for a while, and perhaps overnight.[28] Other papers, including the *Tribune*, were more candid about Jennie's freedom to be out in the evenings socializing, which her mother and sister confirmed.

But in the weeks leading up to the trial, Jennie's family, perhaps out of misplaced guilt or the desire to present her in the "best" light, kept revising her habits over and over. Her sister said she did not know Jennie to drink. Then, when the four suspects were arrested, she said that Jennie had never liked McAlister, and though willing to drink with him, found him "too fast." For many opinion-makers, then, sympathy required a middle-class script of propriety. So either witnesses or the papers themselves would simply change the details. The *Brooklyn Daily Eagle* was a bit more straightforward:

> Jennie was a type of too many of her sisterhood. She had graces of person and was well favoured; she was poor, but had the fondness of her class for finery and display. No greatly dishonoring accusation is made against her, but the eyes of the hyenas were upon her, and her indifference to propriety must be conceded.[29]

---

[28] *New York Times*, "Bosschieter Murder Details Told in Court," January 14, 1901.
[29] Nelson, 1901.

Patronizing as it was, it was hardly damning. Indeed, the description seems to emerge of a pretty girl who was determined to carve out a small sphere of autonomy, enjoyment, and sociability for herself in an otherwise bleak factory town that could not provide her with much more than sporadic work and a crowded, impoverished home where she also has some domestic responsibility. As for fetching baby powder, she would do it, but perhaps not until returning in the morning. In retellings of the story, this matter always drops away. The *Daily Eagle* did condemn the young people of Paterson as engaged in a "condition of immorality" in which young men and women were "mutually corrupting" but does not see Jennie as particularly flagrant in this respect.

The *New York Times* also reported on class politics of the case. An article on the convicts' transport to serve their 30-year sentences detailed the gentlemanly indulgences they were given beforehand, and the taunting of crowds, composed of "factory hands" gathered along their path through Trenton.[30] Local labor opinion sided with the girl's family. In Paterson's socialist paper, Editor Daniel DeLeon frames the murder (and the vicious whispers after) in terms of stark class war, less than a week after the incident, on October 26. Jennie was a factory girl and her assailants "thugs ... of the kid-glove class" and hypocrites who pretend to respectability.[31] At times, sidelining the drugs issue seems important. "Such things have been done before. 'Knockout drops' have not always been administered. Many a girl has been ruined by the liquor which such degenerates have persuaded her to drink. Then, when she was helpless, they have ruined her." Smuggled in Jennie's defense, then, is the assumption that Jennie would not care to drink unless implored by these men—one of them, Death, whom she had previously dated. Nonetheless, in the next paragraph, he defends her right to drink without fear of violation and death—the only publication to explicitly do so. He takes the "capitalist papers" to task for calling her a prostitute and a "depraved girl" in DeLeon's paraphrase, naming the *Sun, Journal, World, Tribune,* and *Herald*. He spares the *New York Times*.

---

[30] *New York Times*, "Hoot Bosschieter Convicts," February 2, 1901, 6.
[31] Daniel DeLeon, "The Paterson Murder," *Daily People*, vol. 1, no. 118, October 26, 1901, 1.

This was a curious interpretation on DeLeon's part. My examination of the coverage of the crime in the *New York Herald*, *New York World*, and *New York Sun* gave me a much different impression.[32] Neither the *Herald* nor the *Sun* implied this, although the *New York World* did seem to insinuate, particularly in its earliest coverage of the case, that Jennie sought out the company of men wealthier than her and that she liked to go out at night.[33] But the tone in the other papers became more uniform once the arrests were made and the stark class elements of the case came into relief.[34] Not only was the coverage in the papers sympathetic to Jennie and her family, it devoted a great deal of attention to the vicious reputation of Walter McAlister in particular and continuously returned to the allegations that his companions were unsavory characters at best, and scandalized by what it called McAlister's "haughty" behavior in the courtroom.

The papers often seemed to share a sense of urgency that they attributed to citizens, indicting the police and prosecutor for moving too slowly on a number of fronts, and underscoring the popular fear of Paterson's working-class residents that the affluent young men who were accused would find some way to buy their way out of just deserts. The *New Haven Register* described McAlister—known as "Sporty" to his friends—as a man of "fast horses and big diamonds."[35] The papers were the ones who sought out other women who said they were drugged by McAlister. The *Herald*'s only suspicion of popular outrage—and this was more a matter of tone than strong advocacy—was against the assemblies that gathered daily outside the jail and courthouse, which the *Herald* took as a possibly menacing sign of impending vigilantism.

Indeed, the *Herald*'s and the *World*'s investigations of the case seemed to turn up a history of personal threats to Jennie around every corner,

---

[32] The New York papers the *Times*, *Herald*, *World*, *Tribune*, and *Sun* are available for most of the relevant dates in archive form, while the *Journal* is not. The *Times* maintains its own archive, and the *Herald*, *World*, *Tribune*, and *Sun* are available at the Library of Congress.

[33] *New York World*, "Quick Justice for Mill Girl's Slayers," October 26, 1900, 1; "Jury Hears of Bosschieter's Death," January 14, 1901, 2.

[34] *New York Sun*, "Paterson's Murder Case," October 30, 1900, 10.

[35] *New Haven Register*, "Slayers of Girl Confess; Mill Girl was Drugged and Done to Death by Four Men," October 24, 1900, 11.

reporting on previous incidents where suitors treated her roughly, or threatened her in a letter. Of course, these threats, discovered as second-hand stories, came from her peers. It also saw Jennie's murder in the context of the "mashers" like McAlister who hung around the drug stores and preyed on girls like her. Then again, DeLeon believed the case represented an indictment of current society. "What sort of a system is it that can make the depravity of a child an excuse for such savagery as only a moribund civilization can bring to light?" Jennie represented many conflicting things to the press, partisan and mainstream, even sometimes within the same article.

But the matter of "depravity" on Jennie's part seemed in dispute. The commentary I saw in the newspapers clearly used the term to refer to the accused rather than the victim. Indeed, it is DeLeon who sees the possibility of the drinking girls' "ruin" through drink itself, if not drugging. The prosecutor's summation also seemed to imply that the panicked men's small-hours flight with Jennie to Drs. Wiley and Townsend was an action that potentially made the situation worse: if either had successfully revived her, she would then know she had been cruelly abused. Death in the field, he said, was the true mercy. One wonders if Bosschieter's friends and family felt the same way. The idea that drugging assaults are merciful while being still depraved may have started early, but it has not disappeared.

In the end, though, attempts by the defense to paint Bosschieter as the unlucky fun-seeking girl were thwarted by the presence of chloral hydrate. For this, the defendants had no explanation, or at least any that they dared introduce as theories, for fear of introducing material that could be countered. The defense could only argue on the uncertainty associated with chloral's dangers compared with those of alcohol and absinthe particularly. Had it really killed her? What if it had put her into a manic state instead? What was it that they had intended? The defense never conceded that their clients had administered chloral, but Death and Campbell said initially—during their contested station house confessions—that McAlister had dosed her drink. Though they later claimed coercion and that police fabricated portions of their statements, this possibility is lessened by the fact that Campbell was known to Officer Titus—and on the stand at trial, Titus broke down and cried at the reminiscence of the moment he realized that young Andrew was involved in such a thing.

The Bosschieter case allowed speculation, then, about Jennie's role under the influence, not just because the law at the time represented retrograde views of sexual violence, but because the whole question of action and reaction between persons under the influence of drug and alcohol remained an open question. Even death at the hand of a surreptitious chloral dose was understood to be harm, but not yet fully confirmed as on-its-face evidence of intent to kill.

Campbell, McAlister, and Death were convicted of second-degree murder only on January 20, on the same day that the case of Dr. Elster's drugged robbery in Newark was reported.[36] It is fair to say that crimes involving drugs had become quite newsworthy. A day later, a San Francisco newspaper reported on a New York death that "may rival the Jennie Bosschieter affair," while a Los Angeles paper said it paralleled the "Paterson Murder Case."[37] Two young people, a man and a woman, checked into Trabold's Hotel uptown under the age-old tryst identity, Mr. and Mrs. Smith. At some later point, they ordered sherry and then were oddly quiet in the hours after. The manager eventually opened their room to find the young woman dead, and the young man crouched in the corner, holding the woman's hat, muttering incoherently and occasionally shouting "she's gone to hell!" Both were fully clothed. Chloral in the drinks was suspected by investigators. The papers speculated that Clarence Davis had attempted to drug Margaret Travis, and then when she died, took the chloral himself. The underlying assumption was that he was attempting suicide; the alternative theory was that they had made a suicide pact and he had survived. No one considered the possibility that they had taken chloral together without suicidal intent.

Dr. Rudolph Witthaus continued to have a successful professional career as a sought-after expert witness and moved from Columbia University to Cornell University. He died in 1915, at age 69. Within the

---

[36] The convictions carried a penalty of up to 30 years—the maximum prison sentence at the time. Kerr, who had successfully petitioned for a severance of trials from the other three (his presence at Saal's could not be established, and therefore neither could his knowledge of the drugging), pled *non vult* on January 29 to rape, which Judge Dixon remarked seemed to contradict the second-degree murder convictions of the other three. Kerr was sentenced to 15 years, serving 11 of them.

[37] *San Francisco Call*, "Mystery Veils A Girl's Death," January 22, 1901, 3; *Los Angeles Herald*, "A Parallel to Paterson Murder Case," January 22, 1901, 3.

year, the *New York Times* reported that his will was challenged by relatives who accused his companion, Jennie Cowan, of continuously plying him with a "large amount of whisky, gin, and other intoxicants" that caused his incompetence and then his death. Cowan eventually defeated the challenge in 1919.[38]

Mary Paige Case: Brooklyn, New York, 1901

At this time, perhaps owing to the notoriety of the Scofield and Bosschieter cases, drugging and malicious adulteration of foods and beverages became a common speculation for the unaccounted time of people gone temporarily missing, and for the vulnerability of crime victims. Just one day after the verdicts in the Bosschieter case were delivered, the *Brooklyn Daily Eagle* reported that the wife of prominent doctor Russell Fowler had been drugged and forced into a cab, a claim later recanted.[39] On the same day that the Mary Paige story broke, an actress named Rose Tiffany resurfaced, telling a remarkable tale of misfortune. The Tiffanys were from New York, but Rose was first reported missing from Chicago by her mother (also a stage actress, Annie Ward Tiffany) on March 12, after she failed to show for a production of "Monte Cristo."[40] On the 14th, the *Des Moines Daily News* described what they called a "weird story"—Tiffany said she was lured to the Auditorium Annex restaurant by someone claiming to be a friend of her mother's and "induced" to eat a lobster salad, raw oysters, and claret, after which she was dispatched to Joliet.[41] The *Minneapolis Journal* article reported that Rose had returned with a terrific headache, after a sleepy sojourn to Joliet via train with this stranger, an older "richly dressed" woman. She returned to her boarding house unable to relate much else about the episode, other than that she apparently slept for a day after renting a hotel room. Drugging and drink spiking was a kind of available account to explain absences and ellipses

---

[38] *New York Times*, "Dr. Witthaus' Will Attacked in Court," September 22, 1916.
[39] *Brooklyn Daily Eagle*, "Queer Tale of Adventure Related by Mrs. Fowler," January 19, 1901, 1.
[40] *Minneapolis Journal*, "Actress Abducted: Rose Tiffany's Strange Story of her Disappearance," March 13, 1901, 2.
[41] *Des Moines Daily News*, "Actress Comes Back," March 14, 1901, 5.

in the continuity of personal time. And much like contemporary news accounts, no further reports in the media ensued to clarify what had happened to the young actress, despite her family's developing fame in US theater.

But no drugging and assault case brought greater notoriety on the heels of the Bosschieter case than did the case of the young Mary "Mamie" Paige, age 16, as victim. The first print news account of the crime against Paige, appearing on March 12, 1901, noted that "[a] case which closely parallels that of Jennie Bosschieter ... is engaging the attention of the police of the downtown Adams Street station this morning."[42] The case received widespread publicity, with wire accounts appearing as far away as Atlanta and Des Moines, the latter probably intrigued in the absence of closure of the Scofield case.[43] In national coverage, the view of the Paige case as a "copycat" crime to the Bosschieter case was established. In this case, the three accused were boys, 17 to 18 years of age, and as in the Bosschieter case, the victim already had made their acquaintance. One of the defendants, George Abbott, was described by his parents as "a cheap novel fiend. They ascribe his present position to this fact."[44]

Local papers carried frequent updated coverage on arrests, Mary's condition, and court hearings. By the time of the trial in May, attention to the crime was so intense that the proceedings at the Adams Street Courthouse were closed to all but "witnesses and friends." By this time, battle lines were drawn between Mamie's advocates and defenders of the accused boys. The trial reports reflect a set of reworked accounts that differed from earlier ones given by the victim, the victim's family, and the suspects.

On Sunday evening, March 10, Mary Paige left the home of a close neighbor, Mrs. Cahill. Paige said that she had left to attend the nearby Catholic Church. On the way she met one of the accused, an acquaintance named George Abbott, 17, on the street and exchanged pleasantries. Paige said that Abbott then grabbed her and dragged her to the back of Chapel Alley, into a stable owned by his father, the proprietor

---

[42] *Brooklyn Daily Eagle*, "Girl Victim of Drugs; Three Men Accused," March 12, 1901, 1.
[43] *Atlanta Constitution*, "Girl Drugged and Assaulted," March, 13, 1901, 1; *Des Moines Daily News*, "Held for Awful Crime," March 15, 1901, Evening Edition, 3.
[44] *Oswego Times*, "Young Girl Drugged," March 13, 1901, 8.

of a junk dealership. Abbott then let two other boys in, Edward Gleason and David Patterson, also boys Mary had known a year or so through her brother. Paige reports that they gave her some liquid in a tea cup and forced it down her throat. "She declared she was dizzy after drinking the fluid and there was a burning sensation in her throat and on her tongue. It tasted bitter to her."[45] After that, she remembered nothing and awoke to find herself alone in the stable. By then, it was Monday morning.

Mrs. Laura Abbott, the accused's mother, found Mary sobbing and moaning, with torn clothing at about 8:00 a.m. She says she gave the girl whisky and water to revive her. A child witness, Michael Hannaway, first alerted Mary's parents to her whereabouts when he saw her Monday morning, wrapped in a blanket at the Abbott's junk shop.[46] Mrs. Abbott says Mr. Paige arrived at noon and took his daughter away. The *New York Times* claims he did so "without inquiry."[47] By Tuesday, Mary's physical condition had deteriorated. Dr. Gideon Hobart, the attending physician, described her condition as precarious, as she suffered from a high fever and likely the effects of a powerful narcotic. Dr. Hobart had examined her and was, according to the *New York Times*, under the "impression that she had been assaulted." It was then that Mrs. Paige notified the police.

Had anyone been concerned that Mary had not been home that night? Mrs. Cahill said at trial that since Mary did not return Sunday evening, she assumed she had gone to stay with a girlfriend, which implies that Cahill expected her to return there rather than home. Yet the *Eagle*'s first article said that Mary "had never been out all night before" and that her parents "were worried all night Sunday when she did not come home" but did not know how to go about reporting her missing. Instead, they said, they launched an unsuccessful search.

This version of the overnight is contradicted by the account of Michael Hannaway to Magistrate Brennan. The young boy said that Gleason and Patterson had approached him on Monday and asked him to let Mary's parents know that she was "fainting" at the Abbott's. Hannaway reported

---

[45] *Brooklyn Daily Eagle*, "Mary Paige Testifies Against her Assailants," May 7, 1901, 20.
[46] *Brooklyn Daily Eagle*, "Mary Paige's Assailants Have Made Confessions," March 13, 1901, 1.
[47] *New York Times*, "Brooklyn Girl is Drugged and Ill-Used. Mary Paige, only Sixteen Years Old, Found in Alley," March 13, 1901, 1.

that Mrs. Paige would not come "because her husband was angry because Mamie had been out all night." Hannaway then informed Mrs. Cahill. Cahill arrived to find her in a "terrible state" with scratches and dirt on her face, unable to communicate coherently. Returning to the Paiges, he said, Mrs. Paige asked him to "dress Mamie and bring her home."[48] When Hannaway returned, Gleason and Abbott, along with Mrs. Abbott, were trying smelling salts on Mary. Hannaway was sent for Mr. Paige a third time. Laura Abbott stated at trial that Mr. Paige then arrived at the shop angry at Mary for staying out all night.

At home, Mary's health deteriorated. When she spoke to her mother on Tuesday morning, she relayed a somewhat different account than the one she would eventually tell at trial.[49] She said that Sunday night she was out walking and met the boys and consented to go with them to "some resort" to take a drink. After that, all is a blur except being taken to the stable. This version of events was conveyed to a reporter from the *Eagle* that called upon the Paiges on Tuesday afternoon. She was able to name the three boys involved and they were arrested.

Wednesday's *Eagle* report differed a bit, and moved partially toward the story Mary would tell at trial.[50] Mary said she had met Abbott on the street at about 8:00 p.m. on Sunday and strolled with him near the church. It was then, she said, that he forced her into the alley. Gleason and Patterson were already there, and forced on her what tasted like "strong liquor." Abbott, she says, assaulted her first, and then she became unconscious.

The accused maintained their innocence. Naturally, their stories are different than either of the above. Yet news reports of the accused's statements also conflict. The *New York Times* says that Abbott claimed that he had not participated in the assault, but had witnessed Gleason and Patterson doing so.[51] Gleason and Patterson told officers that if there had been an outrage, she had made no objection and spent about an hour and a half with them, Abbott included. They denied drugging her and

---

[48] *Brooklyn Daily Eagle*, "Mary Paige's Assailants Have Made Confessions," March 13, 1901, 1.
[49] *Brooklyn Daily Eagle*, "Girl Victim of Drugs; Three Men Accused," March 12, 1901, 1.
[50] *Brooklyn Daily Eagle*, "Mary Paige's Assailants …" 1901.
[51] *New York Times*, "Girl's Assailants Held," March 14, 1901, 5.

said she had been "seized with a fit and they gave her brandy to revive her." They told police that Mamie was a girl with a neighborhood reputation. They corroborated Mary's claim that Abbott had gotten to her first, and claimed that after the fits started, they remained with her all night, trying fresh air, water on her face, and eventually brandy, which they did admit forcing on her after other methods of reviving her failed.

During the week of the arrests, Mary's condition worsened. By Thursday, Dr. Hobart told the *New York Times* that he was positive she was "not suffering from the effects of a drug." By Saturday, March 16, Dr. Hobart diagnosed Mary with pneumonia, and later with the symptoms of either heart failure or pleurisy.[52] It was not certain she would survive, but she did eventually recover. Later, when Dr. Hobart was called to the stand, he stated that Mary was under the influence of something, "he could not tell what," an impression he formed from her condition and "the history of the case."[53] A grand jury was impaneled, and the accused were arraigned on charges of abduction, rape, and assault.

Despite the changing accounts, the newspaper accounts were highly sympathetic to the victim and damning in their depiction of the defendants, despite the considerable amount of public support that had been mounted in their character defense. One editorial in the *Eagle* described the defendants as "stupid, ignorant street loafers."[54] The *Eagle* noted that the case has stirred "indignation … and a number of letters of condolence have been received by the mother of the girl from strangers in all parts of the city."[55] Thus, a close follower of the coverage might have been shocked to learn of the heavy support that had been generated on behalf of the defendants—and how, ultimately, that support influenced the case's outcome—light custodial sentences for all three, after Gleason and Patterson pled guilty only to assault. When Judge Hurd imposed sentences on Gleason and Patterson—remanding them to the Raymond Street jail to serve sentences of six months each—he told them, "I realize

---

[52] *Brooklyn Daily Eagle*, "Paige Girl Said to be Worse," March 15, 1901, 1; "Not Yet Out of Danger," March 17, 1901, 1.
[53] *Brooklyn Daily Eagle*, "Story of Mary Paige Told by Her in Court," March 26, 1901, 1.
[54] *Brooklyn Daily Eagle*, "Editorial: Reckless Sale of Poisons," March 16, 1901, 4.
[55] Brooklyn Daily Eagle, "Paige Girl Said to be Worse," 1901.

there was a great temptation in your way and on account of your previous good character I am disposed to be lenient."[56]

George F. Abbott was tried separately, found guilty of first-degree rape on May 7 in the court of Judge Joseph Aspinwall. He was sentenced as a juvenile on the 13th to Elmira Reformatory, an adult correctional facility, for an indeterminate sentence, with a maximum of 20 years. He continued to maintain his innocence. Aspinwall told Abbott and those assembled at sentencing that he might not be a "bad boy" and that he had received a variety of petitions and pleas for mercy from well-respected members of the public.[57] In less than five years, the Abbott property went up in flames, and his father, George Sr. was found shot in the head along with an employee in the ruins. His mother, Laura, was repeatedly arrested for theft.[58] George Jr., released from the reformatory for ill health, had already died in Florida.

What Does Innocence Look Like?

Here, as in more modern cases, intimations of drugging seem to take a central role in defining events. The mere possibility of drugging (and in this case, given Mary's serious and quick onset of pneumonia, the amount of alcohol she was given, and Dr. Hobart's uncertainty about how long lasting a drug effect could be, it is unclear) pushes all other cultural tendencies to condemn the victim aside, as it did in Jennie's case. Throughout the trial, allegations about Mary's association with young men in the past were continually raised, and the most damning thing that the court was willing to say was that girls like Mary would not protect themselves, so the court would. Judge Aspinwall plainly told George that his sentence was meant to send a message in this regard. So there was no sense in which the openly aired—and conceded—complaints about Mary's reputation made the outcome for Abbott, as ringleader, light per se.

---

[56] *Brooklyn Daily Eagle*, "Judge Hurd's Mercy Tempers Sentences," June 14, 1901, 2.
[57] *Brooklyn Daily Eagle*, "Abbott Sentenced to Elmira Reformatory," May 13, 1901, 20.
[58] *Brooklyn Daily Eagle*, "Two Victims of Murder in a Squalid Junk Shop," July 12, 1904; "Mrs. Abbott Arrested on Shoplifting Charge," June 28, 1906, 5. Some sources erroneously report that Paige died during the assault.

But in the press, depictions of Mary are more charitable, if nonetheless conciliatory toward the norm of chastity expected of true victims, even while cognizant that the facts do not enable young Mamie to fit this rigid expectation. No defense of Mary's right to socialize without fear of violence is raised. Instead, much as with the Bosschieter case, Mary's activities on the night in question must be constantly transformed into a scene of a young girl going to church and dragged, caveman-style, into an alley and drugged. Her family must also be repictured as one that acts the part of the traumatized, rather than initially indifferent, angry, or reticent until the story hit the papers. That is the cost of defending Mary in the public eye.

In some sense, it is the drugs that save Mamie's reputation, because they trump the claims of consensual sex made by the defendants. Though drugging was never proved in court—it was implied, but the alcohol was talked about as the means of her insensibility—Mamie, it seems, is seen as a flawed personification of another societal symptom, and much of the work of the coverage, particularly in the very local *Eagle*, centers on the popularity of the case as a cause. Mamie's and Jennie's main value are as symbols of the drugs and saloon menace. "Since the Bosschieter case," the *Eagle* editorialized, "it is a matter of public knowledge, or at least common report in print and out of it, that chloral is freely used for just the purpose to which the young ruffians put it or some narcotic like it." The early initial comparisons between the Paige and Bosschieter cases—multiple offenders, sexual assault, previous acquaintance, and so forth—underscored a persistent theme of poisoning and the conjectured role of chloral remained. Even the pulmonary complications that Mary developed were attributed to a drug, until an infection developed. That an already existing infection might explain her vulnerability, or that her subsequent many hours of exposure in frigid temperatures after the boys left her unconscious, appears to be a less favored, in fact wholly absent, explanation.

The editorial further claims that the availability of this "narcotic poison" is an "outrage which is more serious, even, than the life or death of the poor girl."[59] It is an unusually candid claim which is nonetheless reflected in other articles and commentary, and echoes some of the

---

[59] *Brooklyn Daily Eagle*, "Editorial," 1901.

extreme claims made by the prosecutor in the Bosschieter case. Drugs trump everything, even the stark chauvinism of the time. In doing so, however, they reinforced the idea that, in their absence, everything about a young woman's absence from home was suspect. As working-class girls, Jennie and Mamie's leashes were too slack for comfort, and Mabel's pedigree made her independent living suspect, perhaps as much to her killer as to the press. The *Eagle* editorial closes with a plea, via stricter chloral regulation, to impede the threat to "hundreds of girls all over the city." Papers in Des Moines, eager to keep the Scofield mystery alive while the police delayed arresting the suspect they had chosen early—Charles Thomas—took note of the Paterson and Brooklyn cases. It probably influenced Des Moines prosecutors' decision to hold out for accomplices before going after Thomas.

Conclusion

Through three deadly cases of drugging and rape of young urban women in the early twentieth century, we can learn a lot about how the presence of drugs in sexual violence shapes our view of who is a victim—ironically narrowing it by rewriting the stories of actual drug assault victims. These famous cases also set the somewhat distorted prototype of the drugging victim for decades to come, persisting up and through today's concern about date rape drugs. In parallel to today's warnings, the threats are both exaggerated ("freely used") and, even with regard to real drugging cases, distorted as to the likelihood of circumstances.

The tavern setting of the Bosschieter case might seem at first glance to fit the stereotype, but in fact, Jennie only sat and drank with the men because she knew them. A similar betrayal of trust characterized the Paige and Scofield cases. As with any sort of serious violence, social trust, not anonymity or saloons, presented the greatest risk. Nonetheless, publicity about the cases emphasized the out-and-about quality of the young women's demise. In this way, these and other drugging incidents were seen as signal events underscoring the social purity and anti-saloon movements gaining strength at the time, despite the fact that drugging was often used as a competing explanation for the adverse effects of alcohol.

Helen Benedict's study of modern press coverage of sex crimes suggests that "a sex crime victim tends to be squeezed into one of two images—she is either pure and innocent, a true victim attacked by monsters ... or she is a wanton female who provoked the assailant with her sexuality."[60] After reviewing a number of high-profile modern cases, she notes that actual factual distortion and transformation toward the "virgin script" may take place at the hands of sympathizers and advocates, thus reinforcing the dichotomy rather than undermining it or "whitewash[ing] a rape victim in order to protect her." In these turn-of-the-century cases, the desire to transform the victims in this way goes well beyond sympathizers and advocates—it characterizes even the mainstream press, despite the high social standing of the accused in the Bosschieter case and the community support for the accused in the Paige case. Even when used as weapons, drugs are redemptive tragic magic. They shift away blame, shield the victim from knowledge of her own betrayal, and when present in a particular case, cause other elements of the event to be transformed.

---

[60] Helen Benedict, *The Virgin and the Vamp: How the Press Covers Sex Crimes*, (New York: Oxford University Press), 1992, 18–19, 255–257.

4

Baby, It's Cold War Outside: An Era of Pharma-Ubiquity

The Effects of Prohibition

Late American Temperance's focus on vice and the perils of the saloon illustrated precisely Gusfield's assessment that ultimately Prohibition "marked the public affirmation of the abstemious, ascetic qualities of American Protestantism."[1] Were its proponents really trying to stamp out drinking? Maybe some were. But Gusfield argues instead that the broader aim (that explains the astounding fact of Prohibition's victory and 13-year reign) was instead simply to extract "ceremonial deference" to a middle-class culture under siege; a reassertion of this culture's political dominance amidst a rapidly diversifying, urbanizing, and developing country.

If press interest is any indication, drugging fear seemed to fall off well before the onset of the war and Prohibition. The *Washington Post*'s use of the term "choral" peaked in 1907 with 51 articles for that year; the term "knockout drops" had peaked earlier, in 1901 at 22 articles. The decade following 1900 was the peak period for drugging articles in the *Post* with 89 articles; between 1910 and 1920, there were only 35, and then only a

---

[1] Gusfield, 8.

© The Editor(s) (if applicable) and The Author(s) 2016
P. Donovan, *Drink Spiking and Predatory Drugging*,
DOI 10.1057/978-1-137-57517-3_4

handful after that.[2] And so a distinctive, time-bound beginning and end can be seen with the turn-of-the century drugging scare. There were a few likely factors involved.

Once Prohibition went into effect, the specter of drink spiking may simply have been overshadowed by the new roulette dangers of drinking. The federal government was busy itself tampering with alcohol—adding methanol to industrial-purpose alcohol formulas, along with a host of other toxins.[3] The Anti-Saloon League had famously argued against labeling such bottles and vats as poison. Diverted, nonetheless, as it naturally was by both bootleggers and amateurs, and often ineptly remediated, it killed people. There was no moral obligation, in the drys' triumphalist view, to make breaking the law any safer. Absolutists of this sort assumed that their unique and dramatic political victory had put an end to any legitimate claim that one could drink socially or moderately without a problem; didn't everyone now agree this stuff was poison anyway? Essentially, in its antialcohol zeal, the government was not only failing to protect people from a public health harm, it was facilitating it. And it was increasingly aware of the toll.

Why, though, did the press seem to lose interest in knockout drops and chloral crime in the first place, before Prohibition? Partly because the concerns about drugging and drink spiking had been co-opted by the social purity movements of a decade earlier, in particular the antiprostitution and anti-saloon forces. Canalizing every last concern into the threat of alcohol itself and saloon culture obviated other threats as essentially secondary ills. Also, the *protected narrative* of that time required a visible place with an invisible threat—the corner saloon in particular. During the early decades, papers ran reports of men as well as women being drugged.

---

[2] I used ProQuest Historical Newspapers database to search the *Washington Post* from 1900 to 1969, after which nearly all of the scant references were metaphorical. The term "chloral" only appeared to replace the term "knockout drops" up until 1907, then also fell off. The *New York Times* rarely used the term "knockout drops." Using their own index, I found only 10 such references up until 1914, after which the term "chloral" or "chloral hydrate" is used exclusively: 139 such references between 1900 and 1910, 39 from 1911 to 1920, 41 between 1920 and 1930, and then significant declines after that.

[3] Nelli, 153; Deborah Blum, "The Chemist's War," Slate.com, February 19, 2010. Retrieved January 19, 2016. http://www.slate.com/articles/health_and_science/medical_examiner/2010/02/the_chemists_war.html.

Drugging was an extreme outcome pressed into the service of proving everything that was wrong and dangerous about nightlife. It was a provocative place in that it was allowed to exist. Little attention was even given to drugging in other settings.

But even though the press' interest in drugging crimes covered both men and women, it is not as if Prohibition did not change the gender drinking norms that undergirded drink spiking fears. Drive the saloon underground, as Prohibition did, and you instead have young women who are making their intent to transgress clear. No longer the thirsty or unchaperoned girl preyed upon by the bar spiker and predator; she is now the one that goes with her friends and dates and knows the secret knock for the speakeasy. Given the callous attitude by the dry forces toward people who would transgress, there may have been a decline in abstract chivalry at work.

But what about peer word of mouth? Even if elite agendas precluded keeping the drugging threat as a go-to news peg, wouldn't ground-level concerns about it remain? Cultural indications of outright skepticism about the protected narrative emerged, as well. Even before Prohibition, there had been some criticism of the white slavery narrative. In 1921, the muckraking Upton Sinclair doubled down on the protective narrative to explain the sex trade in his book, *The Book of Life: Mind and Body*.[4] He did so with an acknowledgment that the concern was passé:

> In the "movies" you see girls lured into automobiles and carried out into the country, or seduce by means of "knockout drops," and you think this is just "melodrama" but it is happening all the time. In every big city of our country the police know that hundreds of young girls disappear every year.

Sinclair's form of address indicates that the kind of progressive people who read his books might by now have a skeptical view of the protected narrative, simply recognizing that drug, alcohol, and prostitution problems were more complicated than that.

---

[4] The book is an odd combination of practical political proposals, some dodgy storytelling, projections into the features of a future utopia, and self-help physical health and nutrition advice. Upton Sinclair, *The Book of Life: Mind and Body*, Los Angeles: Library of Alexandria, 1921.

Then again, with the roulette problem of bathtub gin, why bother to worry about being drugged? Prohibition also popularized the practice of *drinking fast* before the Feds showed up; for this reason, spirits grew in popularity at the expense of beer at nightspots. Drinking fast is a recipe for ill-effects; it can be downright dangerous with spirits. Drinking had gone from being a fairly normal practice at least in certain settings to being an edgier practice: disasters were expected, not surprising. So much so that any heavy symptoms were likely to be attributed to the suspect manufacture of the drink—why worry about drugs? And drinks tampered at home have never—to this day—been able to conjure up the same fears.

Prohibition in the 1920s, paradoxically, enabled women to drink socially, and sometimes to excess, as they never had before.[5] Speakeasies and private parties were mostly co-ed, whereas saloon culture had been almost exclusively male, although some larger saloons had "side parlors" in which it was acceptable for women to drink.[6] In general, drinking became increasingly privatized as Prohibition set in. Home drink hospitality spawned the now time-honored American cocktail: the better to disguise the nasty taste of whatever spirit you could get your hands on. Naturally, women as hosts slipped into the purveyor role easily. "Signifying a style of consumption removed from the saloon's aggressively masculine atmosphere," Lori Rotskoff notes "mixed-drinks epitomized an avant-garde, heterosocial culture of leisure."[7]

The run-up to World War I saw the fruition of many social purity movements in the USA, but none so dramatic as Prohibition. To the many problems, one universal solution was offered. The influence of dry and sober movements in the USA had always been stronger than that of Europe or Canada, but the rapid move toward enforcing a dry America was still fairly breathtaking on its own terms. Harry Levine and Craig Reinarman, who have written extensively on antidrug and alcohol movements, note that in the USA in particular, drug scourges stand in for a

---

[5] Nelli, 146.
[6] Lori Rotskoff, *Love on the Rocks: Men, Women and Alcohol in Post-World War II America*, (Durham, NC: University of North Carolina Press), 2002.
[7] Rotskoff, 38–39.

host of other problems; the implication is that stomping out the menace will in turn cure the other problems without addressing them directly or acknowledging their complexity or scope. Temperance perhaps set the tone. "From the beginning, temperance ideology contained a powerful strand of fantasy. It held that alcohol was the major cause of nearly all social problems: unemployment, poverty, business failure, slums, insanity, crime, and violence (especially against women and children). For the very real social and economic problems of industrializing America, the anti-alcohol movement offered universal abstinence as the panacea."[8]

And this was probably its animating spirit—the political drive toward the Volstead Act was unimpeded by the large number of people who wished to keep drinking. And some of those people wanted to be stopped by a force larger than themselves. Something less than obvious was operating; the emotional resonance of an uplifted "clean living" America seemed to weaken opposition. Although historians are still trying to explain how the "noble experiment" ever succeeded in the first place, and remained in effect as long as it did (1920–1933), there are some more practical explanations. Although rural areas were not immune from Prohibition's enforcement effects, the "home brew" loophole (whereby it was legal for people to manufacture wine or cider at home for their own consumption) meant that homesteaders did not feel nearly as threatened with suppression of their own drinking. Alcohol—particularly its excesses—were portrayed as an urban working-class vice. Additionally, perhaps middle-class and wealthier Americans already knew they would find the means to keep drinking in their own socially approved way. And they were right.

Ultimately, Prohibition failed to deliver. Circumstances seemed to ridicule its every pretention. In place of prosperity, the Great Depression. In place of the disciplined and thus obsequious workforce that elites desired, labor militancy, socialist movements, strikes, and riots. In place of order and peace on the streets, machine guns and syndicate heavies. In place of clean government, corruption at every turn. The nicest thing you could say about the law was that it was unenforceable, and that it was depriving

---

[8] Harry G. Levine and Craig Reinarman, *Alcohol prohibition and drug prohibition. Lessons from alcohol policy for drug policy.* (Amsterdam: CEDRO), 2004.

a cash-strapped government of revenue. In opposition to the increasing number of critics throughout the 1920s who saw the underworld gain strength, sophistication, and power as a direct result of prohibition, the dry forces only saw a period of increased transparency of the already corrupt quality of imbibing culture. But eventually they lost, and decisively. Nonetheless, we continue to be a culture ambivalent about alcohol, even when we are enjoying it.

Peace Pills, Spiking Your Own Drink, and Fighting Goliath for Control of Your Mind

Do drugging scares then track alcohol concerns, whether the open crusade of the anti-saloon movement culminating in Prohibition, or today's commingling of drink spiking and binge drinking concerns? In the aftermath of Repeal in 1933, a halo began to develop around alcohol consumption. Levine and Reinarman noted that "[l]egalizing alcohol and then regulating it had accomplished what most temperance and prohibition supporters claimed was impossible: alcohol moved from being a scandal, crisis, and constant front-page news story to something routine and manageable, a little-noticed thread in the fabric of American life."[9]

Not that anyone thought of excess alcohol consumption as good or righteous, but getting beer back as an ordinary pleasure during the Depression, combined with the joy of seeing the dry scolds defeated, meant that the usual American ambivalence was somewhat muted. And since Temperance forces had previously become so single-minded that they exaggerated the health and social dangers of alcohol to the exclusion of almost everything else, there was a bit of a backlash that perhaps underestimated the trouble that alcohol could cause. There were other reasons for this countervailing blind spot, such as the underdevelopment of epidemiological perspectives, but the return to temperate drinking without public health disaster may have overshadowed the continuing

---

[9] Levine and Reinarman, 2004.

4 Baby, It's Cold War Outside: An Era of Pharma-Ubiquity 89

problems that go with excessive consumption.[10] The habit of throwing out the cirrhosis baby with the bathtub gin was supported by the general cultural milieu, as well.

A considerably more relaxed view of alcohol consumption in the 1930s, post Repeal, also seemed to carry along a lack of interest in drinks tampering problems. Or perhaps the novelty of the worry simply wore off. After Prohibition, the liquor industry sought to redomesticate the image of alcohol as a wholesome accompaniment to a social evening at home. While drinking slowly became more acceptable for middle-class women, the consumption gap of pre-Prohibition returned. In advertising, women were often shown serving alcohol rather than consuming it.[11] In this milder way, women once again were seen as limiters and keepers in alcohol-serving environments—not people who were at risk, except under exceptional circumstances, of overindulging themselves, but not the grim-faced disapprovers of the temperance era, either. A permanent shift had taken place in norms around drinking women's propriety. There was, by and large, nothing now deviant about it.

Beginning in 2012 and reprised every holiday season since, a sort of silly claim has emerged that the 1944 Frank Loesser holiday tune "Baby, It's Cold Outside" is actually "rapey" in part because the dialogue contained the line, "what's in this drink?"[12] In its own context, this actually makes no sense. First, it is clearly not a song about someone genuinely worried

---

[10] B.S. Katcher, "The post-repeal eclipse in knowledge about the harmful effects of alcohol," *Addiction*, June 1993, vol. 88, no. 6, 729–44. Commentary in a subsequent edition of *Addiction* journal (May 1994) criticizes Katcher for overstating his case.

[11] Rotskoff, 19.

[12] See, for instance: Eleanor Barkhorn and Ashley Fetters, "How to Redeem 'Baby, It's Cold Outside': Fix the Lyrics," *The Atlantic*, December 11, 2012, http://www.theatlantic.com/sexes/archive/2012/12/how-to-redeem-baby-its-cold-outside-fix-the-lyrics/266117/#article-comments. Retrieved December 17, 2015. Counterpoints, origins and role variations: Ken Layne, "How 'Baby It's Cold Outside' Became America's Secular Christmas Anthem, Despite People Claiming It's About Date Rape," *The Awl*, December 21, 2012. http://www.theawl.com/2012/12/baby-its-cold-outside; Leslie Kendall Dye, "Warming up to 'Baby It's Cold Outside': What my mother taught me about the guy who wrote the 'date-rape' Christmas song," *Salon.com*, December 6, 2015. Retrieved December 15, 2015. http://www.salon.com/2015/12/06/warming_up_to_baby_its_cold_outside_what_my_mother_taught_me_about_the_guy_who_wrote_that_rapey_christmas_song/#comments. The song also contains the line "the answer is no," but this seems to have attracted some, but considerably less, attention. For a recent role reversal version, with the lyrics intact, find Lady Gaga and Joseph Gordon-Levitt's 2013 version.

about being drugged, but simply someone teasing her companion, and humoring her own increasing desire to stay with him longer. Her quarrels (and ultimately mocking tone) are with the shaming voices that might disapprove. What it does reveal is both a relaxed attitude about her freedom to go or to stay, and about alcohol itself, and the *mild* disinhibition that everyone seeks from it. The drink (plus the "half a drink more" that she asks for) seems to make her go through the motions of propriety, in an increasingly joking way, of the what-will-people-think variety without diverting her from what she really wants. (A number of subsequent renditions also feature some interesting variations of the "wolf" and "mouse" roles.) It is difficult, however, for modern ears to pick this up unless you have an understanding of both transitioning gender roles at the time and perhaps a maybe *too* relaxed attitude about alcohol, drugs, and mixing the two at the time for both sexes. Barbiturates and chloral hydrate still appeared in a number of pharmaceutical products, and at the time, there was still generally too little concern about their mixture.

It is fair to say that wartime and just beyond were a "quiet period" for drugging and spiking scares that lasted through the mid-1960s. While I have suggested that this may have a lot to do with lessening fear of alcohol itself and its rekindled association with sociability rather than social pathology, it also has to do with the techno-utopian view of tranquilizers coming onto the market. Technology, particularly medicine, in recent decades had solved so many other problems that to look to psychopharmacology for answers for broad questions only seemed forward-looking and scientific, not naïve.

The Tranquilizer Revolution

Almost anyone who thinks deeply about the twentieth century's relationship to the altered state—voluntary, willing, secret, predatory, or otherwise—always ends up thinking about W.H. Auden's apt claim that it was an Age of Anxiety. Auden's book length poem of 1947 considered four temperaments of a shattered world, embodied them, and had them meet—where else?—in a bar.[13]

---

[13] W.H. Auden, *The Age of Anxiety: A Baroque Eclogue*. (New York: Random House), 1947.

Anxiety about the fast pace, ominous threats, and—perhaps a new thing—the vast *scale* of the modern world, paired with increasing individualism is a recipe for drug-seeking like, I think, no other. When there is more drug-seeking, there are more drugs. And when drugs are everywhere—on the street, from the pharmacy, and over the counter—their precision might actually decrease. While nearly all cultures integrate some way of altering their consciousness, in a highly dispersed culture, people no doubt take drugs they probably should not. People take drugs in a way they should not, for instance, with alcohol, or with other drugs. People give them to each other—knowingly, unknowingly, and something sometimes in between. The more there are, the harder it is for people to develop shared knowledge about safe use. Here, take one of these. Coming from pharmaceutical companies rather than from illicit dealers, a new generation of "peace pills" seemed they could not be safer, and pharmaceutical marketing undergirded this idea.

The developed world had plenty of raw material out of which to build more anxiety, more sleeplessness, and more agitation in the twentieth century. Medicine promised relief, but gatekeeping on its part was impossible: word-of-mouth spread and the gates were stormed. The historian Richard Davenport-Hines remarks in his book *The Pursuit of Oblivion: A Global History of Narcotics* that the newly minted expectation that we should also *be ourselves* meant that a "subjective and defiant individualism" may have "degenerated into existential angst, self-absorption, and selfishness."[14]

Being ourselves brought options we never entertained before, but it is also a task considerably more angst-ridden than simply *being able* or *being good*. In many ways, the pharmaceutical answers offered to philosophical questions in mid-century mimic the hyper-real and analgesic qualities of synthetic opiates in contrast to traditional ones. Yourself, only better. Not dreamy, but awake, relaxed, more focused. *Refreshed* after a stressful or busy day. Like the appeal of chloral hydrate to the professional men of the late 1800s, the new pills like Miltown (also marketed as Equanil; generic name: meprobamate) promised to take the edge off an ambitious, conventional, and yet just-bordering-on frenetic life.

---

[14] Richard Davenport-Hines, *The Pursuit of Oblivion: A Global History of Narcotics*, (New York: Norton), 2001 300–305.

Enthusiasm and ensuing carelessness about meprobamate is difficult to overstate. Hollywood figures talked to entertainment reporters about how Miltown enhanced their ability to meet their demanding schedules, and these drugs worked their way into jokes and songs. Comedian Milton Berle, in the 1950s, once joked with his audiences that he was planning to change his name to Miltown Berle. There were even Miltown cocktails variations on the Bloody Mary and Martini that required a dose of the stuff. No worries![15]

The rise of general-audience psychopharmacology was resisted at first by psychiatry, which tended to want to reserve drugs for only the most severe diagnoses and was still deeply entrenched in psychoanalysis. The latter might be appropriate for everyone, but not that many patients demonstrated interest in tackling the troubling aspects of an otherwise outwardly ordinary life that way. It was, and in some sense still is, as a standalone modality, very particular in its meaning system, open-ended, time-consuming, and expensive. Rapidly, as historian Andrea Tone documents, patients simply besieged their family doctors for pills instead.[16]

Meprobamate turned out to alleviate symptoms for people with severe diagnoses, such as people who were institutionalized, and smaller doses were then marketed as safer alternatives to barbiturates. And they *were* safer, by and large, than other treatments available at the time. The appeal of these "perfectly safe" pills, however, boomeranged into much greater demand.

New tranquilizers were upstaged by the first benzodiazepines, Librium and Valium, in the early 1960s, then subject to scrutiny by psychiatrists who were increasingly concerned about addiction. By the time Congress held hearings on the emerging concern of that problem in 1966, 80 million Americans had taken meprobamate and the *New York Times* described the brand names as "virtual household names among housewives, businessmen, and others seeking relief from tensions, worries, and nervousness."[17] By the 1970s, the era of pharma-ubiquity, a phase we are still quite deep in, had risen.

---

[15] Tone, 59–65; Elena Conis, "Valium Had Many Ancestors," *Los Angeles Times*, February 18, 2008. http://articles.latimes.com/2008/feb/18/health/he-esoterica18. Retrieved December 16, 2015.
[16] Tone, 88–89.
[17] UPI, "US Opens Inquiry on Tranquilizer," *New York Times*, June 28, 1966, via *New York Times* Archive.

4 Baby, It's Cold War Outside: An Era of Pharma-Ubiquity

I think the increased level of chronic psychic distress in the postwar period was real rather than just an invented collective ailment to which Big Pharma offered an effectively marketed answer. It was not just a kind of diagnosis called into existence by marketing needs, or even more sinister technocratic preferences for a docile population. (Not that Big Pharma and government technocrats were not hopeful, as we shall see.) Instead, this distress is linked to circumstances that people felt they could not easily change. The retrospective idea that they were effectively pacification tools, however, actually belies historical developments. Would the productive unrest of the 1960s have ensued earlier if we had not been so tranquilized? Doubtful—consider how searing and shattering the Depression and World War II had been. Widespread enthusiasm for a quick, easy, technical solution for being ill at ease prevented social upheaval? Apparently not—it was not prevented. Let us remember that Mother's Little Helpers (typically referring to Valium) ultimately did nothing to divert the rise of second-wave feminism.

But the collective worries about "peace pills" began almost as soon as the techno-utopianism surrounding the new generations of sedatives did. Psychoanalysts and cultural critics wondered whether people would lose the ability to abide the ordinary difficulties of life. And what would become of such a population? The specter of being coerced into using drugs is broader than being slipped something; like the idea of being preyed upon by alcohol purveyors, compulsion into drugs, legal or otherwise, appears in different forms. With street drugs, the conceit had always been that purveyors wanted a bigger audience for their wares, and one dependent upon their product. Stolen girls and women were assumed to be part of the spoils. That shadowy world was a thing apart; the object was to keep you and your loved ones away from it. But with pharmaceuticals, a bit of a broader suspicion was needed, maybe a bit of a critical or even conspiratorial state of mind at that. Are "they" trying to drug us into conformity and submission? Are "they" trying to make us dependent on them? What will they make us do if "they" succeed? Paranoia about mass manipulation with drugs, a world of forced docility at the hands of technocrats—well, it turns out to be honestly earned in the postwar era. But not with the drugs we expected.

In 1956, a Manhattan conference was convened to consider the state of therapeutic psychopharmacology. Among the speakers was Aldous Huxley, famously author of the 1932 book *Brave New World*, but at that time more recently, *The Doors of Perception* (1954). He predicted in his talk that a bevy of new consciousness-altering drugs was nigh, and that society should in some way be prepared to have its foundations rocked. Ethics and religion would be subject to greater scrutiny, he said, in an age when our minds can be fundamentally transformed on demand.[18] Coming from the author of *Brave New World*, which casts a rather dim light on the potential totalitarian, technocratic becalming of populations, this was somewhat startling. His endorsement of the peaceful mind that might emerge from the use of meprobamate was quite explicit—he was a fan.[19]

One of the other parts of Huxley's life story is his foray into consciousness-tweaking drug experimentation. Huxley was one of the original psychonauts, having made a foray into mescaline use. Like many of his generation, he may have been actually optimistic about pharma technology and human evolution. Soma-bad-Miltown-and-mescaline-good is probably not the way he saw it. Rather, the knowledge is here, the drugs are coming—what do we do with this? Some of the distance between *Brave New World* and *The Doors of Perception* can simply be credited to his evolving views on a matter he clearly thought about a great deal. It could also be that he was asking a question—meprobamate seemed to be doing many people some genuine good, but what of the big picture?—without answering it.

Some of the discordance about Huxley's positive views on the tranquilizer revolution only seems sharp from the vantage point of our current dominant cultural messages. Huxley represented a true transitional figure in this regard. The War on Drugs in the USA, beginning in 1981, which reverberated globally, came with some fairly monolithic mantras: *drugs are bad* and *just say no*. Aimed, of course, at substances already made illicit, it also affected how we thought about the drugs that we *are* permitted, and maybe even at times, encouraged to take. Andrea

---

[18] "'Behavior' Drugs Now Envisioned; Aldous Huxley Predicts They Will Bring Re-Examining of Ethics and Religion," *New York Times*, October 19, 1956. Via *New York Times* Archive.
[19] Tone, 62–64.

Tone documents a significant emerging negative view of tranquilizers in the late 1970s that was shared by specific groups all across the political spectrum. "Americans," she notes, "were for the first time politically unnerved by their prescription behavior."[20]

Yet there was only a temporary dip in actual use; mostly, the tranquilizer continued its journey onward and upward. We have taken benzodiazepines in record numbers, yet we mix up no Xanax cocktails and create no Ativan artwork. There is widespread adoption but little open celebration. Simply put, we do not talk about it. Once the medical model of anxiety and acute stress became hegemonic, in the 1980s, it privatized worry about Worry.

Only the strictly sober, we might assume, would see all kinds of mind alteration as inherently suspicious. This turns out not to be the case—some of the most suspicious were the new drug-takers themselves.

Button, Button: The Singular Case of LSD

"A major civil liberties issue of the next decade will be the control and expansion of consciousness. The old values are at stake—academic freedom, freedom of consciousness, the freedom of the nervous system. Who controls your cortex?"—Drs. Timothy Leary and Richard Alpert, in a letter to the *Harvard Crimson* student newspaper, 1962.[21]

"So I'm glad they did it to me, because now I can feel free and honest and virtuous about not having made the decision myself ... I'll never think of it again."—the narrator of *Go Ask Alice* (1971), a fictionalized teen girl's diary of psychedelic ruin, on being surreptitiously dosed with LSD.

Although we do not normally consider stimulants when we thinking of drink spiking or drugging, that is, surreptitious administration of a drug, the singular case of LSD can—like smaller doses of the substance itself does to human perception—sharpen, highlight, and make more vivid the underlying dynamics of drugging and its attendant fears.

---

[20] Tone, 176.
[21] Leary and Alpert, "Letter to the Editor," *Harvard Crimson*, December 13, 1962. http://www.thecrimson.com/article/1962/12/13/letter-from-alpert-leary-pfollowing-is/. Retrieved December 21, 2015. Leary and Alpert were dismissed in 1963.

The *actual* history of LSD deployment, as a potential weapon or defensive substance in war and espionage, potentiates our fear of chemical submission.

In other words, we do actually know what is possible when some entity as powerful as a government sets its sights on drugs as potential weapons to control, coerce, or evade—because the USA and UK went well beyond dabbling in such matters. That such investigations were eventually abandoned tells us only about the limitations of this particular mercurial substance, derived from ergot, and nothing about any theoretical limits to strategic mass drugging under the right circumstances. In the later revelations in the 1970s about this period of experimentation, critics wondered whether we were all potentially part of a power play we could only dimly see. By then, though, the postwar technocratic consensus had worn off in any case.

Not long after the US government, particularly the Central Intelligence Agency (CIA), lost interest in it, LSD's proselytizers eerily echoed the same fears. They loved acid, and yet they were often the most vocal about its potential dangers in the wrong hands.

In the 1960s and after, which saw a genuine and long-lasting uptick in illegal drug use, antidrug forces, like anti-saloon forces before them, have tended to overestimate the amount of prodding, coercion, and deception needed to interest people, particularly the young, in using alcohol and drugs. What first emerges as a moral but ultimately self-determined dilemma—to indulge or not—oftentimes turns to at first submerged, then finally open, accusations that the feared substance is in some sense forced upon the unsuspecting; that the voluntary nature of their participation is illusory, that puppet masters control the user, scheming in advance. This theme is, of course, apparent in the trajectory of the Temperance movements of the 1800s, in its transition from the original self-help-oriented Washingtonian pledgers to the aggressive, outwardly restrictive Anti-Salooners and outright Prohibitionists, who describe inebriates as slaves to the drink and to those that manufacture, serve, and share it. But this has happened with other drugs, too. A variety of immigrants and conjured foreign villains have been held responsible for flinging the drugs we liked at us: opiates, cocaine, marijuana.

And drugging tales of chloral hydrate only emerged when its attractions become interesting to a wider audience, and when word of mouth made it widespread as a sleep aid, analgesic, and soporific. "Everyday worriers," as historian Andrea Tone characterizes them, had never taken no or "stiff upper lip!" for an answer and aggressively sought out the relief they had heard about.[22] Themes of coercion in the era of chloralism came when the addiction and misuse problem spread beyond the elite audience for it—at first only doctors, scientists, and businessmen trying to combat insomnia and perhaps neurasthenia, an elusive and era-bound condition with which ambitious, professional men were diagnosed when they became unable to work due to stress or emotional paralysis.

But things would get a little bit weird, coercion-wise, with regard to LSD.

Drugs and the Postwar Decline in Drug Stigma

In the postwar era, nonmedical drug use shed some of its shadow and stigma in general. Contrary to the usual claims, I would like to suggest that this was down to more than the oft-cited nexus of youthful baby boomers, affluence, and cultural rebellion. It was also about a resurgence of scientific optimism that developed its own flourishes in both mainstream and counterculture trends. There is no better illustration of these themes than the singular case of LSD. It became an avatar of both limitless liberation and the ultimate psychic enslavement, often in the same conversation. There are, it turns out, plenty of coercion themes that emerge about LSD—both careless and malicious spiking stories, allegations of authoritarian cult control, and suspicions about government puppet mastery that go back to real intelligence and military experimentation with it.

To summarize a story widely told: in 1938, a research scientist named Albert Hofmann, working at Sandoz Laboratories in Switzerland, was studying ergot, a naturally occurring fungus often found on stores of grains like rye. Already familiar with historical cases of ergot poisoning,

---

[22] Tone, 21.

he sought out synthetic, more stable forms. Somewhat by accident five years later, he dropped one particular formulation (lysergic acid diethylamide, or LSD-25) onto his hand and discovered its qualities—both its ecstatic, transcendent qualities and its unparalleled terrors. Properly speaking, Hofmann reported that it was a potent hallucinogen. Yet that was merely its classification. There was more, and Hofmann seemed to quickly understand its potential. "There was to my knowledge no other known substance that evoked such profound psychic effects in such extremely low doses," wrote Hofmann, "that caused such dramatic changes in human consciousness and our experience of the inner and outer world."[23] Sandoz went on to market Delysid in 1947. By the 1950s, the field of psychology took a great interest in it. It was sporadically used in a variety of mental health settings, ranging from an adjunct to psychoanalysis to curing alcoholism to using it in research settings as a kind of artificial schizophrenia. It was promising to many—and experimentation with therapeutic aims seems to have been choked off mainly because of its poor timing—in the increasingly negative run-up to its prohibition in 1966.[24]

And—here's where the well-earned paranoia sets in: the drug was also explored for a number of years by military and intelligence agencies, so in this case, the idea of a drug as an incapacitating weapon of pacification had a real-life official precursor, rather than being built out of a series of one-off anecdotes and isolated reports. Unlike therapeutic settings of the early 1960s, military applications sought tactical advantage through it; the potential to control, cajole, or just discombobulate others. Ideas included the possibility of using it to reduce resistance during armed conflict and thus the need for lethal force.

Intelligence agencies, including the CIA, experimented with the drug (and a host of others, including concentrated marijuana extract and scopolamine). In 1953, Allen Dulles, then director of the CIA, inspired by mind control techniques used by the opposing side on prisoners of war (POWs) in the Korean War, thought that the drug might be useful as a

---

[23] Albert Hofmann, *LSD: My Problem Child*, Los Angeles: J.P. Tarcher, 1983.
[24] Erica Dyck, "Flashback: Psychiatric Experimentation with LSD in Historical Perspective," *Canadian Journal of Psychiatry*, June 2005, v.50, #7, 381–387.

"truth serum" and tested it out on unwitting prisoners, staff, and civilian men lured into brothels.[25] The project, labeled MK-Ultra, lasted about ten years. In 1963, the Inspector General's office found out about the project and was troubled by the risks to civilians and recommended the discontinuation of the testing. But it may have ended simply because the drug had proved unwieldy anyway.[26]

Military intelligence also ran what they called "psychochemical experiments" beginning slightly earlier with the mission to possibly replace conventional weaponry with pacification. "Material Testing Program EA 1729" unloaded LSD and other substances onto unwitting test subjects.[27] Raffi Khachadourian's *New Yorker* article on the projects described the program's beginnings at the Edgewood Arsenal in New York State, which housed a psychiatric institute. At some point, the residents there and agency staff were too cognizant of previous experiments, and Operation Third Chance then decamped to Europe and East Asia, where ally agencies cooperated in finding naïve test subjects. Particularly, the thinking about LSD was that it might be of use in interrogation—both extracting the truth and resisting it, "such as discrepancies in previous testimony, evidence of dissembling, and weaknesses, or 'soft spots,' where the assets could be emotionally worn down or broken by harassment."

The results were harsh and harrowing, yet yielded little in the way of applied science. Extremely high doses of LSD, combined with gaslighting,

---

[25] Joe Holley, "John K. Vance; Uncovered LSD Project at CIA," *Washington Post*, June 16, 2005. Retrieved December 14, 2015. http://www.washingtonpost.com/wp-dyn/content/article/2005/06/15/AR2005061502685.html. At least one staff member, Frank Olson, committed suicide. He and three others were apparently drinking spiked Cointreau at a meeting weeks earlier and he lapsed into a sudden, intractable depression, notoriously crashing out a New York hotel room window. Kim Zetter, "April 13, 1953: CIA OKs MK-ULTRA Mind-Control Tests," *Wired Magazine*, April 3, 2010. http://www.wired.com/2010/04/0413mk-ultra-authorized/. Later, they thought it might be used as a kind of intentional mind-gibberish generator foisted on an enemy, perhaps Fidel Castro.

[26] UNITED STATES SENATE, NINETY-FIFTH CONGRESS, FIRST SESSION, *Project MKULTRA, The CIA's Program of Research in Behavioral Modification, Joint Hearing before the Select Committee on Intelligence and the Subcommittee on Health and Scientific Research of the Committee on Human Resources*, AUGUST 3, 1977. http://www.intelligence.senate.gov/sites/default/files/hearings/95mkultra.pdf. Retrieved December 17, 2015.

[27] Raffi Khachadourian, "High Anxiety: LSD in the Cold War," *New Yorker*, December 15, 2012. http://www.newyorker.com/news/news-desk/high-anxiety-lsd-in-the-cold-war. Retrieved December 17, 2015.

accusations, isolation, and denial of food and sleep, sometimes resulted in permanent damage and suicides. Much of this came to light as the result of a series of investigative reports and subsequent fact-finding and Congressional hearings in the mid-1970s.[28] The uncovering of military and intelligence experiments in later decades represented only a filling in of details and an acknowledgment of casualties, not a full revelation: it had been discussed already in the media and acknowledged by government officials in both the USA and the UK in the 1960s.

Call it whatever the opposite of an open secret is, in a sense. The only serious ethical or social analyses of the experiments at first were in the scientific journals—but they were there, in plain sight, if anyone wanted to look, by the early 1960s. When the Congress' Church Committee in 1977 considered the details of the experiments, *then* we were shocked, because now we understood—through a decade of either hearing about or experiencing recreational use—what LSD was, and realized that the much now distrusted government had once been all over it as a potential tactical weapon.

One of the plain-sight commentaries appeared in 1962 when psychiatrist E. James Lieberman published an article in the *Bulletin of Atomic Scientists* titled "Psychochemicals as Weapons."[29] He described the emerging drug research, particularly with psilocybin, LSD, and methedrine. In sum, Lieberman understood the proponents' claim that using drugs in a war, riot, or uprising was surely more humane than conventional weapons, but it raised both ethical questions about medicine's ability to participate and a more general concern that the nonlethal and reversible quality of the emerging drugs might foster what we today call *mission creep* in military ventures or *net widening* in criminal justice.[30] With such options in our arsenal, would restraint be exercised? Would legitimate and nonviolent protest be targeted for longer-term political ends? Would

---

[28] UNITED STATES SENATE, NINETY-FIFTH CONGRESS, FIRST SESSION, *Project MKULTRA* ...

[29] Lieberman, E.J. (1962) Psychochemicals as Weapons, *Bulletin of the Atomic Scientists*, January 1962, Vol. XVIII, no. 1, 11–14.

[30] Specifically, about the ethics of medicine, Lieberman meant that, because scientists already know that indiscriminate use of drugs can cause harm and paradoxical effects, the Hippocratic Oath might well enjoin participation of those who understand the potentialities of the drugs the best.

the new power to shape and control, as opposed to merely constrain or suppress, be resisted? Lieberman was skeptical. If indeed the juggernaut qualities of such a mass scheme were lessened, and the effects thus somewhat more predictable, then another ethical problem emerges:

> Virtually complete control of the individual may come to rest with governments, or with whoever possesses the weapons. Under such circumstances a government could outwardly uphold the noblest statutes of political freedom, while subtly extinguishing the actual expression of individual liberty.[31]

At roughly the same time as the USA, the UK engaged in similar LSD experimentation with the same aims, and dosed soldiers, and later civil service employees, at the Porton Down military installation with what they were told was a cold remedy.[32] However, it appears that widespread knowledge of the MI6 experiments did not surface until the late 1990s, with an official inquiry into a much larger set of drug and chemical experiments on troops, although isolated reports surfaced as early as the late 1960s.

The curiosity that did exist in the early 1960s about these drugs was centered around clinical experimentation for therapeutic purposes, and historian Erica Dyck notes that medical journals all around the world carried articles on Delysid trials by the early 1950s.[33] Canadian researchers working with volunteers suffering from severe emotional problems and alcoholism were openly optimistic. Sequestered within psychiatry at first, it then moved into lay and research psychology. Even when the genie escaped the bottle, there remained boundary issues. Timothy Leary and Richard Alpert, both professors of psychology at Harvard, ordered experimental supplies of psilocybin and acted as experience coaches, eventually seeing themselves as benevolent journey guides for those who volunteered for their early, authorized experiments. Harvard was tolerant

---

[31] Lieberman, 13–14.
[32] Andy Roberts, *Albion Dreaming: A Popular History of LSD in Britain*, (Tarrytown NY: Marshall Cavendish), 2012, 46–60. Only part of Roberts' book deals with government experimentation, but the bibliography contains references to the official inquiry reports as well as news coverage of the scandal, more broadly known as "Porton Down."
[33] Erika Dyck, "Flashback: Psychiatric Experimentation With LSD in Historical Perspective," *Canadian Journal of Psychiatry*, Vol. 50, No. 7, June 2005, 381–389.

of the emerging discussions of the spiritual dimensions of the chemical experiments; after all, in circles like Huxley's and among various progressive theologians, this was an open discussion. Harvard severed ties with Leary and Alpert only when it seemed that research had turned to proselytizing, and garnered too much undergraduate involvement and curiosity. Closed settings, in one way or another, were thus imagined to ideally envelop the hallucinogen experience—an invisible guardian trust for chemical seekers and shaman alike. Of course, it depended on who you trusted with such power and who you did not.

Consider, for instance, an ominous warning by John Kobler in November of 1963 in the middle American publication, the *Saturday Evening Post*. It conjures, for perhaps the first time in popular nonfiction literature, the risk of totalitarian control through drugs like LSD which were then, of course, still legal, albeit harder to get from Sandoz.[34] In his lengthy article on "The Dangerous Magic of LSD," the author describes Timothy Leary and Richard Alpert's post-Harvard wanderings with fellow LSD enthusiasts, whom he largely regards as "cultists." Fun, imaginative cultists, possibly reckless—the tone Kobler takes is almost resentful. Playing to his magazine audience, he emphasizes the audacious cultural elements of the story. Heiresses providing funding, unconventional communal living, feeling released from responsibility, leaving prestigious careers at Harvard, making philosophical pronouncements—details that seem designed to both titillate and irritate. The accompanying photographs are sensual, joyous, and exotic—without the text, the photo array looks like a brochure for a resort that offers lectures and spa services.

Kobler provides a round-up list of casualties, while being vague about therapeutic successes (grudgingly acknowledging the Canadians). While conceding the therapeutic potential of hallucinogens and that the clinical community differed in their views of the promises and threats of LSD, he did accurately map LSD as on the social verge, about to be unleashed. Switching then to catastrophic mode, he cites Lieberman's passage about "soft" chemical tyranny. It is a provocative juxtaposition. And in the next

---

[34] Kobler is more well known for his 1971 biography of Al Capone. Notable also is his 1968 biography of Henry Luce: *Luce: His Time, Life, and Fortune*, (New York, Doubleday), 1968.

few years, LSD did escape its guild keepers into the general population, particularly the young, who were, as the "Baby Boom" demographic bulge, large in number.

A contrasting view came from Time Life publications at the same time. The promise and peril of LSD was a common topic in news magazines. Features began to appear that straddled fear and scientific curiosity: while wary of youth dabbling in acid, science writers in particular were careful to quote a variety of doctors and researchers who believed it had clear therapeutic potential in the right settings, and emphasized their respectability and conventionality. The Harvard credentials of proponents Timothy Leary and Richard Alpert were reiterated, though by then they had long departed. Theologians added an air of credibility to the speculation that, in the right settings, LSD was unleashing genuine "classic form of mystical ecstasy."[35] Both *Time* and *Life* began to cover the interest in hallucinogens, for better or worse, in the next few years, and the rest of the national press followed suit.

Involuntary Use of LSD Becomes a Civilian Concern

The medicalized coverage of LSD in the mid-1960s was even somewhat soft on the involuntary drugging scenario. Not that anyone approved of it, but it was often described as a dangerous prank rather than a predatory attack. These actions were youthful indiscretions or inadvertently harmful, not the work of would-be puppet masters or sociopaths. This may have been in part due to the loosening of cultural strictures culturally regarding drug use (both licit and illicit, "hard" and "soft") that was not reflected in all cases by loosening legislation.

There had always been marginal concerns about involuntary ingestion. Hofmann alluded to the dangers of spiking, which he knew about from lab pranks early on. "A young doctor" he reported, "whose colleagues had slipped LSD into his coffee as a lark, wanted to swim across Lake Zurich during the winter at −20 °C (−4 °F) and had to be prevented by force."[36]

---

[35] Time, "Instant Mysticism," October 25, 1963, Vol. 82, Issue 17, 106.
[36] Hofmann, 2013.

Apparently, it was not unheard of for hosts of parties and dinners in the swinging London to dose their guests with the LSD they had themselves become enchanted by, and some high-profile instances no doubt planted the idea to others. Patti Boyd told the *Daily Mail* in 2007 that in the mid-1960s, a dentist served her and the Beatles LSD in their coffee without telling them, at a dinner party he hosted. Looking back, she also suspects that the dentist (who died in 1986) used Valium whenever possible in dental procedures, and wonders what might have happened while his patients were under.[37]

While it might be the case that the dinner guests were none too pleased to be dosed without permission, voluntary use by a number of musicians, including the Beatles, led onlookers to minimize this kind of transgression a bit, echoing the almost tolerant "naughty prank" tone of public conversations about LSD dosing incidents. And of course, the question of who asked for what may have been disputed, or at least mired in confusion. Michael Hollingshead, who founded the World Psychedelic Centre in London, once was thought to have coated the surfaces of an apartment in NYC with acid, failing to tell the numerous guests at the party. After returning to London, he did the same thing to a punch bowl there.[38] In the early years of psychedelic experimentation, it appears that some unintentional dosing resulted from miscommunication of the "everyone thought everyone else knew" variety.

---

[37] Patti Boyd, "Patti Boyd: The dentist who spiked my coffee with LSD," August 5, 2007. http://www.dailymail.co.uk/tvshowbiz/article-473207/Patti-Boyd-The-dentist-spiked-coffee-LSD.html#ixzz3xhajgRdM. Boyd, *Wonderful Tonight*, (New York: Three Rivers Press), 2008, 101–103.; Martin Lee, And Bruce Schlain, *Acid Dreams: The Complete Social History of LSD; the CIA, the Sixties, and Beyond*, (New York: Grove/Atlantic), 1985, 180.

[38] Hollingshead came to be regarded suspiciously by Leary and friends, who were still at Harvard, but he had a great deal of high-quality product and may have actually been first among the psychonauts to try LSD. See Lee and Schlain, 84, 98, 116. Hollingshead does not appear to address the "coated doorknobs" claim in his writings, though he notes in his own book that, in London, "[t]he place was a centre for all kinds of psychedelic experimentation, and it was only a matter of time before someone complained or turned me in. There had been a number of 'incidents' surrounding the history of this flat, such as a party attended by some eighty guests who got accidentally turned on via a spiked fruit-and-wine punch, amongst whom were some police spies masquerading as hippies." At the time, LSD was not yet prohibited in either country. Michael Hollingshead, *The Man Who Turned on the World*, (London: Blond and Briggs, 1973). Available online at http://www.psychedelic-library.org/hollings.htm, see chapter 7.

4 Baby, It's Cold War Outside: An Era of Pharma-Ubiquity

But the initial press cautions were raised about illicit users more directly dosing their peers without consent. The idea was treated more as a youthful (albeit serious) error in judgment rather than a desire for power over a victim. *Life*'s science editor, Albert Rosenfeld (1966), put together a question-and-answer article that included a number of fatalities linked to dosing. "A woman in Europe, into whose drink a prankster dropped some LSD, thought she was going crazy and committed suicide … Anyone who drops LSD into someone's drink and thinks it is fun should not be surprised if the jury thinks it is murder."[39]

The Sandoz patent expired in 1963, and by 1966, the company had decided not to manufacture it anymore. In its April 29, 1966 issue, *Life* magazine prominently editorialized that their decision to pull the plug altogether on Delysid was "regrettable" given its medicinal potential and the likelihood that the emerging acid-manufacturing underground would produce precisely the dangers of alcohol Prohibition—unregulated, unmeasured, and easily usurped by criminal elements with no ethical commitments beyond profit. Indeed, the drug easily cast off its moorings—both clinical and subcultural—particularly rapidly after its prohibition. In October 1966, California was the first state to prohibit its sale, but many more states followed, along with US Congress by the end of that year.

The early counterculture's concern about unintentional ingestion was palpable, if ultimately futile. Augustus Stanley (better known as 'Owsley') manufactured LSD in Berkeley even before it became illegal, and rumor had it that he endeavored to color-tint his batches to signal strength and avoid unintended ingestion. Owsley maintained that, in fact, the batches were all the same; the attributions of differences between them were really projections, which in turn shaped user experiences.[40] This was a kind of supra-personal acknowledgment that the drug was a bit of a juggernaut even if you included its potential psychic benefits.

Though plenty of advocates desired to position themselves as sentinels and helpers for more vulnerable psychedelic explorers, the fascination

---

[39] Albert Rosenfeld, "A Remarkable Mind Drug Suddenly Spells Danger: LSD, The Vital Facts" *Life*, March 25, 1966, vol. 60, no. 12, 28–30D.
[40] Lee and Schlain, 147.

quickly overran the capacity of the babysitters and the imagined soft landing provided by a supportive counterculture. Leary, for at least a time, was as publicly incensed by the new genie-out-of-the bottle problem as the drug's detractors and traditional prohibitionists. Already regarded suspiciously by the established experts, Leary testified before a Senate committee in May 1966 that LSD was out of control, particularly on college campuses, as the *Washington Post* characterized it. He argued against prohibition but in favor of licensing and regulation; legislation that would permit responsible adults to experiment with it.[41] Most of the rest of the testimony was about its positive qualities, yet it did betray an unease with unguided use. Not long after, according to biographer Robert Greenfield, he came up with a more concrete proposal about regulation through a blue-ribbon commission and staffed Psychedelic Center clinics.[42] Looking back, it may have seemed naïve to think that social and interpersonal backstops could manage access to and ingestion of the drug in optimal settings, but it was not a foregone conclusion at the time that regulation would be rejected in favor of flat-out prohibition.

Life Magazine, well into the expansion of youth interest in the drug, in March 1966, presented a cover story on LSD which hewed fairly closely to the Promethean view, with a tinge of positive curiosity.[43] The feature article interspersed photographs of young people in the throes of ecstasy and misery at the hands of acid. Testimonials from emergency room workers said that when it all went bad, it went really bad. Young enthusiasts

---

[41] "LSD Use Out of Control, Says Dismissed Doctor: Out of Your Mind Disturbing Incidents," *Washington Post*, May 14, 1966, A8. Via ProQuest Historical Newspapers.

[42] Robert Greenfield, *Timothy Leary: A Biography*, (Orlando, FL): Harcourt Books, 277; Jean White, "Leary Proposes a Ban on LSD Except in 'Psychedelic Centers'" *Washington Post*, May 27, 1966, A2. Via ProQuest Historical Newspapers.

[43] Stephen Siff's study of the early era (1954–1968) shows that the Luce publications covered LSD more extensively, that is, more frequently and more in-depth, than its competitors. The affection of the Luce family, owners of Time-Life Incorporated, for LSD as a psychotherapeutic and spiritual adjuvant has been widely discussed, particularly as it seemed to affect their magazines' positive, at times or at least not uniformly condemning, view of LSD's rising popularity. Jack Shafer, "The Time and Life Acid Trip," *Slate.com*, June 21, 2010, Retrieved January 19, 2016. http://www.slate.com/articles/news_and_politics/press_box/2010/06/the_time_and_life_acid_trip.html; Stephen Siff, *Acid Hype: American News Media and the Psychedelic Experience*, (Urbana, IL: University of Illinois Press), 2015.

said when it went well, it was irreplaceable, spiritually and emotionally. In the mainstream press in these early years, the roulette metaphor became fairly routine.

Despite whispers to the contrary, an incident in Marina del Rey in 1970 marks the first official case of a mass hallucinogenic spiking. *Time* reported on a party at which approximately 200 guests were present, and 40 ingested LSD without their knowledge, 16 were hospitalized. *Time*'s framing of the incident was from the viewpoint of the world-weary suburbanite, besieged:

> Psychiatrist Louis Lunsky, who treated many of the trippers, called the Marina del Rey incident the first documented case of mass hallucinogenic poisoning. "The frightening thing is," he adds, "that it could happen again." These days, if an American escapes being hijacked in an airplane, mugged in the street or sniped at by a man gone berserk, he apparently still runs the risk of getting accidentally zonked by the hors d'oeuvres at a friendly neighborhood cocktail party.

The arrestee, 31-year-old Donald Henry, told the court he dosed the potato chips only because he wanted to add a little life to the party, which the *Los Angeles Times* and *Time* averred was actually a "swinging singles party."[44] Henry was sentenced to six years in prison, and his case opened up a news peg for the sporadic, apparently random, spikings nationwide that followed. In 1971, two diners eating spaghetti at a restaurant in California were dosed with LSD that came from a cheese shaker.[45]

LSD spiking, though apparently a rarity, loomed as yet another world-gone-mad threat on the quiet suburban street. In 1973, Dr. Lester Coleman's syndicated column "Speaking of Your Health" ran a letter from a man who ingested LSD-spiked food at a dinner party and had a resulting experience he described as "ghastly." Coleman's response is instructive— he responds that doctors "all around the country" are treating such cases

---

[44] "Metropolitan: Man admits guilt in LSD cases," Los Angeles Times, February 4, 1971, A2; "Acid by Accident," *Time*, April 20, 1970, Vol. 95, Issue 16.
[45] "LSD in Cafe Hospitalizes 2," *Washington Post*, April 15, 1971, A3; via ProQuest Historical Newspapers.

which reflect spikers' "pseudo-sophisticated game plan."[46] Again, a kind of resentment creeps in where ordinary public health concern might be. Referring back to the Marina del Ray case, he notes that "victims suffered from his [Henry's] sadistic pleasure." The strange thing is that the column contains little advice for the letter writer, and no scientific information beyond noting that small doses of LSD can be highly potent. It is not even entirely clear where information he imputed about Henry's motivations came from. Gone were the reckless but nonmalicious dosers of Rosenthal's cautions in the early years of acid.

In the young adult, diary-format book *Go Ask Alice*, published anonymously in 1971, the narrator is drawn into a life-shattering course of wandering and drug-seeking by a single event: being dosed with acid spiked in a bottle of cola at a party, where a game of "Button, Button" is in progress.[47] She experiences unprecedented beauty, wonder, insight, heightened senses, and very little terror. "Wow" she writes, "am I glad I was one of the lucky ones."

Touted when first published as a true diary, it is currently listed as fiction by Beatrice Sparks, and its origins remain ambiguous. The party marks just the beginning of an odyssey with drugs, running away, hippie counterculture, heroin addiction, periods of renewal and reform, but finally death. One hit, it seemed, and you could write the rest of the sad, sad script easily. At one low point, the narrator and her friend find themselves in a heroin haze, thinking perhaps despite their own multiple drug quests, they have been offered it at a particular party to be sexually exploited by San Francisco's most "elite" denizens of the drug scene who, strategically, took speed instead.

Drug seeking and fear of being drugged are often biographical neighbors rather than opposite temperaments. This twinning will become more clear in a later chapter on toxicology. But it is important to realize that "drug lore" is often facilitated, elaborated, and passed on by aficionados as well as by scared, straight society and fearful parents. *Go Ask Alice*

---

[46] Lester L. Coleman, "Speaking of Your Health: Letter from Mr. H.H.," Version published in *Washington (PA) Observer-Reporter*, September 10, 1973, C-2. Via Google News: Newspapers. Retrieved December 30, 2015. https://news.google.com/newspapers?nid=6w2ZCmoKEM0C&dat=19730910&b_mode=2&hl=en.
[47] Beatrice Sparks, writing as Anonymous, *Go Ask Alice: a Real Diary*, (New York: Simon and Schuster), 1971.

has been enormously popular among teens, despite its subtext as an antidrug tale. Among subcultures of drug-takers, allegations of manipulation, poisoning, and malfeasance—and how to avoid being victimized by them—take on a kind of solidarity-building quality and a flirtation with outer boundaries of acceptable practice. Unscrupulous home manufacturers were thought to use strychnine, and while this may not have been as widespread as folklore had held, Albert Hofmann reports that he confirmed a case of strychnine poisoning in a powder represented as LSD.[48]

The voluntary audience for acid would generally remain relatively small compared to that for more conventional stimulants (the various forms of amphetamine and cocaine), marijuana, and alcohol. And so it is hardly surprising that as in previous "onset" drug eras, anxiety about the matter became funneled into folkloric treatments and suspicions of coercion, dosing, and deceit.

Skulduggery

The convergence of the now-stigmatized youth culture's embrace of acid and its potential as a weapon naturally emerged within the political skulduggery of the Nixon administration. Desiring to "neutralize" the leaker of *The Pentagon Papers*, G. Gordon Liddy brags in his memoir that he and Howard Hunt schemed to dose Daniel Ellsberg's soup with LSD to disorient him at a fundraising event, to make it seem as if he were just another half-coherent rebel doper. Liddy also says he considered killing columnist Jack Anderson by coating his steering wheel with LSD.[49] Liddy was probably conversant with military and intelligence interest in and experimentation with the drug, but he was also the prosecutor of Dutchess County, New York, a few years earlier, during its surveillance and raids on the Millbrook estate, where Timothy Leary and several hundred revolving friends had holed up to continue their LSD experiments after being run out of Harvard.

---

[48] Albert Hofmann, *LSD: My Problem Child*, Jonathan Ott, trans. (Oxford: Oxford University Press), 2013, 57.
[49] G. Gordon Liddy, *Will: the Autobiography of G. Gordon Liddy*, (New York: St. Martin's Press) 1980; Rick Perlstein, *Nixonland: the rise of a president and the fracturing of America*, (New York: Simon and Schuster), 2008. On Millbrook: Lee and Schlain, 1985.

All of the emerging "sadistic" possibilities only underscore how much LSD had come to seem like an inevitable force for destructive mania, which could be tactically inflicted, rather than the criticism of otherworldliness and detachment it had faced earlier. Not to be outdone in the category of refiguring LSD as a weapon of mass discreditability, some Manson family associates, amidst the group's murder trials, attempted to neutralize a prosecution witness by megadosing her hamburger.[50]

Though LSD as a cloak-and-dagger political weapon turned out to often be less than the sum of its parts, the prospect weighed heavily across cultural milieux. Not only had acid reached the suburbs, it was represented like an invading military force, an occupying army, intent on the submission of the good citizen. There was plenty of reason to associate it with zombification—the government had gotten a hold on it first, after all. If you were part of the counterculture that liked it, that was part of the cosmic joke—grabbing what was studied as a psychoweapon and turning into a tool of psychic liberation. But if you knew very little about it other than what you read in the press, it just seemed like a menace. When it came to being dosed with acid, you could, depending on where you found yourself on the cultural map, fear the government, fear a cult leader, or fear your neighbor, bountiful bundt cake, new formica kitchen, and all. As with most such scares, these one-off events somewhat camouflaged the voluntary and recreational taste for the drug among suburban teens and a few adults too, which climbed upward in the early 1970s.

As the legal suppression of the drug increased and hostility to the psychedelic culture rose, acid dosing became a more palpable fear. Even in its earliest sequestered form, in the labs at Sandoz and in intelligence-meeting settings, there appeared to be an unusual temptation to slip the drug to one's confederates, sort of for the hell of it. Exquisitely sensitive to this growing fear in the USA, youth activists churlishly threatened to dump great tons of it into the drinking supplies.[51] To them, such an action would be half aggressive and half benevolent, and completely vaudeville. In 1969, National Guardsmen were warned against taking food from civilians as it had been reported that protesters had been offering them

---

[50] UPI, "4 Manson Followers Jailed in LSD Case," *Washington Post*, April 17, 1971, A1.
[51] PBS, "Independent Lens: Chicago 10," [broadcast documentary], 2008; Lee and Schlain, 1985.

oranges spiked with LSD at demonstrations.[52] While acid blended for a time in the culture of rebellion, of political dissent, of remaking the world, and of escape from any variety of convention, the embrace of it was ambivalent; the strong belief even among advocates and permissive onlookers about its disquieting qualities was also clear.

Puppet Masters of the Hip Scene

Spiking would always be difficult to confirm since LSD is not detectable in the body and its ingestion can only be inferred by behavioral symptoms and circumstances. Conversely, though, paranoia is a common, though typically transient effect of LSD experiences, causing some users to regard even their closest companions suspiciously. Like its more positive emotional effects, it well may linger, and collectively shape broader suspicions. Probably the single most feverish paranoid fantasy of LSD totalitarianism was the 1968 film "Wild in the Streets," which had cross-generational appeal.[53] A series of political maneuvers causes the US government to be taken over by youth. Those over 30 are rounded up on buses and sent to reeducation camps, where they are fed LSD, to quell their historically destructive tendencies. They wander around in peace-sign blue robes, in their Paradise Camps surrounded by barbed wire, and slowly go insane. Those under 30 are apparently trusted to live freely, and LSD apparently empowers rather than diminishes them.

The Controlled Substances Act of 1970 made LSD a Schedule I drug, subject to the draconian punishment scheme of narcotics. Demand, nonetheless, increased through the early 1970s, and illegal supply kept pace. Predictably, the contamination of street acid with other drugs, such as amphetamine, increased the likelihood of adverse effects as its onset was different than expected. Profiteering had arrived. It is possible that dosing and drugging scares among hippie and other countercultures of

---

[52] UPI, "Students Spiking Food, Guardsmen Are Warned," *Washington Post*, Jun 12, 1969, A7. Via ProQuest Historical Newspapers.
[53] Stephen Tropiano, *Rebels and Chicks: A History of the Hollywood Teen Movie*, (New York: Random House), 2006.

this period serve as a kind of cautionary tale about delinking community and drug proffering and taking.

It was the death of more than a closed guild in consciousness enhancement, however. Many of those who had been on the scene for a while saw much that seemed ominous around them—the rise of speed, the apparent entry into the acid trade of underworld profiteers who "enhanced" blotter acid with all kinds of adulterants. Subterfuge was suspected. The mob was blamed. The CIA was blamed. But it was that the world left behind simply reintruded: street entrepreneurs, confidence men, predators, thieves, and other ordinary skells of the American scene saw opportunities. One of the more famous reflections on the death of acid dreams came from Hunter S. Thompson, who felt that Timothy Leary and his crowd had "crashed around America selling 'consciousness expansion' without giving a thought to the grim meat-hook realities that were waiting for all the people who took him too seriously."[54]

A newly identified figure arose—the "acid fascist" whose emergence on the scene represents a key element in the "death of the dream" trope on both mainstream and countercultural magazines that took hold as the sixties drew to a close. David Dalton, a reporter for *Rolling Stone*, began along with other writers a series of exposes of communes and cults that used LSD to create what they felt were zombies—kids searching for existential or spiritual answers who fell under the spell of acid-feeding villains.

The Manson murders represented to the counterculture a finality to the increasing recognition that like most mind-altering substances, LSD had no "implicit moral direction" as Lee and Shlain put it, but rather a potentiator of what lies beneath instead. Nonetheless, there did appear to be a pattern: a charismatic leader would convince a bunch of heavily dosed followers that he was some variation on the Savior.[55] All other endeavors in followers' lives would cease; the welcome ego death once associated with LSD itself then appeared to transfer to complete egoless devotion

---

[54] Hunter S. Thompson, *Fear and Loathing in Las Vegas: A Savage Journey to the Heart of the American Dream*, (New York: Random House), 1971.

[55] David Dalton, Robin Green, *Mindfuckers: a source book on the rise of acid fascism in America*, Straight Arrow Books, 1972; Bruce Chatwin, *What am I doing here?*, (New York: Penguin), 1990.

to said leader, who inevitably had some sort of grandiose agenda. Charles Manson was perhaps the most notorious of these, but there were several other authoritarian and fairly successful such cultural entrepreneurs, only lesser known for having not graduating to ritual murder in the way Manson's protégés did. In many ways, the acid zombie was a kind of transitional figure between the freewheeling hippie experimenter of the mid-1960s and the "brainwashed" cult member of the 1970s.

But not all feared acid dosing was as instrumentally minded as that of the acid fascists.

Acid and the "First Break"

A retired psychotherapist told me that many schizophrenics he encountered who were more or less in the appropriate generation attributed their "first break" with reality to being surreptitiously dosed with LSD. I naturally thought it interesting that they cited a coerced, rather than a voluntary, acid trip as the culprit. So is it possible that LSD—whether taken voluntarily or not—could induce a psychotic disorder, or that it can "trigger" schizophrenia, per se? The research literature on the intersections between schizophrenia, episodes of psychosis in people not previously known to be schizophrenic, and the use of LSD is characterized by a host of complications, not the least of which is the changing norms of diagnosis in the 50-plus years that researchers have been looking at the drug.

Several inferences, though, exist if the connection between schizophrenia and LSD is weak or nonexistent, despite clients' claims to the contrary. Coerced ingestion suggests an onset of illness set in motion by a single drugging rather than by internal processes or genetic predisposition. It may also reflect an internalized belief initially created by someone else, such as heartbroken parents struggling to explain the onset of schizophrenia in a young adult—the coincidence problem that bedevils all manner of public conversation about causation in medicine. It could reflect paranoia. It could also be a way to feel closer—or more similar to—peers that they encountered while they were in custodial care. Those peers, suffering from psychotic reactions to drugs, for the most part came to an end of the episode and its aftereffects and were released. Redefining schizophrenia as "merely" a strong psychotic reaction can be seen as a hope for an eventual end to the problem.

Further complicating matters is "comorbidity," that is, substance abuse problems and mental illness at the same time. Boutros and colleagues examined the problem historically and epidemiologically in Connecticut and noted:

> Once a chronic psychotic syndrome starts, it is almost impossible to decide whether a particular patient was destined to develop the disease without substance abuse playing any role or whether substance abuse may have caused the disease to emerge in a person who otherwise would have never developed such a disease. It is, of course, also quite possible that a patient with low-level genetic loading for schizophrenia may manifest the disorder only after exposure to the toxic effects of drugs of abuse.[56]

Nonetheless, using data about psychiatric hospital admissions, the authors believe that a peak and decline in drug-related admissions in the early to mid-1970s is followed strikingly by a peak and decline of schizophrenia and paranoia admissions in the late 1970s, which also has a notable "age fit" feature.[57] It would seem unlikely that many of those diagnosed with chronic psychosis in the late 1970s were dosed by others as opposed to themselves. The recreational interest in LSD declined after the early 1970s peak, in a fairly consistent downward pattern. But urban scarelore attached to it—of the malicious dosing type—continued to appear and become elaborated. Unlike the peer-dosing scares of the 1960s, the 1980s and after saw the rise of malicious acid spiking against children and total strangers using phone booths.

---

[56] N.N. Boutros, M.B. Bowers, and D. Quinlan, D., "Chronological Association Between Increases in Drug Abuse and Psychosis in Connecticut State Hospitals," *Journal of Neuropsychiatry and Clinical Neuroscience* 10, February 1998, 48–54.

[57] It was not—due to the research design—the same young adults who showed up on the hospital steps dissociating a few years later; rather, the authors used the early spike in drug admissions as a kind of proxy for an overall use surge in Connecticut (and which was, of course, matched by a nationwide trend).

The Blue Star Tattoo Legend

This urban legend was one of the first—but one of the most durable—legends associated with involuntary LSD ingestion. And as such, it was a fairly extreme allegation, even in comparison with other antidrug panics. The rumor (often supported by photocopied flyer warnings) was that acid dealers were giving drug-laced tattoos to children, which they mistook for ordinary temporary tattoos, festooned as they were with appealing icons like Mickey Mouse, blue stars, or Bart Simpson. Upon contact, it was alleged, the drug would penetrate the skin and a kiddie acid trip would begin. Echoing the claims of Temperance ranters about the motives of grog sellers, this practice was attributed to the desire among dealers to create new customers through addiction.

From a strictly pharmaceutical standpoint, there are several problems with the plausibility of the story. The first is that LSD is not addictive, though it can be reasoned that any mind-altering substance can create psychological craving or dependence. The second is that while in sufficient pure doses, acid can penetrate the skin, it is unlikely in recreational doses. The fiction-to-reality bridge here is that kids might use their mouths to moisten a tattoo to lift the ink rather than water—which would actually be an effective delivery system.

Several common-sense problems emerge as well. Involuntary ingestion would be unpleasant to a child in all likelihood—hardly something worth repeating. Finally, anyone who knows anything about retail illicit drug markets would recognize that risk and reward ratio here would be highly unfavorable. To engage in such activity would have to stem from sheer moral perversity, rather than a profit motive. However, many people who place great salience in such social malfeasance legends tend to believe that the mere existence of malign intent and bad actors in the world is enough to justify any scare story.[58]

As many debunkers have pointed out, some elements of the story probably were hatched from misunderstanding true aspects of retail LSD methods. Liquid LSD is often soaked into, and then dried, on blotter paper which is "stamped" row by row with little icons delineating individual doses.

---

[58] Donovan, 2004.

Visually, these papers may have looked like temporary tattoos, though they are often too small to be visually appealing to children.

But it is important to look at how this story fits into the drugging scares. It contains most of the major elements. The victims of the dosing are complete naifs—literally children, in this case. The stories often center around school buildings, suggesting that the kids were engaged in virtuous behavior—school attendance—at the time of the dosing. The drug "blends in" with acceptable recreational activity in that specific social context, literally hiding among kids' peer culture of icons and tattoos. Jean-Bruno Renard, who has studied the career of this urban legend in France and Belgium, notes that it shares with other contamination rumors the theme of a startling contrast: the tattoos are represented with iconic images that make the dangerous objects "between innocence and perversion" attractive to children.[59]

Various motives are actually attached to the warning. The most common is to foster addiction, as if the drug in question were not appealing enough on its own to voluntary drug-takers. The other, seen in some versions, is the malicious prank for personal amusement—wouldn't it be funny to see children tripping? And here, of course, is the thematic displacement—if parents insist upon thinking that their own children have no interest in the drugs "out there," then naturally any drug fear will be transferred onto a phantasmagorical, involuntary ingestion scenario.

New Hybrid Legend: Pay-Phone Dosing

A newer version of the "dosing people involuntarily through the skin" began to appear in the 1990s. This time the target was adults—unsuspecting users of pay phones whose handsets had been coated in LSD. When the user picks it up to make a call, the acid seeps through their palms, or their fingers when dialing. Surprise!

As the debunking website *Snopes.com* quipped about this rumor, "Apparently the recent two-pronged attack on American society by gang members and drug addicts hasn't fared as well as they'd hoped, so now

---

[59] Jean-Bruno Renard, "Les décalcomanies au LSD," *Communications*, 52, 1990, 11–50. doi:10.3406/comm.1990.1781

they've joined forces."[60] Tongue very firmly planted in cheek, the author also wonder if the cellular phone industry was not behind this legend. (The timing was curiously accurate, and a number of other pay-phone danger legends appeared at the same time—mid-1990s—coinciding with the increasing popularity of cell phones.)

LSD dosing scares underscore the need to recognize the diverse set of motivations for spiking—not all such attempts are in the direct service of crime or personal control over another. Here is the best illustration of the imagined coercive spiker, just randomly messing with the public. Or dosing a friend to turn them on to acid's insights—like Helen of Troy's gift to Telemachus and his men. Real scientific forays into mass psychological pacification, forced spiritual evolution, pranking which is amusing at least to the doser, fantasies about weaponization, and just plain mischief animate both real and feared cases of acid spiking. LSD turned out to be too anarchic in its manifestation to be used well instrumentally, though it was often a good way to explain behavior—particularly more delusions or more drug-seeking—after the fact.

After Acid and Before Ecstasy

The Return of the White Slavery Legend

LSD dosing was not the only spiking scare of the time. By the late 1960s, the Progressive reform era's white slavery legends returned with a vengeance, too, now fueled not only by narcotics but also by the easy access to the whole pharmaceutical candy shop that sprung up around the ill-at-ease company man and his bored housewife. Andrea Tone's history of tranquilizers underscore the shift to unease about the ubiquity of peace pills—now viewed in current affairs as a problem rather than a solution, seen perhaps through the harsh light of younger people's emerging street drugs epidemic.[61]

---

[60] "Payphone Poison," *Snopes.com*, 2011. http://www.snopes.com/horrors/mayhem/payphone2.asp. Retrieved December 30, 2015.
[61] Tone, 176–187.

In sociology, there is the landmark study of sociologist Edgar Morin, *Rumor in Orléans*, about the outbreak of a drugging-and-sex-trafficking rumor panic in that French city-suburb in 1970s. The rumor that spread was that dress boutique owners were drugging their young female customers, rendering them unconscious and selling them into forced prostitution abroad. The rumor attached in particular to the city's Jewish shop owners and thus the rumor panic took on anti-Semitic overtones fairly quickly. Civic organizations and the municipality stepped in to quell the rumor and stigmatize it. But did it work? Morin's analysis is that the embers of suspicion still remained; they just became unacceptable to voice.

Another version popped up in a scare about the same scenario at US shopping malls. This time, the girls were captured from restrooms by procurers using injected narcotics, it was alleged, for local prostitution rackets. Folklorist Jan Harold Brunvand terms this legend "The Attempted Abduction" and notes that, while it was routinely debunked in local newspapers during the 1970s, it has maintained its basic narrative structure.[62] The revised version usually carried no information, at least not explicitly, about the ethnic background of perpetrators, which is of considerable curiosity considering the legend's weighty scapegoating history of more than a century as basically the white slavery tale. Sometimes, Brunvand suggests, the belief in the tale is a bit partial: more "good to think with" about the dangerous world than to verify or act upon.

Notably absent in these 1970s versions, also, were the Progressive era's chivalrous men who intervened and rescued the girl. Something of an amalgam version of the new sex slavery tale using drugging and abduction made its way into popular exploitation books like Stephan Barlay's *Bondage*, in 1968.[63] Evidence was, as usual, elusive. But it seemed to fit with a larger theme of wild Western girls on the loose snatched up by an elusive international exploitation machine. Implied was the idea that drugs certainly held no allure to youth on their own and had to be forcefully administered.

---

[62] Jan Harold Brunvand, *The Choking Doberman and Other Urban Legends*, New York: W.W. Norton and Company, 1984: 78–92.

[63] Stephan Barlay, *Bondage: the Slave Traffic in Women Today*, New York: Dell, 1969.

As in Morin's example, one way of understanding how this fear gained traction was the newness of the mall as modern consumer crossroads at that time and the decline of Main Streets. But the rebounding interest of young people in both street narcotics and diverted pills also must set the context a bit.

Resurgence of the Narcotics Problem

Before Ecstasy earned the title of "love drug" in the 1980s, that crown was held by newcomer methaqualone—first marketed as Quaalude in North America and Mandrax in the UK.[64] Advertising, especially as a sleep aid, emphasized its mild side effects and its nonbarbiturate status.[65] Some formulations also contained a dose of diphenhydramine. Most people are familiar with the latter as an antiallergy drug used at roughly 25–50 mg[66]; higher doses, however, particularly combined with alcohol, can produce effects that mimic heavy narcotics: blackouts, heaviness in the limbs, and disorientation. Also popular among nightclubbers, methaqualone was also known as the "lude," "mandy," or "disco biscuit."

The explosion in psychoactive drugs, each of which tends to enjoy an initial respectable phase when prescribed to the anxious and restless middle class, helps foster an environment where pills are quite easy to get to divert for one's own recreational or self-medicating use, but also potentially to dose someone else with. And with such things so widely prescribed, the origin of any bad pill episode becomes shadowed by uncertainty. Did he spike her drink? Did she take it on her own? Did someone give it to her under a false pretext, like another drug the taker approves of?

Consider what we now know about Bill Cosby's alleged serial predations with methaqualone, diphenhydramine, and probably some other pharmaceuticals, which he has denied. Cosby's is accused of offering young

---

[64] By Rorer and Company in North America and Roussel Laboratories (Sanofi-Aventis) in the UK.
[65] Victoria Bekiempis, "Do People Still Take Quaaludes?" *Newsweek*, August 2, 2015, Retrieved January 16, 2016, http://www.newsweek.com/do-people-still-take-quaaludes-357914.
[66] The best-selling brand in North America is Benadryl, made by Johnson & Johnson; internationally, the name "Benadryl" is also licensed to other, nondiphenhydramine preparations.

women drugs, in some cases purportedly to cure minor ailments such as headaches, and then sexually assaulting them. A great deal of media attention has been devoted to the allegations as they span several decades of Cosby's long entertainment career.[67] Cosby admitted via his lawyer in July 2015 that he sometimes gave women methaqualone, but insisted they knew what they were taking—a claim that most of his accusers dispute.[68] But a "passing pills around" counterclaim on Cosby's part is very consonant with the relaxed attitude about methaqualone and benzodiazepines at the time.

Methaqualone in the 1970s proved a bigger menace than anticipated. Young people believed the safety hype put out by the industry, particularly that it was nonhabit forming, and liked the subjective effects. Like Rohypnol later on, it seemed to balance sensual or sexual disinhibition, at least for some users, with relaxation; for other users, it was reported to aid in sleep—just as it had been advertised. Owing in part to a tendency in nightclubs to readily mix it with alcohol, the effects could sometimes be dangerous. Reports of addiction and adverse effects began to filter in by the early 1970s.[69] In the USA, it was removed from the market in 1982, and it was made a Schedule I drug in 1984.

---

[67] Over 50 women have made such claims. See Amanda Holpuch, Jessica Glenza and Nicky Woolf, "The Bill Cosby sexual abuse claims—57 women and the dates they went public," *The Guardian*, UK Edition, December 31, 2015. http://www.theguardian.com/world/2015/dec/31/bill-cosby-sexual-abuse-claims-57-women-dates-public-accusations. Most of the incidents took place too long ago to result in prosecution. Attempts at civil remedy remain possible in some of these cases. More recent allegations have not resulted in prosecution. Sam Levin, "Bill Cosby will not be charged in two sexual assault allegations in LA County," *The Guardian*, UK Edition, January 6, 2016. http://www.theguardian.com/world/2016/jan/06/bill-cosby-will-not-be-charged-in-two-sexual-assault-allegations-in-la-county. For his part, Cosby has filed defamation suits against some of his accusers: Amanda Holpuch, "Bill Cosby files defamation suit against women who accused him of assault," *The Guardian*, UK Edition, December 14, 2015. http://www.theguardian.com/world/2015/dec/14/bill-cosby-defamation-lawsuit-women-sexual-assault. One criminal prosecution is currently ongoing, related to similar claims of misconduct lodged by Andrea Constand in Pennsylvania. See Holpuch, Glenzam and Woolf, 2015.

[68] Graham Bowley and Sydney Ember, "Bill Cosby, in Deposition, Said Drugs and Fame Helped Him Seduce Women," *New York Times*, July 18, 2015. http://www.nytimes.com/2015/07/19/arts/bill-cosby-deposition-reveals-calculated-pursuit-of-young-women-using-fame-drugs-and-deceit.html. Retrieved January 19, 2016.

[69] Darryl S. Inaba, George R. Gay, John A. Newmeyer, Craig Whitehead, "Methaqualone Abuse: 'Luding Out,'" *Journal of the American Medical Association*, June 11, 1973; 224(11), 1505–1509; Emil F. Pascarelli, "Methaqualone Abuse, The Quiet Epidemic," *Journal of the American Medical Association*, June 11, 1973.): 1512–1514.

Ecstasy and the Company It Keeps

But by then, "love drug" interests had shifted to Ecstasy, which has stimulant and sometimes hallucinatory qualities. The most prominent of the drugs labeled rave, club, or party drugs at the time, Ecstasy (or MDMA [3,4-methylenedioxymethamphetamine], now often referred to as "molly") had a specific appeal to college students. Though some attributed sexual disinhibition to it, users said that the effect was more "sensual." At the time, despite all of the usual detractions from antidrug forces, this claim was more or less accepted. There was no sense of incipient threat of it being used coercively, though it certainly could be, like anything else. Users liked its enhanced sense of social belonging, making the user feel warm and "close and bonded to those around them." Like LSD, it was sometimes used as an adjunct to psychotherapy, before it was made Schedule 1 in 1985. It has, before and after prohibition, been relatively expensive (and consistently so) at $25–40 per dose. As such, adulteration and substitution is very common.[70]

In the early 1990s, it developed a doppelganger in a cheaper, easier-to-manufacture substance called GHB. GHB is not a stimulant but a CNS depressant. The drug is strange in that it seems to feel like different things to different users. It earned the half-ersatz title "liquid X," which enabled its confusion with MDMA. It is sometimes used before a "big night" of drinking because some users liken it to moderate alcohol intoxication. Before it was illegal, it could be found in vitamin stores as it had a word-of-mouth appeal among bodybuilders and athletes. The one thing that it had not yet become—like Quaaludes and Ecstasy before it—was a carrier of the master identity of date rape drug.

---

[70] David McDowell, "Marijuana, Hallucinogens, and Club Drugs," in Richard J. Frances, Sheldon I. Miller, Avram H. Mack, eds., *Clinical Textbook of Addictive Disorders, Third Edition*, New York: Guilford Press, 2005.

5

A "New" Problem Appears in the 1990s: The Birth of the Contemporary Date Rape Drugs Scare

Date Rape Drugs: The Construct

The term "date rape drug" is probably the most misleading moniker a class of drugs could possibly get. The first problem is that hundreds of drugs already on the market—both prescription and over the counter—were perfectly suitable for drugging, given a motivated offender. As our early pharmaceutical history in this book shows, any and every CNS depressant can be used in a predatory way. Other drugs can be surreptitiously administered—stimulants, over-the-counter remedies, even the active ingredient in many eye drops.[1]

As American drug scares go, the date rape drugs scare that emerged in the 1990s, and continues through today, had unusual elements. This was the first time that a drug managed to pick up a core identity related to its occasional (and it turns out, not all that common) role in a violent crime. In decades past, everything from marijuana to phencyclidine (PCP) was associated with committing, or being the victim of, violent crimes. But

---

[1] M.E. Stillwell and J.J. Saady, "Use of tetrahydrozoline for chemical submission," *Forensic Science International*, 221, September 10, 2012, 12–16. doi: 10.1016/j.forsciint.2012.04.004.

none had picked up a classification like "date rape drug." Opium never became, in ordinary parlance, a "white slavery drug." Marijuana, even at the height of "Reefer Madness" depictions, never had its name changed to "youth debauching drug." LSD never became the "murder facilitation drug" despite it being blamed for playing a prominent role in the Tate–LaBianca murders, which were otherwise widely framed as the death knell for a playful or earnest view of hallucinogen experimentation.

Even the most fervent antidrug forces, in other words, never managed to shift any illicit drug's core social identity by naming it along the lines of its worst outcome, either real or in the social imaginary. "Thus, even as previous drug panics have drawn on stories of sexual depravity as part of their propaganda campaigns for criminalizing drugs," Karen Weiss and Corey Colyer note, "at no other time has any drug been so explicitly defined as a weapon of rape, nor has any previous drug-induced crime story been framed so explicitly as a crime against women."[2] Only anti-alcohol forces said what they really thought about the drug they hated: demon rum—and in terms of naming, they convinced only themselves.

And so this is not your mother's or your grandmother's drug scare. It never seemed to be about the dangerous underclasses and their habits, or about the corruption of youth in particular, but about how a group of drugs became labeled "date rape drugs" where they were once sleeping aids or club drugs. And the label "date rape drug" also obscures the other common motives for drinks tampering when it does happen—pranking and robbery. Repositioning a drug as a weapon, as we have seen, does not usually start a drug panic, but rather helps to sustain it from the onset of scrutiny and skepticism a few years in. Indeed, this panic is out of sync with the onset of the War on Drugs and Just Say No campaigns of the 1980s.

How thoroughgoing has the change in drug identity been? For flunitrazepam (marketed first by Hoffman-LaRoche as Rohypnol), it was devastating. It was developed as a sleep aid and regulator, and continues to be available by prescription in Europe, more or less without incident. But in the USA, increased illicit use emerged by the mid-1990s, and in the underground market, it was proffered under a number of names,

---

[2] Karen G. Weiss and Corey J. Colyer, "Roofies, Mickeys, and Cautionary Tales: the Persistence of the 'Date-Rape' Drug Narrative," *Deviant Behavior* 31, 2010, 348–379.

but none more famous than the "roofie." Like other CNS depressants—and flunitrazepam is apparently a very effective kind of heavy benzodiazepine—it will not only induce unconsciousness but often anterograde amnesia, if the person so dosed remains nominally awake for a period of time. This mimics the alcoholic blackout, which is also due to this particular kind of amnesia that inhibits the forming of new memories. Like surgical anesthesia revolutionized in the 1800s, that is precisely what it is intended to do.

It is not entirely clear how a scattering of sexual assault incidents involving flunitrazepam (and then quickly, GHB and ketamine) coalesced into a "new" problem in the eyes of clinics and law enforcement, rather than merely another means of rendering a potential victim helpless. Typically, when there is new street use of a substance, emergency responders will see an uptick in a variety of adverse effects, and certainly public health services become aware of such effects when hospitals and other clinics see patients with acute symptoms that differ somewhat from known drug effects. The press may then help develop the idea that the country (or world) is facing a new scourge in a long line of scourges past and present. In fact, it almost seems as if the slowly inclining knowledge of the attractions and hazards associated with these same drugs when they were still club drugs has been lost or drowned out by their "date rape drug" identity.

When President Bill Clinton signed the "Hillory J. Farias and Samantha Reid Date-Rape Drug Prohibition Act of 2000" for instance, he noted in his signing statement that one of the targets of the bill, GHB, was "a drug that is abused for its psychoactive effects and, less frequently but more perniciously, used as a tool by sexual predators."[3] And because it was occasionally used for such a purpose, the legislative reasoning went, it posed a special danger. Imagine drug war propagandists trying to get the public to reconceptualize alcohol this way, or direct this sleight of hand to any number of the other widely prescribed insomnia drugs, over-the-counter drugs, and antianxiety remedies that have been used to drug people. The bill that resulted in the law was quite unabashed in its desire

---

[3] William J. Clinton, "Statement on Signing the Hillory J. Farias and Samantha Reid Date-Rape Drug Prohibition Act of 2000," February 18, 2000. http://www.gpo.gov/fdsys/pkg/PPP-2000-book1/pdf/PPP-2000-book1-doc-pg280.pdf. Retrieved October 26, 2015.

to essentially assign a new predatory identity to GHB despite acknowledging its primarily recreational use. Establishing its potential dangers primarily through evidence of adverse effects on people who combined it with alcohol, or who attempted to drive while under its very alcohol-like influence, the final bill nonetheless asked federal agencies, including Health and Human Services, to initiate

> a national campaign to educate individuals [in health care and law enforcement]...on the following: (i) The dangers of date-rape drugs, (ii) The applicability of the Controlled Substances Act to such drugs, including penalties under such Act, (iii) Recognizing the symptoms that indicate an individual may be a victim of such drugs, including symptoms with respect to sexual assault, (iv) Appropriately responding when an individual has such symptoms.[4]

While it is certainly desirable that such personnel be up to date on anything that might pose a threat to public health and safety, it is notable that no specific instructions were given about education and training on the more ordinary circumstances of GHB, ketamine, or Rohypnol use: voluntary ingestion—something that they are much more likely to encounter.

By Any Other Name

Before the onset of the date rape drugs era, there were always a handful of cases in which surreptitious drugging was indeed involved—but such cases involved drugs that had not, or not yet, gained a date rape drug label. Take the tried-and-true chloral hydrate, for instance. In 1992, three women alleged that in 1987, in separate incidents, Senator Brock Adams of Washington either tried or succeeded in drugging them with a pinkish liquid. Adams vehemently denied the allegations, but resigned amidst the related publicity in 1992, calling out an overzealous press and

---

[4] 106th Congress, United States, "PUBLIC LAW 106–172—HILLORY J. FARIAS AND SAMANTHA REID DATE-RAPE DRUG PROHIBITION ACT OF 2000," http://www.gpo.gov/fdsys/pkg/PLAW-106publ172/content-detail.html. Retrieved October 26, 2015.

mentioning the possibility of civil legal action.[5] None of the allegations would reach a police file or courtroom; thus, even those sympathetic to the complainants wondered whether this matter, ominously, might be tried entirely in the press. No suits or countersuits did ever take place, and Adams died in 2004.[6]

Lawyers for the women suspected a Bristol Meyers Squibb product called Noctec, which contained chloral hydrate.[7] Chloral has remained on the market since its heralded emergence, and is used in a variety of remedies, but as it became a less popular drug, it was rarely added to routine toxicological screens. As we will learn more about in the next chapter, when toxicology screens do find drugs in patients that they do not remember taking, it is usually not one of the drugs labeled as a date rape drug. As for Adams, he resigned after a total of eight women came forward to the *Seattle Times*, some with similar allegations of drugging and assault over what Adams described at his resignation press conference as a 20-year period.

As this was before the "date rape drugs" era, the alleged events that ended his career were simply labeled "sexual misconduct" and the suspected use of chloral-based sleep aids in this case were simply described in the press as either classic knockout drops or a Mickey Finn. The fact that the more recent term "date rape drug" represents a thoroughgoing misnomer—the drugs so labeled are infrequently used this way, and many other drugs that can and have been used in a predatory way are not prone to the label—is more than just a mistake in categorization that exaggerates their danger and perhaps suppresses knowledge of potential therapeutic uses. More tangibly, the "date rape drug" concept has a life of its own now that it is transforming views of rape, alcohol, and voluntary drug use.

---

[5] New York Times, "Brock Adams Quits Senate Race Amid Sex Misconduct Allegations," March 1, 1992. http://www.nytimes.com/1992/03/02/us/brock-adams-quits-senate-race-amid-sex-misconduct-allegations.html. Retrieved March 11, 2016.

[6] Michael Janofsky, "Brock Adams, 77, Senate and Cabinet Member, Dies," September 11, 2004. http://www.nytimes.com/2004/09/11/politics/brock-adams-77-senator-and-cabinet-member-dies.html. Retrieved March 11, 2016.

[7] Susan Gilmore, Eric Nalder, Eric Pryne, David Boardman, "Pink Liquid Knockout Drug: Chloral Hydrate," *Seattle Times*, March 1, 1992. Retrieved October 26, 2015. http://community.seattletimes.nwsource.com/archive/?date=19920301&slug=1478557.

Media Shapes the "Personality" of a Drug, or Three

Why might a person be found in possession of GHB? In the early 1990s, probably because of the bodybuilding craze that favored its consumption. Yet quickly its occasional surreptitious use on victims of sexual assault transformed its entire identity and that of its aficionados. Now media sources overwhelmingly make this "sole use" assumption in reporting on GHB arrests, even when the quantities seized were so large that any diligent reporter might think to question whether it indicated a mass rape in preparation. In 2004, the *Montreal Gazette* reported that police in the Quebec city of Longueuil had made five arrests in connection with a large drug seizure, including GHB, cocaine, Ecstasy, and marijuana—the total haul having a street value of about $500,000 (CA). Cash and weapons were also seized. The headline? "600 sex assaults averted with drug bust."[8] The article then goes on only to talk about the dosage and potential effects of GHB in a surreptitious drugging situation—nothing of specific interest about any of the other items seized, despite the eyebrow-raising quantities of the other drugs present. The connection between GHB and rape had become so strong that the potentially sensational bust of a crime and drug trafficking ring took a back seat. A year earlier, the Canadian Alliance, a conservative party, proposed classifying "date rape drugs" as weapons rather than drugs because "they are used to victimize other people involuntarily," which accidently gets to the heart of claims about the drugs.[9]

Sometimes, the effect is more subtle, but just as pernicious: in February 2014, the *Hamilton Spectator* newspaper in Ontario ran a headline, "Edmonton police troubled by 'astronomical' spike in date-rape drug seizures."[10] The brief article made no reference to recreational

---

[8] Roberto Rocha, "600 sex assaults averted with drug bust: Longueuil police: Five arrested. Three litres of 'date rape' drug seized in raids," *The Gazette* (Montreal, Quebec), August 6, 2004, A7. Via Lexis-Nexis Academic, Retrieved August 25, 2015.

[9] Tim Naumetz, "Treat date-rape drugs like weapons, MP says: Alliance MP wants tougher penalties for use of the drug," *Edmonton Journal* (Alberta), June 11, 2003, A17; CanWest News Service, "Classify date-rape drugs as weapons, Alliance urges," *Edmonton Journal*, (Alberta) September 24, 2003, A12. Both via Lexis-Nexis Academic, retrieved August 25, 2015.

[10] "Edmonton police troubled by 'astronomical' spike in date-rape drug seizures." *Hamilton Spectator*, February 27, 2014. http://www.thespec.com/news-story/4387399-edmonton-police-

use, instead noting that the quantities seized in recent months was high—"officers coming across 206 litres of the colourless and potent drug—enough for up to 70,000 doses." And then: "Police Chief Rod Knecht calls the GHB spike troublesome, noting that police investigated 330 sexual assault cases last year but have been called in on 334 this year." No link is made to actual drugging-and-sexual-assault cases. A seizure of GBL (gamma butyrolactic acid; an industrial solvent that, if ingested, converts to GHB in the body) in Cincinnati in September 2015 prompted the local Fox affiliate to report that "120 lbs. of drugs linked to sexual assaults intercepted in Cincinnati," though as you can probably now guess, this event was not linked with any sexual violence; the report simply noted that GBL could be used as a date rape drug.[11] The *Times Daily* of South Africa reported on a seizure of a trove of counterfeit drugs—quite a variety, including Rohypnol but also cosmetic and slimming drugs—by noting that "police are investigating whether date-rape cases have surged in the area."[12]

After close to 20 years of experience with such drugs, news sources, college administrations, and occasionally law enforcement agencies nonetheless tend to assume that the presence of such drugs must indicate incipient sexual violence, or a massive number of rapes averted by a timely discovery of a cache of the drugs. The distortion is so deep, in other words, that the primary use of such drugs is obscured, even to those who should demonstrate some expert knowledge about the matter by this point. There is no excuse for such confusion, but it happens all the time. It is commonly assumed by reporters that arrests for the manufacture or possession of GHB simply must have something to do with sexual assault since, after all, it is known as a date rape drug. In circular fashion, then, the reasoning goes that local drug seizures might be implicated in a suspected drug rape.

---

troubled-by-astronomical-spike-in-date-rape-drug-seizures/. Retrieved October 26, 2015.

[11] Brad Hawley, "120 lbs. of drugs linked to sexual assaults intercepted in Cincinnati," *Fox19now.com*, September 9, 2015. http://www.fox19.com/story/29996082/120-lbs-of-drugs-linked-to-sexual-assault-intercepted-in-cincinnati. Retrieved October 26, 2015.

[12] Katharine Child, "Roaring trade in rape drug," *Times Daily*, September 7, 2015. http://www.timeslive.co.za/thetimes/2015/09/07/Roaring-trade-in-rape-drug. Retrieved October 26, 2015.

How the Construct Shapes Other Problems

In this respect, the logical error made in these articles differs little from the generally bad reporting on illicit drugs in general—the tendency not to look skeptically at numbers, or the tendency not to be specific and accurate about the trends in, or the effects of, drug use. But while the date rape drugs scare of the present day shares certain characteristics with scares of the past, there is something unique about it. The "date rape drugs" concept has not only distorted thinking about how these drugs are used, and why they are manufactured and sold, but how we think about rape as well—and the intersection between intoxication and sexual assault. This latter distortion has the potential to unravel decades of social learning about the nature and dynamics of acquaintance rape, by attempting to paint intoxication as involuntary, when this is rarely so.

Reporters even began to raise the possibility of date rape drugs out of whole cloth in obvious cases of acute alcohol toxicity. A reporter for the *Tampa Bay Times* questions the autopsy findings of a Florida woman, Lauren Ortiz, who died after ingesting 4 to 5 rum drinks and another drink with grain alcohol. "On Nov. 19, [the Hernando County Sheriff] got the autopsy, which showed her blood alcohol level between .422 and .436, more than five times the legal limit. The report from the medical examiner said Ortiz died from 'acute alcohol intoxication' and called her death an accident. The detective closed the case." The reporter acknowledged that "Bacardi [rum] 151 is 75.5 percent alcohol, and Everclear, grain alcohol, is so potent it can be used as disinfectant" but still wanted to know, perhaps at the behest of Lauren's disbelieving father, why she was not tested for date rape drugs. The sheriff's office told the reporter that she was not "tested for the date rape drug because there were no physical signs that she had been sexually battered."[13]

This pretty much captures the mind-bending level of confusion about such matters across the board—the dismissal of Ortiz' blood alcohol levels at obviously lethal values, as if this could not have killed her, and the

---

[13] Michael Kruse, "Dead woman's father wonders: What more is there?" *Tampa Bay Times*, April 6, 2008. http://www.tampabay.com/features/humaninterest/dead-womans-father-wonders-what-more-is-there/445091. Retrieved October 25, 2015.

sheriff's office decision not to consider drugs—if there is no indication of rape? Indeed, despite the now-clichéd warning that "alcohol is really the biggest date rape drug," as public health advocates warn, when alcohol is present in a story, there seems to be some disbelief about alcohol toxicity and vulnerability to assault.

In a later chapter, I address in more depth the discomfort we seem to still have about the ordinary circumstance of sexual assaults, which tend to be opportunistic in nature, particularly with intoxicated victims. But in this chapter, I first examine the pathway to the present by looking at the emergence and consolidation of the "date rape drug" idea, beginning in the 1990s, which pushed aside other important concerns about drug use and public health, and culminating in the present, with the insistence upon certain drugs—what I will call the Big Three—as having the sole purpose of incapacitation for the purposes of sexual assault.

The Drug War and the Designer Drugs Scare

Philip Jenkins explains the formation of the "date rape drug" concept as part of a larger broadside against the newest synthetics of the 1980s and 1990s. In his book *Synthetic Panics*, published in 1998, he shows how the media continuously amplified the threat of these substances by transforming them from "party drugs" to "date rape drugs" after a spate of drink spiking stories in 1996. He noted that, by 1998, the new, violence-linked term ubiquitously appeared, even when the news story was clearly about recreational use, accidental ingestion, or trafficking. Jenkins' suspicion was that "party" or "club" drug simply did not sound scary enough for draconian prohibition. By 1998, Jenkins notes, coverage of such spiking incidents in the late 1990s "implied a pervasive threat, with the media advocating defensive measures that appear grossly excessive."[14]

This transformation of club drugs into date rape drugs that Jenkins describes was, in fact, wildly successful beyond 1998. GHB is actually "a naturally occurring endogenous compound found in most mammalian

---

[14] Philip Jenkins, *Synthetic Panics: The Symbolic Politics of Designer Drugs*, (New York: New York University Press), 1999, 161.

tissue."[15] As such, it tends to turn up in all sorts of places. Endogenous levels in the human body vary widely from person to person, and tend to fluctuate. It is found naturally in some plants, foods, some wine grapes, and its chemical precursors (including GBL) are a by-product of industrial processes as well.[16] It was synthesized for potential pharmaceutical use in the 1920s.[17] Once someone obtains a precursor to GHB, a simple chemical mix can produce synthetic GHB itself.

Industrial errors led to a notorious contamination episode in 2006, where a children's craft kit called AquaDots was recalled for GHB toxicity. CNN dutifully reported that this toy was "contaminated with date rape drugs."[18] When in 2015 a lawsuit related to this contamination was finally settled, the press also claimed that the contaminant "metabolized into a date-rape drug" when ingested.[19]

In its Public Safety blotter on May 8, 2008, the *San Diego Union Tribune* reported the hospitalization of a toddler in Chula Vista, California who accidentally ingested her mother's liquid GHB stash.[20] An opportunity to learn more about the attractions and risks of GHB? A chance to examine how kids can get their hands on parents' drugs? Nope. "GHB is gamma hydroxybutyric acid, a colorless, odorless liquid that is often mixed in alcohol. It is commonly used in sexual assaults because it renders the victim incapable of resisting and can cause them to forget what happened."

---

[15] S.D. Ferrara, G. Frison, et al, "Gamma-hydroxybutyrate (GHB) and related products," in LeBeau, Marc and Mozayani, Ashraf, eds., *Drug facilitated sexual assault: a forensic handbook*, (London: Academic Press), 2001.

[16] Simon Elliott and Valerie Burgess, "The presence of gamma-hydroxybutyric acid (GHB) and gamma-butyrolactone (GBL) in alcoholic and non-alcoholic beverages." *Forensic Science International*, July 16, 2005; 151(2-3):289–92. The amounts in wine are too small to have an intoxicating impact on their own, but may, if not accounted for, affect lab tests.

[17] Nora Fitzgerald, K. Jack Riley, et al, "A Report to the Attorney General from the Department of Justice Drug-Facilitated Rape Working Group, Office of Justice Program, U.S. Department of Justice," June 26, 1998. https://www.ncjrs.gov/pdffiles1/pr/181396.pdf. Retrieved September 4, 2015.

[18] *CNN.com*, "Toy contaminated with 'date rape' drug pulled," November 8, 2007. Retrieved October 21, 2015. http://www.cnn.com/2007/US/11/08/toy.recall/.

[19] Emily Mahoney, "Aqua Dots trial: Jury awards $435K to Gilbert family," *Arizona Republic*, June 19, 2015. http://www.azcentral.com/story/news/local/gilbert/2015/06/18/jury-rules-favor-damages-aqua-dots-gilbert-monje-family/28898923/. Retrieved March 15, 2016.

[20] Debbi Farr Baker, "Public Safety, Regional: GHB-tainted bottle sickens toddler; mother arrested," *San Diego Union Tribune*, May 6, 2008, B-2. Retrieved October 21, 2015. http://legacy.utsandiego.com/news/metro/20080506-9999-1m6pubsafe.html.

But in order to look at this question more systematically—did the media's reframing of the Big Three into date rape drugs persist?—I looked at articles published in the years 1998, 2000, and 2008, in the largest US newspapers, searching for the exact phrase "date rape drug(s)."[21] In 1998, I found 118 articles using the term. Just under half of the articles (58, or 49.2%) did not concern drugging and sexual assault but were articles about the "Big Three" drugs concerning incidents such as arrest, voluntary use, drug trafficking, and accidental ingestion. Three articles concerned incidents involving other crimes like robbery. Just over half (60, or 50.2%) were actually about drugging and sexual assault. And so this documents the beginning of the shaping of the "date rape drugs" concept: they are labeled date rape drugs even in cases having nothing to do with this particular kind of crime. No wonder, then, that they developed a core identity as weapons and their other uses were shunted aside—even their more likely potential dangers.

Just two years later, after a significant period of impending legislative reform and restriction, as well as some high-profile cases, the amount of coverage increased notably. In the year 2000, using the same search criteria, 232 articles appeared. Yet only 89 of them—or just under 40%—had to do with either cases or legislation related to "date rape drugs" or concerning drugging and sexual assault together. A surprising number of articles had to do with voluntary use of GHB, including one case of a college athlete charged with possession in Florida, which accounted for 40 article mentions.[22] In contrast, *American Family Physician* (*AFP*), a publication for general practitioners, ran an article on GHB that year focusing mainly on its recreational appeal and its potential dangers using case studies, poison control statistics, and a list of about 40 colorful street

---

[21] Via a search in ProQuest National Newspaper Database, completed in January 2009, for the years 1998, 2000, and 2008. National Newspaper Database has 25 of the largest dailies in the USA; it should be kept in mind that smaller media markets and papers would be excluded, as would weekly magazines and online publications. I used only the exact phrase "date rape drug(s)" and not other phrases or drug names like GHB, drink spiking, etc. As such, this search, designed for comparison over time, is only a partial glimpse of media interest in the topic. I excluded duplicate entries, such as the same article in a regional and national edition of the same publication, or the same wire story in multiple publications when verbatim.

[22] Florida State rookie (at the time) Sebastian Janikowski was arrested near a nightclub in Tallahassee; most of the articles label the drugs he was arrested with as "date rape drugs," but this theme does not dominate—or confuse—the rest of the articles, which are about his football activity.

names it went by. While *AFP* noted in its report that GHB was "even being used as a date rape drug," it rightly did not presume that this was the primary problem doctors would be encountering with it.[23]

Other early cautions that the "date rape drugs" concept might be overblown came from a solicited report to the Attorney General, submitted in 1998 by researchers Nora Fitzgerald, Jack Riley, and associates.[24] Their cautions about responding to a relatively small threat that was dispersed across the vastness of the American pharmacopeia—both legal and illicit—were strongly worded. Questioning the usefulness of increased criminalization of these specific drugs in stanching supplies, they also said:

> The term "date rape drugs" appeared only within the last several years. The idea, however inaccurate, that there are only now drugs available suited to the facilitation of rape, has gained a currency which itself is dangerous by introducing the idea.[25]

Repeating the search for 2006 and 2008 yielded a noticeable drop in total articles mentioning the phrase, 92 and 93 articles, respectively. Again, substantial proportions did not concern drugging and/or sexual assault—35% in 2006 and 45% in 2008. I also compared the USA and the UK data set for the year 2008. Media interest in the UK was remarkably higher: 245 articles versus 93 in the US data set. And the "drifting term" problem was considerably more pronounced in the UK: just over 28% of the articles actually dealt with drugging and/or sexual assault related to GHB; the rest were references to voluntary use, related arrests, dealing, and so forth, along with marginally more use of the term (15 instances) as a metaphor or referent in an unrelated topic. Weiss and Colyer also found that, in general, date rape drug articles were more plentiful in Canada, the UK, and Australia than in the USA, despite the apparent origins of the modern scare in Florida and California.[26]

---

[23] Ted O'Connell, Lily Kaye, and John J. Plosay III, "Gamma-Hydroxybutyrate (GHB): A Newer Drug of Abuse," *American Family Physician*, 62, December 1, 2000, 2478–2482.
[24] Fitzgerald, Riley, et al., 1997. The authors found that the amount of newspaper coverage of date rape drugs decreased after 1996, and leveled off by the time they submitted their report. Of course, it still remained much higher than before 1996.
[25] Fitzgerald, Riley, et al., 1997.
[26] Weiss and Colyer, 2010.

As readers and news consumers became used to hearing the misleading term "date rape drugs" throughout the new millennium, what was the effect? Over time, confusion about the drugs and their use only seemed to increase. Sometimes, of course, this has continued to be a productive confusion for opinion leaders who seek more draconian penalties and surveillance powers as a part of the continuing, and now widely criticized, War on Drugs. But it also distorts discussions about rape itself, which, despite recent controversies regarding its measurement, is without question a genuinely large social problem.

Date Rape Then and Now, and Date Rape Drugs

The transition from "party drugs" or "club drugs" to "date rape drugs" in the mid- to late 1990s emerged on the heels of the first "college date rape crisis," but it does not seem to have sprung forth from it. It was pushed by antidrug forces instead. And it really was not that good of a thematic match to the campus issue, in any case. Those pushing for greater awareness and resources to be directed toward nonstranger rape did not exactly have a surreptitious spiker in mind when they conjured an updated image of the typical assailant. Fitzgerald and Riley noted in their Attorney General's report that while media coverage of "date rape drugs" increased dramatically, the early 1990s saw a scant number of articles related to the intersection of substance use and rape—and they all concerned alcohol.

The term "date rape" is itself a bit of a new term. It appears to have origins in 1980s, during a time of massive reform in rape law across the USA. Among the cultural changes that influenced the movement for legal reform was the recognition that most victims and offenders were nonstrangers and, in many cases, were socializing in some fashion before the assault.[27] Date rape is not any kind of official term, but rather one that

---

[27] In the wake of successful overturning of marital exemptions for rape, a countervailing expansion of unprotected victims to include cohabitants and even "voluntary social companions" emerged in some states. Effectively, such laws sought to limit criminal liability from any assailant who could

aimed to get at the circumstances surrounding more typical incidences of rape. While the US rape crisis movement of the early 1970s—as an outgrowth of ascendant second-wave feminism—challenged very pervasive ideas about rape that held sway beforehand (that it was rare, that women provoked it, that it was mainly at the hands of strangers, that wives and girlfriends could not be raped), it did not directly address intoxicated victims generally, nor women who were involuntarily intoxicated. Support for women who had been raped under such circumstances was unarticulated, but presumably categorical: there are no circumstances that justify sexual assault. But it is fair to say that early second-wave feminism's discussions of rape involved mainly force and threats, rather than incapacitation.

The only specific mentions of intoxication had to do with assailants: men whose sexual aggression increased when they drank and, in some cases, drink was used as an excuse for their behavior. Instead, the informal "victim disqualifying" biases shown by police, courts, and even peers—and then criticized in early literature of the era—were dress, sexual history, and prior relationship with the accused. Alcohol and drug use, voluntary or otherwise, was not addressed, though certainly it was the case that reactions to assault victims who had been drinking were dismissive or another disqualifier, even though the letter of the law said otherwise. While feminist-led legal rape reform efforts have led to remarkable reforms in law (such as rape shield laws, which generally bars attorneys in court from bringing up the complainant's sexual life, past or present), the effect on actual arrests, convictions, and the propensity of women to report rapes has been disappointing in the ensuing decades.[28]

In fact, ephemera from the era suggest that the problem of rape was largely thought of as a street crime problem. In the print materials from one of the first Speak Outs on rape sponsored by New York Radical Feminists, emphasis was placed on public vigilance, self-defense, prevention, and even firearms. As for who rapists were thought to be, mentioned are strangers, authority figures like bosses, and "husbands and boyfriends" but no attention was paid to that latter troubled dyad.

---

reasonably claim to have been such a social companion, encompassing what criminologists knew was a significant portion of cases. These eventually receded.

[28] Cassia Spohn and Julie Horney, *Rape law reform: a grassroots revolution and its impact*, (New York: Springer), 1992.

There was no mention of alcohol or drugs, let alone spiking.[29] Susan Brownmiller's 1975 best-selling book *Against Our Will*, likewise, made mention of alcohol's effects only in relationship to offender use and subsequent aggression.[30] The visible "Take Back the Night" marches on or near college campuses began in 1975, emphasizing the low level of safety of streets and public areas for women, including not just rape but physical assault as well. By default, the emphasis was the stranger-assailant.

Rape crisis centers, or organizations, began in the USA in the early 1970s, and in the late 1970s in the UK and Canada.[31] There has been much written about how these solidarity organizations, over time, became more like social services and developed less confrontational politics and less oppositional relationships with police, courts, and health facilities. It was through such organizations that knowledge about rape expanded beyond what the original organizers may have experienced firsthand or among their peers. The movement's increasing class, ethnic, and racial diversity over time also significantly expanded on-the-ground understanding not only of the context of rapes but also of their fraught aftermaths. This knowledge, in turn, shaped research and legal reform of rape laws. The general trend of making laws more favorable to the complainant has been solid; the effect on society as a whole, and criminal justice practice on the ground, has been slower.

Meanwhile, colleges and universities by and large abandoned *in loco parentis* rules that restricted women's social activities on campus much more than men's. It was then much easier for college women to do as they wished—and with this newfound freedom came increased risk. It was not until interest and research in acquaintance or date rape increased (roughly in the years 1985–1995) that the issue of intoxication and consent was taken on as a central concern in the overall antirape movement. It is how we learned more generally about the role of drugs and alcohol

---

[29] New York Radical Feminists, *Rape Conference for Women Only*, Washington Irving High School, New York City, April 17, Ephemera including handouts and conference agenda, 1971. These documents were later gathered in a published volume: Noreen Connell, ed., *Rape: The First Sourcebook for Women*, (New York: New American Library), 1974.

[30] Susan Brownmiller, *Against Our Will*, (New York: Bantam), 1975.

[31] Maria Bevacqua, "Reconsidering Violence against Women," in Stephanie Gilmore, ed., *Feminist Coalitions: Historical Perspectives on Second-Wave Feminism in the United States*, Urbana: University of Illinois Press, 2008, 163–177.

in both enhancing the vulnerability of victims and opportunistic behavior on the part of rapists with intoxicated victims, on the one hand, and greater specificity about how assailants' consumption of alcohol altered their behavior, on the other.

The popularity of the term "date rape" no doubt stemmed from the need to shift the imagined problem away from the stranger lurking in the shadows, and toward the much more common acquaintance. In many nonstranger cases, the assailant is someone who the victim was socializing with (date, friend, classmate, fellow partygoer) when the assault took place, either by force, threat, or lack of ability to consent.

While I do not think the entire development of a controversy over campus date rape in the 1990s needs to be elaborated here, a few key points of contention would eventually become salient to understanding the subsequent date rape drugs scare. The term "date rape" emerged alongside a highly noted study by Mary Koss and her colleagues, whose results were published in both *Ms. Magazine* and peer-reviewed journals.[32] It was a large, multicampus survey that found that 15.4% of college women had experienced an assault that met the legal definition of rape since age 14; another 12.4% had experienced an *attempt* at this type of assault (attempts are also felonies). Forty-two percent had never disclosed the assault to anyone. Eight percent of college men admitted to engaging in acts that met the legal definition of rape or sexual assault.

Immediately, some confusion emerged among both advocates and critics: some erroneously thought that this meant that one in four college women had been assaulted while in college. Others did not realize that respondents had described incidents to the interviewers, and then the interviewers categorized the incident as an assault, using legal definitions. Some critics seemed to object to researchers making these decisions, but also seemed to object to women themselves calling something "rape." Subsequent surveys found similar numbers from year to year, so it is unlikely that the methodology was faulty. Neame's review (2004) of this

---

[32] M.P. Koss, C.A. Gidycz, N. Wisniewski, "The scope of rape: Incidence and prevalence of sexual aggression and victimization in a national sample of higher education students," *Journal of Consulting and Clinical Psychology*, 55, 1987, 162–170.

period of backlash points out that as sound social science, the research has not been challenged.[33]

Most of the backlash, however, was a reaction to the impact of the research in the broader culture. Some argued that the feminist movement had become so preoccupied with violence against women that it "infantilized" women and saw them only as potential victims rather than adults with some ability to self-regulate. (This critique was not entirely limited to antifeminists.) Conflating a set of perhaps irritating cultural turns with what the social science research actually said, there emerged a distinctive trope—the young, relatively privileged collegiate who drank too much and regretted an encounter with a probably equally drunken bedmate, so much so that she called it rape. In this scenario, at least in its typical form, the hapless male is unfairly accused by a vindictive female. In a postfeminist age, where the female is no longer required to be chaste as an ideal, her inability to chalk up a regrettable or objectively ambiguous night makes her a kind of flawed, agenda-driven crusader and thus, the critics alleged, the campuses were thrown into a tizzy for no good reason. Thus, it was that the controversy began to center on ambiguities in consent.

This is one of those strange areas where the law, as written, has always been way out ahead of cultural mores. If a woman willingly consumes enough to make her incapable of consent, or if she knowingly consumes drugs that produce a similar impairment, and she is then subject to sexual activity, sober critics and even moderate drinkers can make judgmental glances, but there is simply no legal ambiguity: a person who cannot consent is presumed to not consent.

The devil, however, is in the details; specifically: evidence. As with most sexual assault allegations, only the victim and assailant are present. Assailants can *always* counterallege consensual relations. When we say "too drunk to consent," what do we mean? And here a genuine lack of consensus emerged. Any alcohol? Too drunk to drive, but not too drunk to walk with a companion? Stumbling back to the dorm room? These are the kinds of questions that were asked then, and again in recent years, as

---

[33] Alexandra Neame, "Revisiting America's 'date rape' controversy," *Family Matters*, 68, Australian Institute of Family Studies, Winter 2004.

the campus rape problem has again drawn a great deal of media interest and campus activism.

In the long run, though, the activism and research of the 1990s, however, did succeed in changing perceptions of the typical rape. It appears that at a certain point, though, the gains associated with a more thorough understanding of the commonality of sexual assault among nonstrangers peaked and then stalled. Perhaps too many assumed that once we all knew that this was the more common circumstance than the man jumping out of the bushes, then we would see greater consequences for sexual assailants. But instead, since the 1990s, it appears that neither reporting rates (the likelihood that a victim will report an assault to the police) nor conviction rates have systematically improved. In some ways, perhaps caution was warranted in this matter. Given what we already knew about the circumstances under which women were more likely to report sexual assault to the police (by a stranger, if there were other physical injuries, if the assailant used a weapon), the likelihood that nonstranger rape reporting would increase drastically was low to begin with. Still, the almost complete lack of improvement in reporting is troubling.

It would be tempting to say that the rise of concern about so-called date rape *drugs* constituted a new realm of victimization that might be "owned" by antirape activists acting as moral entrepreneurs, representing a potential new expanded domain of problems to be solved.[34] But this does not appear to be the case, at least not in a sustained way. After initial interest by victim advocates and rape crisis staffers, the drugging scenario is increasingly looked at as a rarity by such forces, and even sometimes as a bit of a distraction. When they talk to the media about date rape drugs, they often try to shift the focus back onto alcohol—albeit not always successfully, since many campus activists equate any mention of alcohol as inherently victim blaming, a problem I will return to later in the book.

---

[34] "Moral entrepreneurs" are, in the words of sociologist Howard Becker, people who seek a wide-ranging change in cultural or social norms and practices by identifying, categorizing, and typifying some sort of disturbing social problem. In the case of crime or violence, such entrepreneurs often pull incidents from existing categories into new ones. When successful, moral entrepreneurs succeed in convincing opinion leaders and sometimes broad public opinion that the problem is urgent, unaddressed adequately, and distinct enough from other problems to be so labeled. See Becker, *Outsiders: Studies in the Sociology of Deviance*. (New York: The Free Press), 1963.

The Co-optation of Date Rape by Drugs

Sarah E.H. Moore's study of the co-optation of the term "date rape" into the "date rape drugs" concept suggests that in the social imaginary, still, we have failed "at the level of culture, to fully assimilate feminist arguments about sexual violence."[35] Her study of the use of the new term "date rape" in the media first documents a rapid increase in mentions in US news sources beginning in 1987. By the 1990s, the amount of coverage, and Rohypnol coverage, increased, too. But the concepts, once merged in the mid-1990s, were forever woven together thereafter. Moore found:

> Of the newspaper reports in 1995 that contained the phrase "date rape," only twenty-two (or 4 percent) mentioned Rohypnol. Of the newspaper reports in 1996 that contained the phrase "date rape," 378 (or 34 percent) mentioned Rohypnol. This was the year that Rohypnol stopped being represented as "teen narco," and came instead to be seen as the "rapist's weapon": of all the newspaper reports that mentioned Rohypnol in 1996, a staggering 92 percent mentioned "date rape."

And by 1998, Moore finds:

> from 1996 to 1998 three-quarters (75.2 percent) of "date rape" cases reported in the news involve the spiking of a victim's drink with a drug.

It is now fairly routine, in fact, to not only describe suspected bar druggings as "date rape" but also use general statistics on sexual assault in general to bolster the significance of the drink spiking problem, in much the same way as the Canadian coverage of GHB seizures did. In a September 2015 article in the *Milwaukee Journal-Sentinel* (Wisconsin), a new organization, Date Rape Awareness Milwaukee, is described.[36] One of the founders drank four beers and then remembers little of her actions

---

[35] Sarah E.H. Moore, "Tracing the Life of a Crime Category: The shifting meaning of 'date rape'," *Feminist Media Studies*, Vol. 11, No. 4, 2011, 451–465.
[36] Marion Renault, "Group builds awareness of date rapes in Milwaukee's bar scene," *Milwaukee Journal-Sentinel*, August 31, 2015.

afterward, though her friends describe "chasing after her as she ran wild." She believes that she was given GHB, and that this was the second time she was drugged. She was not sexually assaulted this time, but this incident prompted her to form the organization and launch its awareness campaigns. For background, the story used general statistics on sexual assault (3500 such reports from law enforcement and crisis centers) in Milwaukee County, and anecdotes from volunteers that were about suspected drugging. The *San Jose Mercury News* (California) reported on two 2013 suspected drink spiking incidents at the Nickel Rose pub in Marin, which this time were indeed followed by sexual assault complaints.[37] The headline, "Police investigate two cases of date rape at Marin nightclub," was a good example of Moore's point: the rapes took place elsewhere, and neither victim remembers being on a date. The fact that it was fairly easy to parse what the article meant—that it was suspecting druggings that took place at the Nickel Rose—only underscores the mangling of the term "date rape." No follow-up reports have emerged about the incidents since in the press, which is typical for such reports. The failure of news outlets to follow up on suspected public-place druggings adds to the fixed notion that the scope of the problem is both distinct yet irresolvable. And yet, weren't their two rape complaints? Why were they no longer newsworthy?

Date Rape Drugs as a Reversion in Rape Thinking

In her 2009 column on the then crescendo-like media obsession with drink spiking, Amanda Hess sarcastically called out the "date rape drugs industrial complex" as fomenting fear about a relatively rare occurrence and trying to shift talk about rape back to the lurking stranger.[38]

There really does seem to be such a complex: a loose grouping of mutually reinforcing claims-makers, including news reporters, politicians,

---

[37] Megan Hansen, "Police investigate two cases of date rape at Marin nightclub," *San Jose Mercury News*, September 27, 2013. http://www.mercurynews.com/breaking-news/ci_24189306/police-investigate-two-cases-date-rape-at-marin. Retrieved October 26, 2015.

[38] Amanda Hess, "The Date Rape Drug Is an Urban Myth. Let's Put It to Rest," *Washington City Paper*, October 28, 2009. http://www.washingtoncitypaper.com/blogs/sexist/2009/10/28/the-date-rape-drug-is-in-an-urban-myth-lets-put-it-to-rest/. Retrieved October 26, 2015.

researchers, campus administrators, entrepreneurs, and self-styled activists, that keep this rather dubious formulation intact. They tend to raise the specter of drugging out of whole cloth, exaggerate the amount of uncertainty about the numbers, or simply piggyback on harrowing rape statistics in general—for reasons ranging from overconfident laziness about the facts to strategic use of the idea to shape events, respond to crises, and put forth policy proposals.

Hess noted the face-saving qualities of the formulation: "Now, society is ready to accept that a rape victim is still a rape victim if she goes out to a bar with her girlfriends and has a few drinks—as long as her intoxication is capped off with a surprise roofie." It is basically a form of victim blaming that manages to look like victim sympathy at first. Many opinion leaders and policy-makers are squeamish about asserting the simple right of intoxicated people (women in particular) to *not be assaulted*, no matter how they got that way. At the same time, public health officials are confronting increased binge drinking, with inclines sharper among women. Inflating the surreptitious drugging threat can provide a more comfortable, consensus-building platform, even as it focuses on a relatively small corner of the alcohol and rape problem.

But after a whole generation of partially successful shifts in understanding and attitudes about rape, why the desire to resymbolize intoxication as involuntary? Why the return of Lurking Man Who Plies the Unknowing Victim as a stand-in for the ordinary case? To some extent, because while acquaintance rape accounts for the majority of cases, stranger rape still happens enough to provide a reservoir of material for forming symbolic (and often preferred) substitutions for the general problem. Bar Spiking Man may be myth in the same kind of way, but there are always a few high-profile cases—or suspected cases—to draw upon. In fact, such cases, rarities though they are, often direct the spotlight to particular drugs, even though their characteristics differ little from other, easily obtained drugs. But there is more than discomfort about drinking here: there is also new iterations of the techno-utopian followed by techno-nightmarish depiction of new drugs. And the always present desire to be in the know about murky things—and the press certainly depicts the spiking problem as much murkier than it really is.

The Rise of the "Big Three": Flunitrazepam ("Roofies"), GHB, and Ketamine

A reminder of sorts is probably useful at this point: there is nothing special in the group of drugs now typically classed as date rape drugs. They are not uniquely effective compared with many other drugs at making potential victims vulnerable. They are not found in particularly high numbers in toxicology tests, especially compared with alcohol or street drugs, but not even in comparison with other diverted pharmaceuticals. The only big factors are that they were new, or somewhat new, as sought-after recreational drugs at a time when many people (not just in the USA, but in other developed countries) began turning a skeptical eye toward the War on Drugs.

Federal and State law enforcement agencies and public health agencies began surveillance on these date rape drugs at a time when they were ripe for relabeling by antidrug forces, who were clearly incentivized to seek new domains at that point. The alcohol, street drugs, widely prescribed benzodiazepines, and over-the-counter preparations most commonly found in those who felt they might have been drugged seemed to be hiding in plain sight—routinely found in toxicology reports but generating little interest and certainly no new, specialized legislation. Same old, same old. But newer drugs as chemical weapons? Excellent potential for hyperbole.

It is worth considering what we know about "the Big Three."

Flunitrazepam (Rohypnol)

Introduced in mid-1970s as a sleep aid in Europe, Hoffman-LaRoche's Rohypnol (flunitrazepam) was never slated for marketing, nor approved, in the USA. The USA, it seems, already had too many potential competitors with similar effectiveness in treating insomnia. Western societies, and in particular the USA, have a great deal of chronic sleeplessness, and increasing knowledge of the mechanisms of sleep beginning in the 1960s enabled a boom in insomnia treatments.[39]

---

[39] John W. Shepard, Jr, Daniel J. Buysse, et al., "History of the Development of Sleep Medicine in the United States," *Journal of Clinical Sleep Medicine*. 2005 Jan 15; 1(1): 61–82.

Until 1996, flunitrazepam could be used in the USA only if a patient held a foreign prescription and brought it back. After that, it was restricted in most places until 2000, where as part of the Federal Date Rape Drugs Act, it was pushed to Schedule I—subject to the strictest regulation and for most intents and purposes, a legal classification that amounts to outright prohibition, with the penalties being harsh and codified. This drug, though, eventually lent its name to the more general drugging problem, or fear of it.

It is a benzodiazepine, much like other widely available antianxiety drugs such as Xanax (alprazolam) and Valium (diazepam), but considerably stronger. The regulatory battle over it began in Florida, where, like other southern states, emergency rooms (ERs) and drug treatment centers began to cope with the adverse effects of Rophynol smuggled in through Mexico. Part of its menace was that it was inexpensive, at under $5 per dose, and for a while not hard to get, as it was legal in most of Europe and Latin America.[40] Florida changed its state law to push it to Schedule I in 1996. The drug's effects include rapid drowsiness and disinhibition, though some users experience a paradoxical effect of excitability or aggression. It has a marked propensity to produce anterograde amnesia, which probably figures into the street lore surround it as a "forgetting pill." Mixed with alcohol, it poses grave dangers to respiration and the combination can be fatal.

Sought after by drug users to counteract the lingering effect of stimulants, and by those seeking to boost an opiate high or manage withdrawal symptoms, it generated its most sensational headlines by incidents of suspected drug spiking followed by rape. Hoffman-LaRoche was making $100 million in annual profits from it by the time lawmakers moved to suppress it in the USA in 1996.[41] In an effort to stave off increased regulation and enhanced scheduling, Hoffman-LaRoche launched a "watch your drink!" campaign, which it claimed would alert potential spiking victims to the danger without tipping potential assailants off to a new

---

[40] Mireya Navarro, "In South, Drug Abusers Turn to a Smuggled Sedative," *New York Times*, December 9, 1995. http://www.nytimes.com/1995/12/09/us/in-south-drug-abusers-turn-to-a-smuggled-sedative.html. Retrieved September 4, 2015.

[41] Weikel, Dan, "'Rape Drug' Battle Rages: Amid Growing Evidence of Misuse, Maker Fights Push to Outlaw Rohypnol," *Los Angeles Times*, August 19, 1996. http://articles.latimes.com/1996-08-19/news/mn-35742_1_drugs-rohypnol-misuse. Retrieved October 28, 2015.

method for their madness.[42] The firm also lobbied the Florida legislature hard to counter stricter regulation, and won—at least initially. The Florida attorney general, Robert Butterworth, then used his emergency powers to designate Rohypnol as a Schedule I drug.[43] A serial case in Florida helped solidify the push for greater criminalization as Rohypnol's supposedly distinct advantages as a date rape pill were exaggerated. It also set a template for drugging crime that shaped the discussion of predatory drugging thereafter.

In the early 1990s, according to Broward County Prosecutor Bob Nichols, a Florida man named Mark Perez bragged to his bar buddies that he had drugged and attacked a number of women using Rohypnol. Nichols used the Perez case to suggest that Rohypnol was a kind of new drug rape weapon, and presented one allegation in particular—the only one that would end in Perez' conviction for sexual battery and a sentence of eight years in prison—as a prototypical scenario. He was convicted in 1995 of an attack on a woman who he did indeed meet at a nightclub.[44] She contacted police after blacking out while still at the club and then for many hours, waking partially during the assault, and awaking in her own apartment.[45] Nichols told the Associated Press and *Newsweek* that police suspected more than 20 such victims, aiding the impression that Perez had become a shadowy supervillain of rape through the *unique* powers of Rohypnol. Perez made no comments to the press.[46]

---

[42] *PR Newswire*, "Hoffman La-Roche offers law enforcement testing capability in fight against Rohypnol misuse; company also intensifies efforts through advanced educational program," June 14, 1996.

[43] Butterworth was also one of the earliest prosecutors to file suit against the tobacco firms, an initiative that eventually went nationwide. In the USA, states may restrict substances at higher schedule levels than prescribed by the Federal government.

[44] Florida Corrections record for Perez: Retrieved September 4, 2015. http://offender.fdle.state.fl.us/offender/flyer.do?personNbr=17868.

[45] Burrell, Cassandra, "Penalties May Increase for 'date-rape' pill use," *Daily News* (Bowling Green, KY), Associated Press, July 17, 1996, p. 7-A. Retrieved March 15, 2016. https://news.google.com/newspapers?nid=1696&dat=19960717&id=a_oaAAAAIBAJ&sjid=u0cEAAAAIBAJ&pg=4891,1516888&hl=en.

[46] In US legal settings, it is not uncommon for criminal defendants to remain silent either before the court or to allegations voiced in the press. This silence is usually on the advice of the defense attorneys, and should not be construed as an admission of guilt.

Press reporting on the case set the stage for Rohypnol's transformation into the quintessential "crime in a pill" despite its primarily recreational use, and its similarity to other strong anxiolytics and sleep aids already on the market. Countering Hoffman-LaRoche's observation that "alcohol is the number one date rape drug," Nichols insisted that "no other drug is as tailored to a rapist's need…We've never come up with a pill that has these specific characteristics," he said. "I know of no [other] pill that erases your memory and takes effect in 10 minutes."[47] Except for all the others, of course.

But the Perez case's timing was certainly helpful in the run-up to increased restriction and penalties. Up until this case, most of the concern voiced by government agencies, including those in Florida, and the press about Rohypnol was about how attractive its cheap price and pharmaceutical origins made it to experimenting teens and partiers.[48] Somewhere along the way, Rohypnol became "roofies" and now "being roofied" still stands in for any surreptitious drugging incident.

In seeking similar restrictive legislation, a California lawmaker, Assemblyman Larry Bowler, opined that "[b]ecause of the rapes, this drug is the only drug known to victimize the innocent"—a claim that marked a subtle, but decisive shift to an era in which the "Big Three" were thought to have a specialized, almost magical role in predatory use, particularly for rape.[49] At the same time, the roofie rape scare smuggled in the revival of some very antiquated notions about both intoxication and rape, much like the Canadian Alliance campaign some years later. The Spitzer Twins case—a 1996 dual assailant, serial drug-and-rape case in California discussed in the next chapter—probably launched the preoccupation with

---

[47] Jackie Hallifax, "Illegal Sedative Used on Rape Victims," *Los Angeles Times*, Associated Press, June 9, 1996. http://articles.latimes.com/1996-06-09/news/mn-13222_1_roofie. Retrieved on September 4, 2015; Newsweek Staff, "Roofies: the Date Rape Drug," *Newsweek*, February 25, 1996. http://www.newsweek.com/roofies-date-rape-drug-180048. Retrieved March 15, 2016.

[48] Moore's 2011 study of media coverage of the topic concurs that Rohypnol was depicted primarily as a menace to young, voluntary drug-takers prior to late 1995.

[49] Bowler quoted in Weikel, 1996. The bill, which sought to make surreptitious drugging an aggravating circumstance which would trigger the "one-strike" felony mandatory penalty scheme in effect at the time, failed based on its various redundancies of existing law.

roofies there. The case was also one of the few reported in the media to have begun with actual dates.[50]

National concern emerged quickly. One of the first appearances of the term was in the *Chicago Tribune* in November of 1995, in the article "New Drug Finds Way Into Date-Rape Scenario," which relied heavily on the Florida scare, saying that Rohypnol had been called (unclear by whom) the "date rape drug" and "the Quaalude of the 90s."[51] *Newsweek* ran a short but apparently impactful article in February 1996 with the headline "Roofies: The Date-Rape Drug." While rape was one of the angles mentioned in the article, it was not the major storyline, which hewed fairly closely to the usual "new drug scourge" script of novel teen abuse and health dangers. The article provided the Drug Enforcement Administration (DEA) data on the disproportionate number of seizures in southern states, owing to the drug's legal status in Mexico and Latin America, and underscored the primarily recreational, self-medicating nature of flunitrazepam's appeals and abuses.

But the term had an immediate appeal, assigning as it did an element of violence to a powerful insomnia treatment—one with very few legal users in the USA—and portraying its underground market diversion as a kind of sophisticated means of systematic rape planning. In this way, the understanding of date rape itself was transformed. *American Speech* recognized the neologisms "date rape drug" and "roofie" the next year.[52] The term moved quickly into more official parlance and labeling. In the US Congress, hearings on greater restriction at the federal level took place in 1996.[53] Terence Woodworth, Deputy Director at the DEA's Office of Diversion Control, gave Congressional testimony attesting to the primacy of roofies in thinking about date rape drugging. "Untold numbers of unsuspecting young women are being victimized

---

[50] Sue McAllister, "Jury Convicts Twin Brothers in Date Rape Drugging Case," *Los Angeles Times*, June 18, 1998. http://articles.latimes.com/1998/jun/18/local/me-61130. Retrieved November 2, 2015.

[51] "New Drug Finds Way into Date-rape Scenario," *Chicago Tribune*, November 27, 1995. http://articles.chicagotribune.com/1995-11-27/news/9511280007_1_roofies-rohypnol-date-rape-drug. Retrieved October 29, 2015.

[52] John Algeo and Adele Algeo, "Among the New Words," *American Speech*, v72, #2, 1997, 185

[53] Federal drug scheduling provides a minimal level of regulation at the state level in the USA, but not a maximal one.

and abused by criminals who spike their drinks with Rohypnol, so much that Rohypnol has gained notoriety as the 'date rape' drug."[54] As with most aggressive claims of uncertainty up through the present day, the number of such incidents was "untold" only in the sense that they were relatively rare and therefore without much help in substantiating such claims. Voluntary ingestion by illicit users had, however, created by this point a well-evidenced public health problem. The Clinton administration, using existing FDA exclusions, in 1996 ordered US Customs to eliminate the "personal use" exemption for travelers bringing Rohypnol back from abroad, and gave full seizure powers at Customs.

In 1997, Hoffman-LaRoche reformulated the pill so that any contact with liquid would turn the liquid blue. While approving of the company's actions, the District of Columbia Rape Crisis Center expressed concerns that the singling out of Rohypnol and GHB as date rape drugs would cause people to ignore other drugs, including alcohol. It asserted the typicality of acquaintance rather than stranger rapes. In the same statement, however, they reinforced the bar-spiking scenario, with the usual list of drink surveillance, night-out cautions.

The drug was prohibited altogether in the USA as a Schedule IV Controlled Substance (the designation that Hoffman-LaRoche had originally hoped for), but with Schedule I possession and trafficking penalties akin to those for heroin and LSD. At this level, no exceptions are made for therapeutic use. Today, flunitrazepam is almost never found in toxicology screens or drug seizures in the USA, and it should be if it is indeed being used this way. Toxicological evidence of flunitrazepam is easier to come by than GHB: it is detectable in blood for about 24 hours, in urine for five to ten days, and can be found in hair samples for weeks.[55] The temptation is then to assume that draconian prohibition was effective in preventing drug rape. But most other countries continue to make it available

---

[54] The growth in Rohypnol trafficking cases was real but lacked the galloping epidemic quality hinted at: "Between 1985 and 1991, DEA had three cases or less each year involving Rohypnol. In 1993, that number climbed to 15, primarily in Texas and Florida. By 1995, DEA had 38 Rohypnol investigations. By March 1996, DEA had initiated 108 cases, and the United States Customs Service had 271 cases." (Terence Woodworth, The Abuse and Trafficking of Rohypnol, DEA Congressional Testimony, US Congress, July 16, 1996)

[55] Adam Negrusz, "Detection of 'Date-Rape' Drugs in Hair and Urine, Final Report," National Institute of Justice, Office of Justice Programs, Document 201894, 2003.

by prescription and penalize nonprescription use or trafficking. The drug (in generic form) remains available for limited therapeutic purposes in Europe, yet it appears that predatory use of it rarely has happened there. The UK did not find a single such case confirmed until 2007, though other sedatives have occasionally been found in assault victims.[56] The UK was one of the first countries to restrict it, in 1985, as a Class C controlled substance, and National Health Services (NHS) prescriptions were stopped in 1992. In the USA, flunitrazepam continues to be smuggled in primarily from Mexico and Canada, and though teenagers have reported a slight decline in use since 1996 (when the high school survey, *Monitoring the Future*, first added a Rohypnol question), it continues to have a small but steady interest for recreational use.[57]

Since being roofied now appears to be a generic term for being drugged, an element of humor and verbal play has emerged around the term, as was the case with chloral and ether in the nineteenth century. In 2009 was released the movie *The Hangover*, which was about a group of friends who go off to Las Vegas for an anarchic bachelor-party weekend, where one of them drugs the others with what he thinks is Ecstasy. He later finds out that he bought flunitrazepam instead, explaining their blackout amnesia. In chatting with his spacy dealer, they both try to figure out why the drug is called "roofie" and not "rapie."

GHB

Many health and public safety websites refer to GHB as a "commonly used" date rape drug. Ambiguous at best, this often makes it sound as if GHB is used this way *often*. It is true that GHB is found more often

---

[56] Jenny Hope, "Drug rape myth exposed as study reveals binge drinking is to blame," *Daily Mail*, February 16, 2007. http://www.dailymail.co.uk/news/article-436592/Drug-rape-myth-exposed-study-reveals-binge-drinking-blame.html. The article refers specifically to the upshot of a drug scare in Wales, discussed in the next chapter; Camber, Rebecca, "Date-Rape Drug Has Never Been Used in a Sex Attack Here," *Daily Mail*, January 31, 2007, 7. Retrieved via Lexis-Nexis Academic, October 27, 2015. This article references the claim by law enforcement that other drugs and alcohol are typically found in lab tests.

[57] See biyearly reports, including the most recent, L.D. Johnston, P.M. O'Malley, et al., "Monitoring the Future national results on drug use: 1975–2013: Overview, Key Findings on Adolescent Drug Use," Ann Arbor: Institute for Social Research, University of Michigan, 2014. http://www.monitoringthefuture.org/.

in toxicology tests than roofies or ketamine, but that does not make the finding "common."

GHB is not difficult to make in a home lab from easily obtained ingredients and an internet recipe. Like Rophynol, GHB was already considered a date rape drug by mid-1990s despite its primary illicit use being voluntary. Some agencies like the National Institute on Drug Abuse (NIDA) continued to describe it as a club drug while acknowledging its newer reputation as a date rape drug.[58] Users cite its pleasant effects that mimic light-to-moderate alcohol ingestion—without the calories, nausea, or hangover. It is often used to "pregame" before going out to save calories and money.[59]

In larger doses, GHB presents very similar severe symptoms to dangerously high blood alcohol levels—in other words, even in crisis situations, alcohol and GHB overintoxication may easily be mistaken for one another, and simultaneous ingestion presents a unique danger in that GHB slows alcohol elimination, thus keeping blood alcohol content (BAC) levels higher for longer, though contrary to internet lore, it does not actually raise BAC levels. GHB and alcohol together can be quite dangerous. Contrary to blanket claims that date rape drugs are "odorless, colorless, and tasteless," GHB is distinctly salty, and its precursor GBL is described by users as stale or putrid. So if a drink is to be tampered, it must be one that can disguise this taste well.

Like LSD, it enjoyed a legal period in which favorable views developed among some scientists and users. It was often available at vitamin stores. Like flunitrazepam, polydrug users often used it as a sleep aid to counteract the edginess left by other drugs, while bodybuilders and athletes used it to accelerate muscle strength improvements (and despite its illegality, some still do). In the USA, a very narrow exception in law exists for prescription Xyrem,[60] a GHB drug used for sleep disorders. Amateur

---

[58] NIDA, *Community Drug Alert Bulletin—Club Drugs*, 2004. http://archives.drugabuse.gov/ClubAlert/clubdrugalert.html. Retrieved October 27, 2015.

[59] Tamar Nordenberg, "The Death of the Party: All the Rave, GHB's Hazards Go Unheeded," *FDA Consumer*, March/April, 2000. Retrieved October 27, 2015. http://permanent.access.gpo.gov/lps1609/www.fda.gov/fdac/features/2000/200_ghb.html.

[60] Xyrem (sodium oxybate) is manufactured by Jazz Pharmaceuticals. In the law's enactment in 2000, GHB was moved to Schedule I, but permitted for limited research in line with protocols from the less-restrictive Schedule III.

manufacture of GHB, like other illicit drugs, is done with varying degrees of care. Since GHB use and the internet grew up together, we have more recreational user reports available about the effects of this drug. Around 1–3 g is the typical dose. Like Ecstasy, it is sought after because it creates a warm and sociable feeling, and users report reduced inhibition. The slippage between reduced inhibition and vulnerability to sexual assault that often appears in legislative and media accounts of both Ecstasy and GHB are notable and troubling—it is as if these states of being are the same thing. Like Ecstasy, GHB is sometimes described as an aphrodisiac, which is imprecise—both are simply disinhibitors; GHB is occasionally associated with bizarre behavior or aggression, as well. Alcohol, of course, has these same properties.

As euphoric feelings may overlap, it should be noted that there are key differences between the drugs. MDMA is a stimulant which acts on serotonin levels in the brain, while GHB is a CNS depressant. But GHB is also different in that it produces different adverse effects. GHB is more likely pose an acute threat right away, with peak levels at roughly 30 minutes, and once the threat has passed, effects are minimal. The adverse effects of MDMA are usually long term and more chronic in nature: users sometimes report a rebound effect of severe depression, anxiety, or paranoia.[61]

ERs saw a rapid increase in GHB-related cases in the late 1990s, which should have been concerning enough on its own. Visits soared from less than 20 cases in 1992 to over 700 in 1997.[62] Studies looking to examine the validity of self-reported drug use in ERs and clinics have found GHB a particularly difficult drug to decipher in terms of intentionality. Its mimicry of other street drugs makes it unclear what the patient intended. It indeed may be that some individuals may misremember what they have or have not taken, or may be confused about what was offered to them on the dance floor. GHB and Ecstasy are both club drugs, and one indeed might readily end up with the former while assuming one was getting the latter.

---

[61] Explanations range from prior self-selection in drug seeking to what appears to be damage to serotonin-balancing mechanisms in the brain.
[62] Nordenberg, 2000.

5 A "New" Problem Appears in the 1990s

Since Ecstasy is expensive, there is some indication that in casual illicit sales, GHB is not uncommonly passed off as Ecstasy to new users. To complicate matters, GHB is sometimes referred to as "Liquid X" or "liquid ecstasy."[63] The list of street names from *American Family Physician* in 2000 also revealed that GHB was often marketed and sold as a close alternative to other drugs, such as "nature's Quaalude," "ever clear," and "cherry meth"—suggesting that GHB has a more divergent perception of effects than many other street drugs. GHB, it seems, is a bit of a shape-shifter. Thus, with GHB, it is very hard to figure out who intended to do what, for what reason, when someone tests positive for GHB. The assumption that it is typically a "near miss" prelude to a sexual assault—absence of evidence of that intent—is not grounded in reality.

In Congressional hearings preceding revisions to the Controlled Substances Act in 1998, Rep. Bill McCollum related his frustration that the dangers of these drugs did not appear to be getting through:

> The Associated Press reported yesterday that two Penn State students were rushed to a local hospital after intentionally ingesting gamma hydroxybutyrate, popularly known as GHB. The director of the University's Office of Student Health Services was particularly upset, since Penn State's students are warned about potential date rape drugs at orientation. GHB is one of the drugs discussed at that orientation, and yet the message clearly did not get through.

The threat of sexual assault was quickly taking over any other concern about adverse physical or psychosocial effects of drug use. The possibility that dressing GHB up in date rape drugs clothing might not be much of a deterrent to voluntary users was not considered.

In 2005, researchers noted that GHB combinations were becoming more common and deliberately sought after, and that users describe the experience as a smoother version of Ecstasy. Dutch researchers Uys and

---

[63] GHB is a popular club drug, and since purchase of either MDMA or GHB is an illicit transaction, users must rely on street dealers, who may substitute one for another due to fluctuating supplies or costs. Beginning with its rise in popularity in the 1990s, dealers might commonly substitute the cheaper GHB or one of its analogs. Judith C. Barker, Shana L. Harris, and Jo E. Dyer. "Experiences of Gamma Hydroxybutyrate (GHB) Ingestion: A Focus Group Study," *Journal of Psychoactive Drugs* 39.2, 2007, 115–129.

Niesink suggest there are indeed underlying differences in psychoactive effects that may enhance satisfaction with the experience. "The 'sleepy' feeling of GHB is diminished by the stimulating activity of MDMA without MDMA taking away the 'alcohol-like' feeling of GHB." GHB users are also quite likely, more often than not, to use it in combination with other drugs and share GHB experiences with people they already know.[64]

Given the problems presented by a new underground drug that seemed to elude characterization and seemed to be called a lot of things—it often seemed like not-quite-that-other-drug—it was surprising that the "dangerous new drug attracting teens" did not suffice. Instead, there was a persistent attempt to shoehorn GHB's threats into a sexual assault framework. Consider the young women who gave their names to the landmark Federal date rape drugs legislation—Samantha Reid and Hillory Farias.

Samantha Reid, age 15, of Michigan attended a small house party with friends. She and at least one other teen were given GHB in their drinks, most likely without their knowledge. A third girl asked for alcohol and was served some. Others present said the girls who were given GHB began vomiting and lost consciousness. The young men holding the party (and who spiked the drinks) refused to take them to the hospital or call an ambulance at first, and instead left the house to get cleaning supplies. When they eventually brought the girls to the ER, they pretended the girls had been elsewhere. Four of the men were eventually charged with involuntary manslaughter and served terms of several years each.[65] Reid died at the hospital; the other girl, Melanie Sindone, recovered. None of the girls were sexually assaulted. Though the ensuing publicity about Reid's death made it sounds as if the girls were "lured" to an apartment,

---

[64] Joachim D. K. Uys & Raymond J. M. Niesink, "Pharmacological aspects of the combined use of 3,4-methylenedioxymethamphetamine (MDMA, ecstasy) and gamma-hydroxybutyric acid (GHB): a review of the literature," *Drug and Alcohol Review* 24, July 2005, 359–368; Zsófia Németh, Bernadette Kun, and Zsolt Demetrovics, "The involvement of gamma-hydroxybutyrate in reported sexual assaults: a systematic review," *Journal of Psychopharmacology* 24, 9, 1281–1287, 2010.

[65] Jackie Harrison Martin, "Remembering Samantha Reid: 10th anniversary of teen's GHB death," *News-Herald* (Downriver, Michigan), January 16, 2009. Retrieved October 28, 2015. http://www.thenewsherald.com/articles/2009/01/16/news/doc4970e3f098507043714937.txt.

the boys who they were hanging out with were trusted friends, according to Melanie, and her sense of betrayal was profound.[66]

The Farias case from Texas is even more peculiar. Hillory, age 16, went to a party where she drank two sodas. At least one was shared with a friend without incident. She came home, went to sleep, and failed to regain consciousness. At some point in the early morning, she suffered a cardiac arrest. She arrived at the hospital in cardiac arrest and was pronounced dead there at 12:40 p.m. Though initial tests were inconclusive, a later test found GHB in her system. The case is unusual—and has raised some questions—because GHB's acute adverse effects present themselves very quickly, within an hour or so. Some critics of the case point out that the amount found in Hillory's system would have been unlikely to kill her.[67]

Here's the version that Rep. Sheila Jackson Lee related at the Congressional Hearings 1998:

> Witnesses said that Hillory consumed only soft drinks while at the club. Not long afterwards, she complained of feeling sick and having a severe headache. A friend took her home and she went to bed. The next morning Hillory's grandmother discovered her lying in bed unconscious and not breathing. She rushed her to the hospital, but Hillory never regained consciousness.[68]

---

[66] Melanie Sindone, "One Sip Can Kill," *Scholastic Choices*, Nov/Dec2000, Vol. 16, Issue 3. Via EBSCO Academic. The magazine is aimed at secondary schoolers.

[67] According to the account of Farias' death—of wide interest as it was thought to be the first documented GHB fatality—the Centers for Disease Control and Prevention (CDC)'s *Morbidity and Mortality Weekly Report* of April 4, 1997 says that Farias' serum level of GHB was 27 mg/L. "Gamma Hydroxy Butyrate Use—New York and Texas, 1995–1996," 281–282. Recreational and therapeutic users routinely ingest 2000–8000 mg, and it was suggested by critics that 27 mg/L was too low to have been fatal and may have been endogenous. Ruth Rendon, "Two Mystery Deaths, Same Pal, no breaks," *Houston Chronicle*, December 14, 1998. Joye Carter, then the Chief Medical Examiner of Harris County, Texas that investigated Hillory's death, told Congress in the 1998 Hearings that the staff analysts recognized the serum amount was low, but attributed that to the passage of time since she had purportedly ingested the drug in a soda. Carter also reiterated the large number of substances involved in "date rape." Transcript of 105th United States Congress, "Controlled and Uncontrolled Substances Used to Commit Date Rape. Hearing Before the Subcommittee on Crime of the Committee on the Judiciary, House of Representatives, 2nd Session on H.R. 1530, July 30, 1998."

[68] *Ibid*.

Raul Farias, Hillory's uncle, at the same hearings:

> Hillory came home around midnight. Grandma was waiting for her, as usual, and she told Hillory to go brush her teeth and go to bed for the following day, and Hillory complained of a headache. She took some aspirins, went to sleep and never woke up.

GHB's generally rapid onset of effect, at approximately 15–20 minutes, and quick peak would likely preclude it as the cause of her death; some now suspect natural causes related to a heart defect. The case remains mysterious, since there are varying endogenous levels in healthy bodies and increased levels toward the time of death. Toxicologists and medical examiners know this now, if they are experienced with GHB problems, but these confounding factors were less known then, and still today sometimes create false positive results.

Farias was not sexually assaulted either, and there is little to indicate that their fatal ingestion of GHB was linked to such intent. Some in Farias' family have also questioned the conclusion that Hillory died of GHB ingestion.[69] Yet to this day, the specific law related to Date Rape Drug prohibition (in the periodically updated Controlled Substances Act, Public Law 106–172) stems from H.R. 2130, the "Hillory J. Farias and Samantha Reid Date-Rape Drug Prohibition Act of 2000."

While GHB is now illegal, its component parts, often referred to as precursor chemicals, are easily obtained and can be used to experience some of the same effects. GBL, for instance, an essential part of its manufacture, is an industrial solvent and used in a number of consumer and agricultural products. The USA and Canada attach criminal provisions to their use outside these realms, but in Europe, only GHB itself is prohibited; the precursors are not. (In the UK, GBL is one precursor that was banned in 2009, but others were not.)[70] Synthetic drugs are much more versatile

---

[69] Ruth Rendon, "New Tests have Family Asking if 'date rape' drug really killed teen," *Houston Chronicle*, February 7, 1997 and "DEA Disputes Family's Claim about Drug Test," *Houston Chronicle*, February 8, 1997.

[70] GBL is described by the *Enfield Independent* (UK) as a drug that "helps sexual predators take advantage of young women" and does not mention its primary recreational use. Elizabeth Pears (2009), "'Date rape' drug banned following MP's campaign," August 30. http://www.enfieldindependent.co.uk/news/4572216.print/. Retrieved October 15, 2015.

in their composition—and thus more easily amenable to substitutions by underground chemists. Moreover, many of the precursors are used in industrial and construction solvents and as such are difficult to ban or restrict, even when new legislation prohibits personal use.

Beyond the variety of circumstances that can lead to unwitting GHB ingestion, GHB toxicology testing is complicated by a number of factors. First, the precursors rapidly metabolize into GHB itself after ingestion. Fluid tests administered after 12 hours are bound to be inconclusive, as small (though variable) amounts are present in the human body naturally, and present in some wine grape varieties as well as some other foods. GHB levels are also known to spike around the time of death. While the amounts in food and in drinks are too small to be psychoactive, careless lab processing can fail to account for these other nonpredatory sources of GHB.[71] Hair testing can be done for weeks, but this test is not routine.

The Productive Uses of GHB's Uncertainties

The drug's close mimicry to alcohol and its tendency to be undetectable in urinalysis after 8–12 hours has created a disturbing tendency for prohibitionists to suggest that there are likely to be a vast number of "hidden" cases out there. In a 2004 testimony before the US Sentencing Commission, Jodi Avergun of the DEA used all of the typical sleight-of-hand, statistics-citing maneuvers. First, she incorrectly claimed that GHB was uniquely positioned for predatory use, a claim not borne out by existing studies, even then. Second, as is very common in such rhetoric, the general problem of sexual assault, and that of intoxicated victims—a genuine and significant public health and criminal justice problem—is amassed to "stand in" for all of the missing data on predatory drugging:

> How large is the problem of drug-facilitated rape, and how often is GHB the tool of sexual predators? Reliable data are simply not available.

---

[71] A number of scientific articles have cautioned lab personnel about this problem. See, for instance: Simon P. Elliott, "Gamma hydroxybutyric acid (GHB) concentrations in humans and factors affecting endogenous production," *Forensic Science International*, vol. 133, no. 1, 2003, 9–16; Marc LeBeau, Madeline A. Montgomery, Cynthia Morris-Kukoski, Jason E. Schaff, and Anna Deakin, "A Comprehensive Study on the Variations in Urinary Concentrations of Endogenous Gamma-Hydroxybutyrate (GHB)," *Journal of Analytical Toxicology* 30, March 2006, 98–105.

Because GHB cannot be traced in blood or urine after about 8–12 hours, even tests conducted the day after the incident are too late. The effects of GHB are such that many victims cannot recall or do not realize what happened. However, we can hazard some idea of the scale. Some estimate that drugs are used in 15–20 percent of sexual assaults. It is undisputed from the consensus of field agents and health practitioners that GHB is the controlled substance of choice of sexual predators. DEA has documented 15 sexual assaults involving 30 victims who were under the influence of GHB, and of the 711 drug-positive urinalysis samples submitted from victims of alleged sexual assault, 48 tested positive for GHB. With approximately 95,000 sexual assaults on women each year, it is fair to assume that GHB has been used in thousands of crimes of violence.

The first claim is true, but not what it appears to be in this context: the estimate of "15–20 percent" here reflects mainly voluntary use of drugs (all drugs, including marijuana) copresent with reported sexual assaults, not predatory drugging. However, as health authorities in New South Wales, Australia note, it is unlikely that there are numerous undetected incidents of GHB drugging or spiking lurking just outside the borders of our health and safety surveillance systems. GHB and alcohol together have a very dramatic (because similar) effect, and GHB's effect (both pleasurable and acutely frightening) is also relatively quick. Thus, ERs and medical examiners' offices should be seeing more people with acute toxic effects than they apparently do.[72] Remember that GHB is often manufactured in amateur ways, and with no easy strength control like ketamine, flunitrazepam, or other benzodiazepines. There is not that much room for error between a pleasant dose and a highly symptomatic one. Lower doses that pose less danger are unlikely, conversely, to produce symptoms that would cause concern to a drinker or voluntary user of GHB.

But positive GHB tests, too, have to be looked at with caution. People may end up getting GHB when they thought they were buying and using something else to get high. Cheaper, easier-to-use "date rape drug" tests often produce false positives. In 2007, a man carrying a bottle of Dr. Bronner's Peppermint Sage soap was arrested on narcotics charges

---

[72] Drug Info, New South Wales (2014) GHB. http://www.druginfo.sl.nsw.gov.au/drugs/list/ghb.html. Retrieved September 14, 2015.

in California after the soap tested positive for GHB, "a date rape drug" according to the *Los Angeles Times*, and spent three days in jail.[73] In fact, many natural soaps will test positive for GHB using certain kinds of field kit tests. I once got a positive GHB test with a "date rape drug detector" sheet using a popular brand of imported mineral water (I unsealed it myself), which is not surprising, since many of these detector kits aimed at consumers are just acid-alkaline tests. If there were an iceberg under this tip, we would know it by now.

Ketamine

Of the Big Three, it would be fair to say that ketamine probably gets the smallest amount of attention. The reason it was propelled into the group of now-suspect CNS depressants that came to be labeled "date rape drugs" was likely because of its emergence in the club and rave scene of the 1990s, where it was known as K or Special K. Ketamine's ill-effects are *genuinely* distinguishable from other drugs and from alcohol, much more easily so than GHB (which mimics alcohol and sometimes other chosen drugs) or benzodiazepines (which have overlapping but not completely the same symptoms as heavy alcohol intoxication).

Discovered in the early 1960s and first produced by Parke-Davis, ketamine's primary current use is as an animal anesthetic, although in some circumstances, it is still used for human anesthesia. It was used on US soldiers in Vietnam. Some countries permit small doses to be sold over the counter as a pain reliever. It has a more dissociative quality than either GHB or Rohypnol. It has been known as a recreational drug since the late 1960s, but its popularity as a club drug increased in the 1980s, where it was sometimes mixed with Ecstasy.[74] It can have mild-to-moderate hallucinogenic effects, and seems to have a less sedating effect than benzodiazepines or other anesthetics. As a club drug, it had a more

---

[73] Roy Rivenburg, "Soap tests clean, so punk rocker won't face charges," *Los Angeles Times*, April 17, 2007. http://articles.latimes.com/2007/apr/17/local/me-soap17. Retrieved October 29, 2015.

[74] "Emerging Drug Trends, Lancashire Drug and Alcohol Action Team (LDAAT) project," Lancaster University, http://www.lancaster.ac.uk/fass/projects/clubresearch/emergingdrugtrends.htm. Retrieved October 28, 2015; CESAR: Ketamine, University of Maryland, http://www.cesar.umd.edu/cesar/drugs/ketamine.asp.

mixed reputation—sought after by some but avoided strongly by others. Psychedelic effects are reported at about one-tenth to one-quarter of an anesthetic dose.[75]

According to researcher David McDowell, "[t]he drug causes a dose-dependent dissociative episode with feelings of fragmentation, detachment and what one user has described as 'psychic/physical/spiritual scatter.' Use of ketamine imparts a disconnection from awareness of stimuli from the general environment. These stimuli include, but are not limited to, pain."[76]

Amnesia is common at moderate dosage levels, as is a loss of time sense.[77] Lower doses impair memory and cognition. High doses are potentially fatal; at high but nonlethal doses, hallucinations are common and similarities to PCP are noted.[78] Low doses appear to only operate as an analgesic. At moderate doses, ketamine users report a distancing or out-of-body experience (a there-but-not-there, a self-but-not-self) that may feel either relieving or relaxing, on the one hand, or terrifying or paralyzing, on the other. This drug, when used surreptitiously on someone, is probably the one that comes closest to realizing our fears of chemical automatism.

Chronic users may develop paranoia and/or grandiosity in a manner similar to other drug-excess syndromes. Frequent users who then stop their regular usage may experience a "k-hole," which is described as a very unique kind of acute severe depression, "characterized by social withdrawal, autistic behavior and an inability to maintain a cognitive set." However, in recent years, experiments in psychiatry have demonstrated potential therapeutic potential for depression with ketamine.[79]

The potential for its use in a predatory manner comes not so much from its hallucinatory effects (which may be either pleasant or terrifying) as its potentially paralytic ones. In line with its use in surgery, some users report feeling unable to move. In a surgical setting, the aim is have the

---

[75] Simon Willis, *Drugs of Abuse*, 2nd edition, London: Pharmaceutical Press, 2005, p. 208
[76] McDowell, "Marijuana, Hallucinogens, and Club Drugs," 2005.
[77] Willis, *Drugs of Abuse*, 209.
[78] Hallucinations: the drug may cause genuine misperception of people, places, and circumstances, as opposed to the pseudo-hallucinations often associated with LSD, psilocybin, or MDMA, where users experience illusions or visions but are often aware, at least at moderate doses, that they are illusions or imaginative impressions facilitated by drugs.
[79] James Gallagher, "Ketamine 'exciting' depression therapy," *BBC News* (online), April 3, 2014. http://www.bbc.com/news/health-26647738. Retrieved September 14, 2015.

patient both unconscious and not moving; but street use often splits these effects such that a person may be conscious yet unable to move. Indeed, treatment for acute problems related to ketamine ingestion often involves benzodiazepine sedation to have the patient sleep until the effects of ketamine wear off. It is detectable in fluids testing 7–14 days after ingestion. Heavy hallucination, of course, does complicate the ability of victims to account for the details of the assault, albeit in a different way than for unconscious victims.

Ketamine was implicated in the case of Richard Esposito, convicted of multiple rape counts in Queens, New York City, in 1985.[80] It was legal to possess at the time, and with it, Esposito drugged at least two women, by causing forcible inhalation, and assaulted them. Ronald Siegel, a drug expert that consulted on the case, describes how the case came together when one victim had been paralyzed during the attack but did not hallucinate.[81] It turned out that the cranberry juice that she drank beforehand suppressed this element of the drug effects; the witness thus was able to describe details of the multiassailant, multivictim assault. Esposito was sentenced to a minimum of 68 years in prison, belying the distortion put forward by some that drug rape prosecutions are an outcome of stricter, targeted penalties enacted in the late 1990s. Police suspected that there were many more victims, but no follow-up appeared in the press. Press coverage simply explained what Esposito did as a serial rape case that involved drugging.

Much like GHB, ketamine can be unknowingly ingested when a drugtaker is led to believe that they are buying MDMA, or it can be sought after in a mix of drugs.[82] But much like GHB and flunitrazepam, news coverage of cases involving possession, theft from animal hospitals, and trafficking tends to search for a sexual assault angle, even when the quantities involved suggest regular street use, and nearly any public health website attests to its primarily recreational appeal.

---

[80] Jonathan Ferziger, "Man convicted for rape and sodomy," *UPI Archives*, November 13, 1985. http://www.upi.com/Archives/1985/11/13/Man-convicted-for-rape-and-sodomy/8412500706000/.

[81] Ronald K. Siegel, *Fire in the Brain: Clinical Tales of Hallucination*, New York: Dutton, 1992.

[82] Karen Joe-Laidler, Karen and Geoffrey Hunt, "Sit Down to Float: The Cultural Meaning of Ketamine Use in Hong Kong," *Addiction Research and Theory*, June 1, 2008, 16(3), 259–271. doi:10.1080/16066350801983673.

Ketamine was brought to Class C level in the UK in 2006, and then owing to reports on chronic users' development of severe bladder problems, upgraded to a Class B substance in 2014 (methamphetamine and cannabis are Class B drugs). A possession charge carries a penalty of up to five years of prison time. This time around, the impetus for the law was health impacts rather than drugging.

Named Drug Legislation of the Late 1990s: When All Else Was Beginning to Fail

Significant federal legislation emerged in 1996 Controlled Substances Act and then was strengthened in 1999. The UK in the ensuing years criminalized and enhanced penalties for these same drugs. Certainly, as Jenkins argues, and as we have seen in parallels from previous eras, drugs thought to have uniquely predatory characteristics are bound up as much with overheated drug warrior rhetoric as the politics of sexual assault. But there are a few mysteries about these developments that remain. First, why were the deaths of Samantha Reid and Hillory Farias linked to the predatory problem, rather than the "threat to teens" antidrug theme that is more or less always available when a new drug appears that interests young people? Second, why did pharmaceutical interests so easily accede to the strictest prohibitions of Rohypnol and GHB without the kind of resistance they showed initially to pseudoephedrine regulation? The quick co-optation of the term "date rape" by drugs is truly astonishing—why was that term pressed into the service of the bar-spiker scenario?

The bill was signed by President Clinton in February of 2000 year. In his signing statement, Clinton noted that the law imposed on the Department of Health and Human Services the obligation to "collect data on the incidence of date-rape drug abuse and report the information annually to the Congress."[83] Yet dedicated statistics still do not exist—they have to be pieced together from sexual assault surveys, public health reports, and toxicology samples.

---

[83] William J. Clinton, "Statement on Signing the Hillory J. Farias and Samantha Reid Date-Rape Drug Prohibition Act of 2000."

Early Expert Suspicions That Drink Spiking and Drugging Were Overestimated

On the heels of intensified legislative efforts in the 1990s to shape the "date rape drugs" problem, there were attempts to clarify the scope of the drugging problem by toxicological investigation. In 1999, Hoffman-LaRoche commissioned a study (based on reports and samples that they had solicited from forensic labs around the country) on suspected date rape drugging to determine how prevalent the problem was, particularly in comparison with other substances. The resulting ElSohly and Salamone study has become one of the more widely cited studies, though both its strengths and weaknesses are often ignored.

Only ElSohly and Salamone's 1999 study attempted, at that point, to address the real prevalence of date rape drugs *where they were suspected*, using toxicology screens. The sample they used, therefore, was highly purposive: to confirm or refute suspected drugging cases from around the country, and they came in from various sources: law enforcement, rape crisis, and health-care settings. Forensic toxicologists Negrusz and Gaensaellen warned against using the ElSohly sample as indicative of the underlying problem:

> 60% of all samples tested were positive for one or more drugs. GHB was detected in about 4% of samples. About 8.2% of the specimens had confirmed benzodiazepines of some kind, but flunitrazepam was seen only in few cases (about 0.5% of these specimens). This data does not square with the "anecdotal evidence" which would have us believe that drug-facilitated "date" or "acquaintance" rape is common.[84]

Their article suggested that newer, more sensitive tests down the road could be used to detect these drugs. The article also pointed to the problem of extrapolating findings from this particular sample, since "statistically based, systematic sampling procedure was not employed, nor is it

---

[84] Negrusz, Adam and Gaensslen, R.E. "Analytical developments in toxicological investigation of drug-facilitated sexual assault," *Analytical and Bioanalytical Chemistry*, Vol. 376, No. 8, August 2003, 1192–1197.

clear how the originating laboratories selected the cases for submission in the first place." A reasonable assumption was that when Hoffman-LaRoche solicited the samples, those who responded used different criteria for inclusion.

But what ElSohly and Salamone's study did suggest was that many who thought they had been drugged were not. And with these particular sampling flaws, the numbers of positive results actually should be *higher*, since these cases seem to have been more vetted as potential drugging cases rather than being drawn from any naturally occurring, single-context sample, such as whoever might have come into a particular ER in a particular time interval. Indeed, in the ensuing years, even smaller percentages were found, despite more sensitive tests being available.

It appears that many in the field assumed that more sensitive assays, and more rigorous sampling, would produce more confirmed cases of drugging. Certainly one of the practical advantages to such advances would be to aid litigation in involuntary intoxication cases. Yet beyond this it is unclear why belief in a large "dark figure" of unconfirmed drugging was so tenacious among researchers.

As early as 2001, training organizations attempted to counter the claims that the Big Three were unique as rape weapons, and that they were responsible for a new kind of crime. It is clear that a number of prominent experts involved in rape crisis centers, clinic aftercare, and sexual crimes investigation in law enforcement were becoming uneasy with the characterization of "date rape drugs" as a discrete entity. Emphasizing the role of alcohol and general drug use, as well as the vastness in power and reach of the modern pharmacopeia, the National Center for Women and Policing disseminated a training briefing that year that seemed to express the committee's frustrations with the focus on the Big Three.[85] It reiterated the overwhelming role of voluntary alcohol consumption and widespread voluntary drug use in sexual assault, and expressed its wariness of the overemphasis on a small number of surreptitious drugging cases. The Center felt this threatened to reinforce the good girl/bad

---

[85] The National Center for Women and Policing, "Successfully Investigating Acquaintance Sexual Assault: A National Training Manual for Law Enforcement," May 2001. Retrieved November 2, 2015. http://www.mincava.umn.edu/documents/acquaintsa/participant/drugfacilitated.html.

girl dichotomy by making date rape drugging "real rape" in legal scholar Susan Estrich's term and everything else...well, you know:

> Voluntary drug use should not be seen as a basis for questioning the validity of the victim's allegation....If the victim says that she voluntarily used alcohol or drugs and indicates that her assailant took advantage of her vulnerability, the successful investigator will therefore frame her use of alcohol, or other drugs, as corroborative evidence. This evidence should therefore serve as a way to support rather than challenge the victim's credibility.[86]

Fifteen years on, we still find an enormous discomfort, culture wide, with this eminently humane approach that better reflects reality.

Doubling Down on the Big Three as Rape Weapons

The insistence that the Big Three only exist as rape-facilitating chemicals was grandly reasserted in the 2014 election cycle as California voters prepared to consider Proposition 47, a criminal justice reform referendum that would, among other things, roll back potential penalties for nonviolent drug possession cases. The goal of the law was to ease crowding in the state's overcrowded correctional facilities, both by diverting (and releasing) low-level offenders. Among the drugs included whose possession was to be bumped down from felony to misdemeanor were the Big Three. Naturally, the organization "No on Proposition 47" used the handle @StopDateRape to run a sensationalistic, accusatory feed on Twitter, implying that the possession of "date rape drugs" was tantamount to sexual violence itself. Although the Twitter feed complained about a number of penalty reductions enumerated in Proposition 47, for gun theft and other property crimes as well, it all rolled under the banner @StopDateRape.

---

[86] *Ibid.*

Although sexual assault (or any felony) facilitated by surreptitious administration of an intoxicating substance is already a separate offense under California Penal Code item 222, antidrug forces wasted no time in criticizing Proposition 47 for minimizing the penalties for "date rape drugs," implying that not only were these drugs exclusively assault toxins, but also somehow the law had failed to avenge drugging victims in the past. Code 222 was passed in 1876, and remained consistently enforced, revised as recently as 2011.[87] Like most states, using this particular means to facilitate a felony victimization constitutes a penal code violation separate from any felony charges that constitute the crime itself, and this has been so for nearly a century and a half. Furthermore, the laws pertaining to rape and sexual assault themselves define these crimes so as to include administration of intoxicating substances as a means akin to force.[88] Some states have less clear definitions of force or incapacitation, but this does not seem to have been a hurdle in filing appropriate charges. Finally, laws against poisoning for any motive can be pressed into such prosecutions, as they typically include drugs. So the idea that somehow rolling back possession penalties for the Big Three was going to result in minor penalties for rape (or any felony crime) committed by drugging someone with them was pure election season nonsense.

But which kind of nonsense, exactly—the sincere but militantly ill-informed kind, or the cynical, knowing, manipulative kind? It was, it should be said, like most drug hyperbole, bipartisan nonsense. Drug warriors have always been willing to use the threat of drug rape to enhance drug penalties. One can see an interesting alliance here of political bedfel-

---

[87] California Penal Code § 222. "Every person guilty of administering to another any chloroform, ether, laudanum, or any controlled substance, anaesthetic, or intoxicating agent, with intent thereby to enable or assist himself or herself or any other person to commit a felony, is guilty of a felony punishable by imprisonment in the state prison for 16 months, or two or three years." Enacted in 1872. Amended by Stats.1984, c. 1635, § 78; Stats.2011, c. 15 (A.B.109), § 287.5, eff. April 4, 2011, operative Oct. 1, 2011

[88] See, for instance, California Penal Code Section 261–269. In 1986, the US Congress amended its Federal criminal code on rape: November 14, 1986 [H.R. 4745] Sexual Abuse Act of 1986. 18 USC 2241, Public Law 99–654, 99th Congress. Among other changes, barely discussed in the hearings, was addition of "aggravated rape" where stupefying substances are administered by the assailant. Aggravation is accompanied by enhanced penalty to the underlying felony. The influence of this Code on day-to-day rape prosecution is limited in that Federal prosecutions are unlikely; State criminal codes prevail except under extraordinary circumstances. Nonetheless, the Federal Code sometimes serves as one of the model penal codes for states.

lows from across the aisles. The press increasingly presents the Big Three as potential rapes in pill form, often in obvious contradiction to their own routine reporting on arrests and public health concerns with voluntary use of these same drugs. Some law enforcement agencies and court officials eagerly make such claims, too.

In the run-up to the Fall 2014 referendum, opponents latched onto the date rape drugs angle. A Gannett paper serving the Palm Springs area, the *Desert Sun*, withheld its support for the measure because, as the editorial claimed, the downgrading of certain nonviolent offenses would threaten public safety. The editorial said:

> Proposition 47 would reclassify six nonviolent crimes, including possession of nearly all types of illegal drugs, including heroin, cocaine and date rape drugs. We understand struggles with addiction, where treatment is the better option, but we can think of only one motivation for possessing a date rape drug.

The breezy confidence in such a statement—made without reference to evidence, as clearly no one thought it was necessary—is bad enough. The fact that support was withheld from a broad measure whose aims the editorial board otherwise *supported*—diversion to drug treatment and reducing jail overcrowding with nonviolent offenders—is perhaps more so. To be fair, it also objected to downgrading most handgun thefts to petty theft. Of course, the *Desert Sun* neither breaks nor makes any kind of vote outcome on its own. And indeed, Proposition 47 was handily passed, despite similar drug rape warnings in other op-eds and editorials.

After the Proposition passed, the date rape drug angle reasserted itself, but other drug and gun provisions of the law were the main focus of opposition. Indeed, a number of previously incarcerated drug offenders were released all at once in the wake of the new law's implementation, and local law enforcement agencies had to cope with spikes in theft and other petty crimes. The *Desert Sun* also supported bipartisan efforts by state legislators to upgrade to a felony "use of 'date rape drugs' such as GHB, Rohypnol, or ketamine with the intent to commit sexual assault." The bill that passed on September 3, 2015 was actually a bit different than the *Sun* described. It created a new felony for possession of GHB, flunitrazepam, or ketamine with the intent of committing a sexual assault.[89] Only those three drugs, and only for that offense. Not any other drugs possessed for such intent, nor any other felony crimes.

The *Los Angeles Times* seemed, at first, to fall for the idea that Proposition 47 had inadvertently weakened rape laws.[90] They described SB 333, saying that "the bill would plug a loophole created by the passage last year of Proposition 47, which reclassified many crimes from felonies to misdemeanors" and quoted the sponsoring Senator, Cathleen Galgiani (D-Stockton), as saying, "I firmly believe that voters in California did not intend to weaken sexual assault statutes," which, of course, they did not. The *Times*, to its credit, later praised the legislature for seeing through these claims.[91]

Andrew Luster—the assailant in a notorious California case discussed in more detail in the next chapter—was convicted on 86 counts in 2003—of rape by means of drugs, and rape of an unconscious person. This case involved three victims. California's laws, like those of most other states, already offer prosecutors multiple—and potentially stackable—offenses to charge a drugging rapist with, and they are written broadly enough to encompass any intentional act involving either a "stupefying" or intoxicating substance.

Chances are that SB 333s newly codified crime—having to have all of these elements in place—would not be a common charge, and prosecutors might indeed prefer the comprehensive qualities of existing laws in prosecuting drug-facilitated rapes. The history and analysis put forth by the bill's sponsors seems to acknowledge the relative rarity of the surreptitious drug rape problem by looking at currently valid and up-to-date epidemiological and toxicological literature, pointing to the predominantly

---

[89] Owing to the constitutional limits on the legislature's ability to modify a bill passed by referendum in California, like the laws that came from Proposition 47, the state legislature created this new crime instead—an action that is squarely within its powers as a legislative body.

[90] Patrick McGreevy, "State lawmakers approve traffic relief and stricter penalties for sex offenders," *Los Angeles Times*, September 6, 2015. http://www.latimes.com/local/politics/la-me-pol-bills-20150904-story.html. Retrieved same date.

[91] Los Angeles Times, "Editorial: The Naughty and Nice of 2015," December 27. http://www.latimes.com/opinion/editorials/la-ed-christmas-naughty-nice-html-20151225-htmlstory.html. Retrieved same day.

voluntary use of such drugs, even in situations involving assaults. The analysis represents a rare moment of scientific rigor.

But the symbolism of the law is as interesting for what it leaves out as for what it includes. This legislative action may be the first time in which the singling out of the Big Three is actually codified in law pertaining to violent crime, cementing the misperception that they are fundamentally more rape-facilitating than other substances. In fact, it invokes the "interrupted bar spiker" scenario to explain the legal difference between "intent" and an "attempt." (An attempted felony is already just that, a felony.) So this expands the reach of the felony classification if someone spikes a drink with these particular drugs and declares to some other party in advance their intentions to use the spiking as a means to commit sexual assault. Or prior criminal acts could potentially, according to the bill's language, be evidence of current intent. Though the presumption would be that this would mean previous evidence of sexual violence, the legislation does not specify that. Again, all other malign motivations—and all other drugs—would not be covered.[92]

In early October 2015, California Governor Jerry Brown vetoed the new bill, noting that it and other rejected criminal justice–related bills "creat[e] a new crime—usually by finding a novel way to characterize and criminalize conduct that is already proscribed." Placing it in the history of California's notorious tendency to generate byzantine criminal codes to cover nearly every bit of malfeasance without a resulting crime suppression payoff, he said, "The multiplication and particularization of criminal behavior creates increasing complexity without commensurate benefit."[93]

Contrast this pile-on with Australia's swift response to a genuine loophole in criminal law there: there were no laws that covered drink spiking

---

[92] California Senate Committee for Public Safety (2015), SB 333 History and Bill Analysis, April 28. http://leginfo.legislature.ca.gov/faces/billAnalysisClient.xhtml?bill_id=201520160SB333. Retrieved September 6, 2015. Of course, this is redundant in a number of ways described above, but earlier postpassage versions of this bill, SB333/AB46, just wanted to restore more draconian penalties for possessing the Big Three based on their core identity as date rape drugs, or at least reassign them to "wobbler status"—legislative lingo for giving district attorneys the power to charge as a felony or misdemeanor.

[93] David Siders, "Jerry Brown signs racial profiling bill, vetoes date rape measure," *Sacramento Bee*, October 3, 2015. http://www.sacbee.com/news/politics-government/capitol-alert/article37586379.html#storylink=cpy. Retrieved October 10, 2015.

for reasons *unrelated* to other criminal intent, such as rape, robbery, or grievous bodily harm.[94] As the realization gained that many public spikings involved stimulants and no clear motive other than perhaps pranking drink-mates, Australia moved to draw up a specific law in 2006. While it remained difficult to figure out whether someone had in fact had their drinks tampered, and who had done so, the legislative trajectory here was quite different: it acted on *newer* knowledge about the problem, it was *broader* rather than bizarrely specific, and framed it as a general public health problem rather than insisting on the "crime in a pill" scenario.[95]

Although California's post Proposition 47 drama makes the classic mistake of singling out the Big Three and misconstruing their usual circumstances of use, that is not to say that the date rape drug concept cannot be expansive. Not to be outdone by California in the 2014 campaign season, Florida's midterm elections featured Proposition 2, which would ease access to medical marijuana. A group called "No on 2" ran ads and put up a website. "No on 2" claimed that if the medical marijuana bill is passed, teenagers will have easier access to pot. A Twitter picture then asks if the new face of date rape will look like a marijuana cookie.[96]

Press credulity was much lower in this case; the National Broadcasting Company (NBC) local coverage included a doctor acting as a debunker. His dismissal of the rape claim, however, was based on marijuana's ubiquity and his assertion that there was not any rape case linked to pot. This is not strictly true, since if you believe that alcohol can be a date rape drug, that is, if that formulation makes sense to you, you would have to admit pot to that pantheon as well, since it can be found in measurable amounts in people who fear they have been drugged. Of course, in all substance-related intoxication cases, self-ingestion is the most likely means. Predators could indeed potentially put more cannabis in a product (like a cookie) than a target thought she was consuming. Florida failed to

---

[94] Jeremy Gans, *Modern Criminal Law of Australia*, Cambridge: Cambridge University Press, 2012, p. 342. (Crimes Law 1900: 39.)

[95] Janet Fife-Yeomans and Ellen Whinnett, "Jail for drink spiking; Laws revamp plan gets tough on tampering," *Herald Sun*, April 13, 2007, 2nd edit., News 9. Lexis.

[96] Steve Litz, "Ad Tries to Connect Pot with Date Rape," *NBC Miami 6*, August 12, 2014, http://www.nbcmiami.com/news/local/Ad-Tries-to-Connect-Pot-with-Date-Rape-271000431.html. Retrieved October 28, 2015.

pass Proposition 2, by falling short of the 60% yes vote that it needed to amend the law. Generally, however, the "No on Prop 2" organization was alone in raising the date rape drug menace.

Date rape drugging exists as a specter, but in a few notable cases, it exists as a reality. High-profile offenders actually represent an interesting group as they inadvertently demonstrate some of the normal barriers to more widespread drugging. Yet in a peculiar fashion, the lessons to be learned from them in understanding this crime often fail to be heeded. The next chapter considers some high-profile cases, and what we know about perpetrators of predatory drugging. It also considers the local politics of the bar scare, which popped up periodically in the 2000s.

6

Who and Where Are the Druggers?

It is never hard to explain why press coverage of crime would go for the sensational elements of a crime. If press coverage emphasizes the sensational elements of either a single event or a category of events, such coverage can distort our understanding of everyday occurrences of the event. What is harder to explain is why, when you have crimes with *inherently* sensational elements to them, the sensational would be pushed aside and even ignored. This is, strangely, the case with drink spiking and drugging assaults. High-profile cases of drugging have the kind of elements that scream outlandishness: smooth-talking serial offenders, con artistry, videotape, braggadocio, privileged offenders and sometimes privileged victims, and of course, drugs, alcohol, violence, partying, and sex.

In the late 1990s, some very creepy, multifaceted serial cases of predatory drugging emerged. The fact that they got the attention they did probably owed something to our general interest in crafty serial offenders, and well could have stood in for a brave new era of date rape drugging. In reality, they were an unfortunate side effect of changes in night life, where newer club drugs were preferred and newer drugs experimented with. Yet these serial drugging rape cases were not chosen to typify the date rape drug problem in the way that the Reid and Farias cases—apparently erroneously—were. In fact, there was a curious *lack* of attention to the very mediagenic, rife-with-metaphor qualities of real cases, in favor of the rising "epidemic" theme instead.

Submerged as a theme here, too, was the thinking about drink spiking as a form of poisoning or tampering, which was strange since the USA in particular had undergone a convulsive era of product tampering in the 1980s. The largest case, in which seven people in the Chicago area died as the result of cyanide placed in Tylenol,[1] has remained unsolved. Below I consider what the research on poisoning and tampering can tell us about drink spiking.

At this point, it is also worthwhile to examine the existing literature on sexual assailants as they are the excessive focus of concern about drink spiking—the assumption being, as we saw in the last chapter, that every unaccounted-for drug in a drink (or in a drinker) is a rape prepared or foiled. It is not, and it is probable that other motivations dominate this relatively rare event; as we shall see, Australia at the current time seems to have the best grasp of the "prank spiking" problem.

The sexual assault literature is, of course, still relevant. It turns out then, the victims of drugging rape are recruited more or less in the same way as other victims of sex crimes—through basic social trust or a ruse. Nonetheless, the randomness with which tampering victims are affected—their involuntary role in a drama—turns out to have some overlap with the drugging rape victim.

Who Are the Druggers?

What makes a person decide to tamper with the behavior, cognition, and capacity of another individual by drugging them in some manner? Though tampering behavior, as we have seen, can go well beyond drink spiking, we can learn a great deal about drink spikers by looking at the mindset of poisoners and tamperers. Tamperers, poisoners, and surreptitious druggers are not large in number compared to those who seek to

---

[1] Tylenol (made by McNeil Pharmaceuticals) is the leading brand of acetaminophen (paracetamol) in North America.

control or harm others in more straightforward ways, such as physical confrontation or threat. Much like the forensic psychology of rapists, the parallel literature on poisoning is good at generating typologies of perpetrators, particularly serial perpetrators, but it must do so from the relatively small database of those who not only got caught but also submitted to interviews. Otherwise, there is just educated guesswork.

Watchers of crime shows on television, particularly those that depict behavioral profiling, may be aware of useful distinctions in serial offender characteristics (e.g., level of planning, organized vs. disorganized, in vs. out of comfort zone, ruse vs. blitz attacks) but may not be as cognizant of the fact that these themes are extrapolated from a relatively small number of cases. They have to be—these cases simply are not common enough to generate a large database. This analytical problem is also similar to the problem we have when we extrapolate the motives and means of rapists based on those who are convicted or incarcerated for the crime. Nonetheless, to the extent that such typologies can be used as a tool to think about drink spiking and drugging situations, they are useful.

In thinking about sexual assailants in general, the most widely used and empirically explored is the Massachusetts Treatment Center Rapist Typology (MTC-R3), first developed in 1971 and further refined 1998.[2] While rapists share generally certain misogynistic and antisocial traits, they do not behave in exactly the same manner. *Impulsive or opportunistic* rapists are not planners, but rather act when they find an opportunity. Bars and parties are common stalking grounds. Such rapists may be generally impulsive in all walks of life, and do not choose victims for particular characteristics other than their presence and vulnerability. They are indifferent, rather than excited or repelled, by fear on the victim's part.[3] They act instrumentally and are unlikely to engage in more force than is necessary to gain victim compliance.

---

[2] Curt Bartol and Anne Bartol, *Introduction to Forensic Psychology: Research and Application*, 4th Edition, Los Angeles: SAGE Publications, 2014.

[3] These assailants are either Type 1 or 2. Type 1 "becomes" impulsive in adulthood in order to gain gratification as opportunity presents itself. Generally, Type 1 has basic social skills. Type 2 has been consistently impulsive and appears to others to lack self-control from an earlier age, and tends to be less socially competent. Of course, the Type 2 assailant can, in fact, control himself as he can keenly differentiate between situations that present opportunity and those that do not.

Pervasively angry rapists are those who are generally misanthropic, display rage, and may act violently toward both men and women. To others, their physical and sexual violence appears random, though they are often able to identify subjective factors—being able to identify who "deserves" it or who has provoked them—that leads to their aggressive assaults (typically physical against men and sexual against women). High levels of expressive violence are used, beyond what might be needed to gain compliance in a victim or neutralize an opponent in a physical altercation.

Sexually motivated, sadistic rapists engage in extensive fantasy and repetition, and are genuinely aroused by their own aggression toward women and the fear produced in their victims. Paradoxically, a victim who too easily complies may make them more violent as they are aroused by the victim's resistance. They will often describe the violent encounter as a game or contest of wills. The sadistic element may be overt or submerged in fantasy. They may also have a variety of paraphilias such as voyeurism.

Sexually motivated, nonsadistic rapists gain general sexual arousal and gratification by enlisting victims in a fantastic delusion that the victim will succumb to his aggression and enjoy the encounter. He typically only engages in sexual assault against strangers or women who are barely familiar (e.g., observed from a distance first). Physical aggression is low and he may flee if the victim resists as this disrupts the narrative of imagined seduction. The rape itself is aspirational: to become the virile man he really thinks he is, and be reaffirmed in this by the victim. He may, as a part of the delusion, attempt to make contact or continue the "relationship" with the victim and check up on how she is doing.[4]

Vindictive rapists have generally negative but powerful views of women, believing them to be inherently faithless and manipulative. They believe they need to be put in their place, particularly ones who are perceived as independent, strong-willed, or successful. They are more likely to also engage in physical violence against women and their goal in sexual assault—often set off by a difficult encounter with another woman—is primarily to humiliate and degrade the victim. Little erotic gratification is obtained.

---

[4] Types 6 and 7 are distinguished by level of social competence, with Type 6 being reticent and Type 7 being more socially competent; differences in occupational attainment may be relevant.

To date there has not been any systematic attempt to place assailants who specifically use drugs on victims into these categories, but the typologies can illuminate some of the behavior described. (Those who take advantage of already intoxicated victims tend to be *opportunists*.) About surreptitious druggers whose ultimate aim is sexual assault or exploitation, we are learning a few things. They prefer private settings to carry out assaults; they like to be in their comfort zones. But the key factor is being able to successfully manipulate social trust. On a meta-level, this is true of most crimes, but this key factor tends to be ignored in the stereotype of the Lurking Bar-Spiker. In forensic psychiatrist Michael Welner's sample of 34 successful prosecutions of drugging rapists, all were repeat offenders, and videotaping of the assault was not uncommon, nor were accomplices or multiassailant cases.[5] The perpetrators engaged in heavy staging and planning and did not generally use public settings. Offenders lacked adaptability: they had to control everything about the setting—typically a home but sometimes a workplace. They did not just throw drugs in a drink and wait to see what happened—they had access to drugs, and felt that they knew the predictable effects of the drugs on the victim. Not all were superficial charmers; some were quiet and withdrawn—but none were overt or assertive with their aggression toward their mostly female victims. This might explain why they would be trusted enough to be become drink purveyors in private settings. They often denied afterward that any sex took place, or less often claimed that the sex was consensual. Since the prospect of being assaulted without remembering is, to many victims, doubly disturbing, victims sometimes have a psychological incentive to believe him.

Welner did not use the MTC-R3 typologies; the common characteristics he describes seem to fall across categories. Using conventional psychopathology subtypes, he described "malignant narcissism" in perpetrators that gives them a pervasive sense of entitlement that allows them to ignore the rights of others. In this sense, it is almost as if the victim's will has to be neutralized *without consequence* as it would interfere with the offender's fantasy and gratification. This differentiates the offender from one whose dominance and rage must be *experienced* by the victim;

---

[5] Michael Welner, "The Perpetrators and their Modus Operandi," in LeBeau and Mozayani, 2001.

he appears to have little need of recognition from her. Videotaping of sex with incapacitated victims certainly hints at the desire to humiliate, characteristic of the vindictive rapist, but often times, these recordings were secreted away and not shown to others. The lack of excessive violence, too, seems to point instead to the fantasy-bound sexually motivated nonsadistic offender who may, in some cases, harbor illusions about his appeal to the victim. He may minimize the drugging in his mind, because he often uses the same drugs voluntarily.

Looking at the problem from another direction—with drugging assault as a form of poisoning or tampering—there seem to be some thematic overlaps. Tampering cases are often followed by tampering scares, extortion-fraud (trying to extort money based on the false claim that the extortionist has tampered with a product), and sometimes by copycatters. Though the numbers still remain low, publicity about tampering or suspected tampering (and public-place drink spiking would qualify) can provoke repeat cases or scares. Thus, public fear in the wake of such cases is understandable—overall small risk and small numbers alone cannot erase the sense that because anyone is the target, then everyone is. Unlike the common turn of events in crime thrillers, tamperers often frustrate such investigations by remaining silent rather than taunting the press or police through communications.

The most notorious product-tampering case in the USA—cyanide contamination of Tylenol in 1982—killed seven people and remains unsolved. Though more than 270 suspected tampering incidents were reported in the following month, only 36 panned out. There were, however, copycat cases in the years to follow.[6] The motives of perpetrators may be personal and aimed at particular victims, while the collateral damage of covictimization may take place on a larger scale. In 1988, Stella Nickell was convicted of poisoning her husband's Excedrin two years earlier, leading to his death which was originally attributed to natural causes. The court further alleged

---

[6] George J. Church; Lee Griggs and Rita Healy, "Copycats Are on the Prowl," *Time Magazine*, November 8, 1982, Vol. 120, Issue 19. Nonetheless, when reviewing the history of the 1982 Tylenol crisis in 2009, *Time Magazine* used the "270 tamperings" number again: see Dan Fletcher, "A Brief History of the Tylenol Poisonings," *Time Magazine*, February 09, 2009. http://content.time.com/time/nation/article/0,8599,1878063,00.html.; Deal, Marlene, "Product Tampering," in Eric Hickey, ed., *Encyclopedia of Murder and Violent Crime*, (Thousand Oaks, CA: SAGE Publications), 2003, p. 368–370.

that in order to make it look like random product tampering, she simultaneously poisoned other bottles of pain reliever in summer of 1986 as well, killing a stranger who purchased the tainted product in a store, and setting off a frantic search for tainted bottles of medicine in the area's retail shops.[7] Nickell notified the police that her husband had taken Execdrin, too, and Nickell eventually sued Excedrin's manufacturer. Nickell stood to inherit her husband's life insurance policy, and upon her arrest, the court claimed this as motive. They saw the other victim, Susan Snow, as simply a person upon whom Nickell acted, almost in the abstract. Nickell was convicted and sentenced to a 90-year sentence in prison, the first defendant in the USA to be convicted of a product-tampering murder. Nickell maintains her innocence.

Product tamperers appear indifferent to the fate of those they sickened and killed. Their sickness and death is a means to some end in the mind of the offender; they may as well be anyone.[8] The same sort of distancing and indifference takes place in drugged victims of sexual assault; the perpetrator can accomplish what they wish without any acquiescence of the victim—she does not need to submit, display fear, experience pain, consciously enact her humiliation, or acknowledge his dominance. She, like the random tampering victim, is assigned a role without knowing it. This overlapping theme leads us away, a bit, from the vindictive assailant, and again toward the sexually motivated, nonsadistic rapist.

In order to surreptitiously drug someone as a means to an end, every circumstance needs to line up just right—there is a clear learning curve (what criminologists call a "boost") that favors serial offenders. One of the ways we know this is that the ERs are not filled with the rookie-mistake casualties of amateur spikers. Were the spiking tool one that was readily and widely taken up by those intending to incapacitate others, we would know it by now. Drugs are essentially poisons in the right dose. Drug overdoses are categorized as poisonings by the Centers for Disease Control. As such, we really should be willing to learn more from high-profile cases.

---

[7] Barry Logan, "Product Tampering Crime: A Review," *Journal of Forensic Sciences*, v. 38, no. 4, July 1993, p. 918–927.
[8] John Douglas and Mark Olshaker, *Anatomy of Motive*, (New York: Scribner), 1999, p. 125–128.

Instead, we managed to take notice of a few serial offenders who used predatory drugging without managing to carry away any impression of the offense itself. Usually, with high-profile cases, the underlying crime in its more ordinary form is obscured in favor of the idiosyncratic qualities of the newsworthy case. With predatory drugging, the opposite appears true: the media has preferred a "ubiquitous threat" narrative and a shadowy "Any Man."[9] High-profile offenders are reported about on a parallel track, a focus on singular, evil crafty-mindedness—that seems never to inform the more general impression of the crime.

Amnesia and Gaslighting as Weapons

As the date rape drugs concept emerged, the category was rife with potential metaphors already established from the past 150 years. Every element of drugging plumbs a pretty deep cultural well: being compelled to act out a different reality against our will, or sometimes even without our knowledge (automatism), amnesia as both reality and descriptor of lost time and disorientation, the ides of sleeplessness and its treatment, pharma-ubiquity—where our bloodstreams and medicine cabinets overflow with any number of CNS depressants. But it is important to remember that while drugs are, instrumentally speaking, just another means to an end, the way we make meaning of a drugging assault is a bit different. From the viewpoint of the assailant, the victim is made fully compliant—quietly, passively, displaying no fear but simply slipping into involuntary submission. Thus, the feelings of power and control over the victim comes from a fundamentally different place than the assailant who uses force or threat, on the one hand, or the one who opportunistically seeks gratification from an already intoxicated, vulnerable victim, on the other.

In addition to the penchant for videotape and false identities, there is also often a certain element of psychological "gaslighting" of the mark

---

[9] I borrow this term from Sarah E.H. Moore, 2009, whose work I discussed in the last chapter. "Cautionary tales: Drug-facilitated sexual assault in the British media" *Crime, Media, Culture*, December 2009, 305–320.

or victim. While in some cases, this is deployed to the instrumental end of hiding the crimes and evading sanction, in others, it appears to be an integral part of how the assailant interacts with the drugged victim. Victims are not necessarily strangers or mere acquaintances; in some cases, the relationship continues so long as the victim does not find out about being drugged. As always, using drugs as a means to exploit someone is also an act of gerrymandering reality. Full unconsciousness and blackout amnesia are the qualities of such events that we tend to talk about most, but many victims have patchy and even hallucinatory memories of the assaults, too. This is unfortunately confounded by the fact, discovered long ago by the first anesthetists, that some people experience sexual hallucination while consuming these drugs.

This is pretty sensational stuff, and there were some pretty fitting, real-life cases out there to dramatize the drugs-in-your-drink bogeyman. It seems like the only good reason to *not* give it a sensational run is that it makes it seem less ordinary and ubiquitous, which turned out to be the preferred view of the threat. The women in these serial cases were often socializing with the men that attacked them; the men used this to enable the crimes against them.

The Spitzer Twins: Roofies, Videotape, Charm, Abduction, and Sexual Assault

George and Stefan Spitzer of Marina del Rey, California were convicted of multiple charges in 1998 based on the testimony of five victim-witnesses who they attacked between 1993 and 1996. Police suspected many more, dating perhaps back to the 1980s, based in part on a trove of videos they found depicting the brothers engaged in sex with women who appeared to be drugged. The Spitzer brothers were sentenced to 30 and 60 years in prison, respectively.

The victims testified that they had gone on dates with one of the Spitzers, whom they described as attractive, charming, and seemingly successful, career wise. At least one says that she was then forcibly abducted and brought back to their home, where she lost consciousness. She suspected she had been drugged and raped. Police raided their home and found a large amount of Rohypnol as well as the videotapes. Another victim told *People Magazine* that George (playing the role of Italian charmer; he and his brother were actually Romanian emigrés) asked her on a date, met her at an Italian restaurant, and after drinking some wine—and noting to herself that this guy was a braggart and a bore—she remembered nothing until she woke up. George denied they had sex and told her she just passed out; she suspected otherwise and went to the sheriff's office.

People Magazine played up the alleged uniqueness of the drug used by the "Rohypnol Romeos" as they called them: "foreign-manufactured sleep aid and pre-surgery sedative ten times stronger than Valium."[10] Other victims told similar stories—of actual dates with the men, who tried on different identities in luring their victims, followed by memories that are hazy at best. Some told of steady dating and consensual sex for a while with one of the dissembling brothers, only to question later, after their arrest, whether drugging might explain some particular experiences they had along the way. The prosecutor suspected that they also posed as each other, having sex with women who had been on a date with the other brother, calling it the "Spitzer-switch."[11]

Like other convicted serial drug rapists, the assailants were careful, patient, and controlled their environments; for a while, they attempted to control perception of events. Women were charmed by them and some remained in a state of disbelief for a long while; echoing the theme that the blackout experience fundamentally rearranges a victim's sense of reality. Not every victim knows right away that something is wrong—at least something that involves this sort of predation. It was the one particular victim that decided to be examined right away that broke the case; this is generally true of such serial cases.

---

[10] Alec Foege and Jeff Schnaufer, "Trouble, Doubled," *People Magazine*, April 28, 1997. http://www.people.com/people/archive/article/0,,20121960,00.html. Retrieved November 2, 2015.

[11] W. Langley, "Date with the Devil," *Courier Mail* (Queensland, Australia), September 13, 1997, Weekend Edition, 5. Retrieved via Lexis-Nexis, November 2, 2015.

"The Compound": Drugging, Assault, Multiple Assailants

In August 1997, Steven Hagemann and Danny Bohannon were sentenced to 77 and 19 years, respectively, for a series of drugging assaults carried out against 14 women that took place at a converted warehouse they called "The Compound" in Lawndale, California, between 1994 and 1997. After giving the women enough GHB to make them unconscious, the two men photographed the sexual assaults they carried out on them. (On some occasions, they also drugged men who came to The Compound, apparently to neutralize them as intervenors or witnesses.) Greg Krikorian's *Los Angeles Times* article on the sentencing is one of the few I have seen that connects the contemporaneous national scare over date rape drugs with this local case.[12] There was something peculiar about The Compound case—it got relatively little coverage compared with the Farias or Reid cases, which were mischaracterized. But this particular horror also got little coverage compared with the other sensational serial cases of the 1990s, such as the Spitzer twins, or the Perez case in Florida, where the assailant became the go-to example of the dangers of date rape drugs. Judge Robert Perry remarked at trial that The Compound case was "extraordinary for the nature of the crimes and number of the victims" and the fact that one defendant was undeterred in his predation despite being questioned by the sheriff's office upon a complaint by a victim in 1995.[13] Yet only two articles about The Compound case appeared, both in the *Los Angeles Times* at the time of conviction and sentencing.[14] Though information on the case is limited, some of the court of appeals documents hint at why. It was not the narrative the press was looking for.

---

[12] Greg Krikorian, "2 Sentenced in 'Date Rape Drug' Attacks," *Los Angeles Times*, August 6, 1997.

[13] *The People v. Steven Michael Hagemann*, Defendant and Appellant, B155446, Court of Appeal of California, Second Appellate District, Division Two, 2003 Cal. App. Unpub. Lexis 1000, January 30, 2003, Filed.; *The People, v. Danny Richard Bohannon* et al. B115308, Certified for Partial Publication in the Court Of Appeal of The State Of California, Second Appellate District, Division Two, (Los Angeles County Super. Ct. No. YA029963) Filed July 31, 2000.

[14] *Ibid.*, and Krikorian, "2 Guilty in 'Date Rape' Drug Case; Courts: Ten women were drugged, assaulted at warehouse over two years in what is called biggest such crime in state," *Los Angeles Times*, July 4, 1997, B1. Via ProQuest, retrieved November 7, 2015.

The victim-witnesses, according to Krikorian, were permitted to give impact statements before sentencing that explained the dire effects of the trauma on their lives. At one point in the sentencing proceedings, the defense attorney referenced his recent attempts to force a new trial. He attempted to use one victim's involvement in pornography as a foil to—well, it is not clear what. The depth of her trauma? The validity of the conviction on July 3? Apparently once naked on film, always acquiescent to be naked on film? This defense claim was apparently one of the attempted bases for appeal. Favorably, Judge Perry was having none of it. But neither the women exploited by The Compound men nor the narrative was what the press and legislators were thinking about. Many were women who liked to party, in one way or another, who enjoyed going to bars, drinking, staying out all night, and, in some cases, doing drugs voluntarily.

One victim, Gina, along with her date John and his friend Marcus, went to an advertised after-hours party at The Compound in March 1995 that they learned about from a flyer given out at a bar they had been at earlier. Bohannon showed them around the place, a warehouse that served as maybe an ersatz record company, a party space, but also a residence. The hosts gave the guests beers and shots. Bohannon's sister, Yvette, testified that she observed Hagemann pour liquid from a vial she knew to contain GHB into shot glasses for them. Hagemann then motioned to Yvette to not tell. John and Marcus passed out first, and then Gina woke up while being assaulted by Bohannon. When the two men awoke and left, they suspected they had been drugged. Gina reported the crime within a few days. Yvette was also drugged, assaulted, and photographed by Hagemann in either February or March 1995, but she did not know it at the time. One year later, detectives showed both women photographs that the hosts had taken while they were unconscious. Later, the police flipped Bohannon by showing him pictures of Yvette. He burst into tears.

In 1996, Sandy, an exotic dancer, met Bohannon at a party and went with a friend, Brandy, back to The Compound and was offered GHB and Ecstasy by Hagemann as well as some "white putty." She took the Ecstasy but refused the GHB. She woke up bruised and in pain and sought medical attention, and the doctor concurred with her suspicion that she had been raped. Bohannon's DNA was retrieved. The case began to come together then, but it became clear they had been at it for a while. Wendy was one of two women who knew the men for more than a decade and bumped into them at a bar. In a consistent pattern among their victims, she went back to The Compound with several women and lost consciousness after drinking one shot. After awaking on the floor in partial undress, Bohannon convinced her that nothing had happened. Police contacted her to show her photos of herself in summer 1996.

This basic modus operandi held for nearly all the cases: inviting both men and women back to The Compound for more partying, usually in groups, offering drugs, including GHB, sometimes using female confederates to get GHB into the victims after they had refused. They would awake, disoriented, in pain, suspicious but eventually convinced they simply passed out or blacked out. If it were the latter, they simply did not know what kind of sex they had engaged in and whether they had given the appearance of consent. The host usually denied any contact, until in some cases dropping a hint about good times had, months later. It was the photographs collected during a raid in August 1996 that enabled the victims to figure out what had happened. That was the paradox in The Compound case, and in others to follow: the recordings were humiliating and disturbing, but they were what made the night finally make sense to the victims. The photos filled in the blanks, and returned to the victims a sense of cognitive and temporal continuity. It was a double-edge sword. On the upside, they also made great prosecutorial evidence.

The sentencing of Hagemann in particular (against whom there was the most evidence) demonstrated the numerous pathways to punishment of such offenders, already available before the date rape drugs scare. According to a FindLaw summary of the appeal:

> Hagemann was convicted of 43 counts against 14 victims as follows: eight counts of rape by use of drugs (§ 261(a)(3)); seven counts of rape of an unconscious victim (§ 261(a)(4)); five counts of genital penetration by a foreign object of a victim unable to resist (§ 289(e)); five counts of genital penetration by a foreign object of an unconscious victim (§ 289(d)); two counts of sodomy of a person prevented from resisting by use of a drug (§ 286(i)); two counts of sodomy of an unconscious person (§ 286(f)); two

counts of attempted rape by use of drugs (§§ 664, 261(a)(3)); two counts of attempted rape of an unconscious person (§§ 664, 261(a)(4)); four counts of conspiracy to rape by use of drugs (§§ 182(a)(1), 261(a)(3)); and six counts of poisoning (§ 347(a)).[15]

Thus, there was no substance to later arguments by California legislators that the law was in any way weak on intoxication rape, let alone simple poisoning, with these Brave New Chemicals. Law was more than sufficient; yet all of the traditional barriers to rape prosecution remained. The penchant for photos upended the usual calculus in court. The press yawned.

The Andrew Luster Case (2000)

In August 2000, Andrew Luster, the heir to the cosmetics concern Max Factor was arrested in Ventura County, California and jailed in lieu of $10 million bail, on multiple counts of sexual assault, facilitated by GHB. The first victim said that she and her boyfriend both had their water drugged at a Santa Barbara bar, barely remembers being in a car, and has patchy memories of a night at Luster's house.[16] The day before his arrest, the complainant, then 21, taped a phone call at the behest of the police with Luster in which she asked him when and why he gave her "liquid X"—a common street name for GHB. In the phone call, Luster acknowledges giving her the drug, albeit upon her request that night and not in her water at the bar. After listening to the tape, Luster's attorney became optimistic.

"He does admit [that] later they took it together and partied," [Attorney] Isaacson told *The [Los Angeles] Times*. "But not at the bar, absolutely not. And really, that's the thrust of the case. If he was lurking

---

[15] FindLaw, "Court of Appeal, Second District, California; The PEOPLE, Plaintiff and Respondent, v. Danny Richard BOHANNON et al., Defendants and Appellants; No. B115308; Decided: July 31, 2000." http://caselaw.findlaw.com/ca-court-of-appeal/1130862.html. Retrieved November 4, 2015.

[16] Tracy Wilson, "Court Considers Rape Suspect's $10-Million Bail," *Los Angeles Times*, December 3, 2000, B2. Metro. The complainant also says she had been drinking that night, though believes that the drugs were in the water she drank.

around, slipping things into unsuspecting women's drinks, that's pretty bad. But he says he didn't do it, he never did that."[17]

Yes, all observers agreed, that would be pretty bad. But the heart of the complaint was a sexual assault; the alleged means was via drugging. A surreptitious drugging would have the advantage of nearly perfectly demonstrating intent, and in a world where sexual assault rarely results in a conviction, prosecutors were no doubt hopeful that he would simply admit drugging the woman and her boyfriend. But as was quickly demonstrated in this, one of the earliest high-profile GHB cases, it does not necessarily preclude a he said-she said, intoxicated sex defense. More sensational findings would take place after his arrest the next day that encouraged the prosecution.

A search of his home unearthed videotapes of him having sex with numerous, apparently unconscious women. Police analysts suggested up to 15 more victims might be out there. Luster was eventually charged with 86 counts of rape with the 3 initial victims. His lawyer's first parry was that the encounters were consensual—a difficult claim to make when the prosecution was in the unusual sweet spot of having videotape of what appeared to be women unable to consent. But the defense even contested this, claiming that the women had taken GHB voluntarily and were groggy but not unconscious in the videos. Two of the complainants were former girlfriends; one had been sued by Luster for a personal loan debt. The prosecution also emphasized to the press that they had found several vials that they suspected of having GHB in them. The victims were more conventional in lifestyle than in The Compound case, and Luster was a rich man—the press jumped all over it.

The *Los Angeles Times* in the ensuing coverage of the case made a link to the rising scare of drink spiking.[18] Reporter Tina Dirmann noted that area law enforcement agencies and crisis centers were trying to raise

---

[17] Margaret Talev, "Luster Says on Tape He Gave Woman Date-Rape Drug; Courts: But the rape suspect's lawyer says it was at the woman's request," *Los Angeles Times*, September 3, 2000, Metro B.

[18] Tina Dirmann, "Ventura County News; Bars, Police Put Spotlight on Date-Rape Drug GHB; Safety: Agencies look for ways to control its use and warn women about predators who slip it into drinks, leaving the victim vulnerable to attacks," *Los Angeles Times*, August 18, 2000; "Regional Review ... Police Expand Investigation of Man Suspected in Rape," *Los Angeles Times*, July 22, 2000, B3 Metro.

awareness of the dangers of drink spiking with GHB. Luster's arrest was the first in Ventura County. But the *Times* also noted that hotline calls from victims suspecting that they had been drugged had increased in 2000. Santa Barbara's college bar strip had been the site of a "Party Smart" safety campaign a year earlier.

Yet elsewhere, there was a strange disconnect between the 30-something Luster's arrest and the rising panic. Despite a promising headline, "The Great GHB-rape Scare," *Salon*'s Stephen Lemons led with, "Slipping someone a Mickey sounds so retro—like a line of dialogue right out of a '50s B-movie."[19]

The press seized on Luster's jaded arrogance and sense of entitlement, but seemed to resist the possibility that he had exploited and violated his victims precisely *because* they trusted him, and that his social status might have something to do with that. Lemons quoted a victim advocate who noted that "[t]his wasn't some creepy guy living behind a bush someplace," says Grace Huerta, community education coordinator for the Santa Barbara Rape Crisis Center, referring to Luster's alleged crimes. "This is a good looking, wealthy, educated man. As women, we're taught at a very early age to pay attention to who we're with, not to go out alone, not to talk to the guys who give you the creeps. That's fine advice, but apparently he didn't have any of those flags that we've been told to watch for."

The *Salon* article contrasts Luster with the stereotypical stranger-rapist. Lemons' article does not refer to any of the national concerns and legislative crackdowns going on at the time, including the draconian laws being applied to GHB, although he did talk about the drug as a kind of chemical substitute for brute force blitz attacks, hewing as such very close to the "brave new world" trope of drug rape reporting. Lemon said about GHB: "Easy to make and cheap to purchase [...] GHB makes rape much easier. Instead of all the effort involved in abducting someone at gun or knife point, less than a teaspoon of GHB can render the woman of your choice vulnerable to assault within 10 to 20 minutes." No one wanted to face the more complex and nefarious way in which Luster probably exploited his victims.

---

[19] Stephen Lemons, "The Great GHB-rape Scare," *Salon.com*. http://www.salon.com/2000/08/17/ghb_2/. August 17, 2000.

His wealth had a great deal to do with what happened next. His bail was reduced to $1 million dollars, and he was permitted house arrest while he awaited trial. Luster then absconded to Mexico. He was convicted in absentia in 2003 sentenced to 124 years. Later that year, he was captured by notorious bounty hunter Duane Chapman and, after some tangles with Mexican authorities over extradition, returned to the USA to serve his sentence.

Attempting to represent Luster's interests during his absence, his lawyer said that "his client is an aspiring pornography producer and that the women were only acting as part of a script and had consented to the sometimes bizarre sexual acts."[20] Which, if you think about it, is probably the only possible defense here, as counterproductive as it might seem. Luster was openly defiant from the beginning, when he bragged that his ability to hire expert lawyers would make his victims look like "fools."[21] Luster later claimed that he and his victims had taken GHB together, as if this were a good defense to rape of an incapacitated person.[22] It appears that Luster had given a former girlfriend GHB in 1996. She agreed to take it when he represented it as an herbal drug and a psychedelic. She did not remember anything that night after that. Her relationship with Luster continued for a while. She did not realize, she says, that Luster was videotaping her during sex in a drugged state. She ended up being one of the three complainants in the case against him, as was another former girlfriend.[23] The Luster case became a subject of a *Lifetime Channel* movie, having all of the requisite elements.[24]

---

[20] Charlie LeDuff, 2003, "Cosmetics Heir Is Missing As His Rape Trial Proceeds," *New York Times*, January 8. http://www.nytimes.com/2003/01/08/us/cosmetics-heir-is-missing-as-his-rape-trial-proceeds.html. Retrieved October 8, 2015.

[21] Richard Winton, 2013, "Max Factor heir's rape sentence reduced from 124 years to 50," Los Angeles Times, April 16. http://articles.latimes.com/2013/apr/16/local/la-me-ln-luster-gets-50-years-20130416. Retrieved October 8, 2015. Luster's sentence was eventually reduced to 50 years in state prison as the court had not given a reason for the unusual heaviness of the sentence.

[22] Chawkins, 2013.

[23] On Luster's relationship to his victims and their experience with GHB: Tina Dirmann, "Ventura County News: Luster Denies Charges, Adding his Life is now a 'Nightmare'," *Los Angeles Times*, September 3, 2000. http://articles.latimes.com/2000/sep/03/local/me-14846. Retrieved October 8, 2015.

[24] "A Date with Darkness: The Trial and Capture of Andrew Luster," *Lifetime Channel*, August 2003. http://www.mylifetime.com/movies/a-date-with-darkness. See also http://www.imdb.com/title/tt0374600/. Retrieved October 9, 2015.

The resistance to GHB as a club and party drug primarily—that can nonetheless render a victim helpless whether they took it voluntarily or not—remains strong. No matter the means by which the GHB was ingested, the jury, upon seeing the graphic videotapes, saw unconscious women engaged in sex that they could not have consented to.

Australia's John Xydias and Harry Barkas

In other countries, the patterns are remarkably similar. Chef John Xydias of Melbourne was accused of drugging, raping, and videotaping 13 women he had met through work. In some cases, he was introduced to his victims by a man named Harry Barkas, who was, at roughly the same time Xydias got caught, accused of being the "Hot Chocolate" rapist. Barkas approached women as they left nightclubs and offered them a ride home. He then offered them hot chocolate into which he had slipped tranquilizers and sleeping pills, including Rohypnol.[25] Barkas was charged with a string of attacks between 1991 and 2005, and Xydias between 1995 and 2006. Both were in their mid-40s.

Xydias typically met women through the restaurant business, Barkas sometimes did, too. One of Barkas' victims worked at the same restaurant he did and regarded him as "an older brother or uncle."[26] Xydias drugged and filmed many women while dressing them up and assaulting them. Upon sentencing in 2010, when he was convicted of 86 charges relating to 11 victims, he told the court that the women only lodged charges against him as vengeance for not continuing a relationship with them. Like other such serial offenders, he claimed that the acts were consensual and that the women were heavy drinkers and drug users.

While it may be the case that the reason nearly all of the men say the acts were consensual is strictly a legal strategy—when the prosecution has a recording of your raping behavior, there are not that many

---

[25] Elissa Hunt, "John Xydias likely to admit serial sex attacks," *Herald Sun* (Melbourne, Australia), April 2, 2008. http://www.heraldsun.com.au/news/victoria/man-likely-to-admit-serial-sex-attacks/story-e6frf7kx-1111115949193. Retrieved November 2, 2015.

[26] Adrian Lowe, "Brazen rapist jailed for 13 years," *The Age* (Melbourne), May 13, 2010, First Edition, 3.

defenses left—it is possible that pathological fantasy, on some level, has made this claim seem real to the offenders. They often see themselves as decadent nightlife hedonists who push the boundaries—so they think, well, why wouldn't or shouldn't their victims be? As in, I am one and you are, too. As edgeplay, they might even consider it relatively tame—"just" drugs. Xydias' presentence psychiatric report called him emotionally "disconnected."[27] Barkas' report suggested a narcissistic personality disorder; his ability to be accountable for his actions was limited.

There was some question of Xydias' relationship to Barkas. Though they were childhood friends and frequented the same venues, they did not, apparently, offend against the same women. Barkas appears to have been more sporadic with his assaults, with a cluster taking place in the mid-1990s and another right before his arrest, leaving a gap of more than a decade.[28] Although police suspected there must have been more victims in between, that is not entirely clear. Barkas was sentenced to 13 years and Xydias, 28.

Philadelphia and Idaho: The Jeffery Marsalis Case (2006)

The legendary public-place drink spiking, followed by a carry-off and assault, as we have seen, has too many moving parts to really be very common. What we find in its place, much more commonly, is voluntary intoxication followed by misplaced trust, or coevolving with it, and then victimization in a private setting. As with acquaintance rape generally, it is really the moment of *misplaced trust* that is exploited by the assailant. Intoxication helps, of course, in reducing the ability to resist unwanted sex, and as such, is simply another tool to facilitate an act of violence. Drugging can make detail retention hazy enough that the victim questions what really happened, and maybe more reluctant to report it, though this amnesia is not guaranteed any more than it is with large amounts of alcohol or voluntary drug ingestion. Culture then piles on

---

[27] Kate Hagan, "Man jailed for 28 years for filmed rapes of drugged women," *The Age* (Melbourne), July 1, 2009, First Edition, 3.
[28] Lowe, "Brazen rapist …" 2010.

by blaming women who drink for anything that happens after. On both individual and collective level, the gaslighting begins. Some gaslighters are better at this sort of thing than others.

If we are demonstrably uncomfortable accepting that we find ourselves vulnerable to violence and exploitation at times—because we have drunk too much or for any variety of other reasons owing to natural human interaction, like relying on basic social trust—then the pill-spiked drink becomes the ultimate beneficiary of general misdirection. It must have been drugs. How else do we explain our unacceptable vulnerability, or our misplaced trust in an individual we find ourselves alone with? We are always expected to be vigilant, and therefore only the most clever of ruses can get past us. This amounts to a denial that this person, who is clearly dangerous, could have accomplished this in any other way.

If you were looking for a poster boy of scheming, precise, skilled drink spiking rapists, you could do worse than the notorious case of Jeffrey Marsalis, who assaulted a number of women in Philadelphia and in ski resort towns in Idaho, all the while inhabiting a series of false biographies. Marsalis at various times convinced people that he was a secret intelligence agent, a surgeon, and an astronaut. He obtained false credentials and used them to enhance his various phony identities. He used his false prestige and genuine good looks to charm women and pilfer money. He also apparently assaulted a string of women who were not used to being fooled in this way. He was, in fact, an on-and-off nursing student who moved around quite a bit, and got by on his various schemes. He was charged with raping seven women and drugging them; he was convicted on two counts of sexual assault in Pennsylvania and one count of rape in Idaho.

Because the press and perhaps the courts, too, became preoccupied with his tricks, and how he finessed his postassault relationships with the women who would eventually accuse him of rape, little attention was paid to how Marsalis' story compared with the "drugging is everywhere" claims increasing in the press. It almost seemed to be a thing apart, somehow *not* what one thinks of when one thinks of drink spiking, not at all connected to that problem, but instead its own thing: Marsalis, the criminal master of imposture. In Idaho, by contrast, the first press release by law enforcement regarding charges against Marsalis there said,

"She had experienced sudden memory loss, impairment inconsistent with the amount of alcohol consumed, blacking out for an extended period of time, waking up feeling something had happened and short flashes of memory about the incident.…All of those experiences are consistent with having ingested a date-rape-type drug." And while the claim of "inconsistent with the amount of alcohol consumed" was like most such claims, exaggerated and overly subjective—forgetting that alcohol under the right circumstances can do this, too—it at least connected the incident with a specific person and event.

The drink spiking allegations against Marsalis were presented at court but not proven; no positive toxicological evidence was obtained. Some press coverage, like Dwight Ott's at the *Philadelphia Inquirer*, was circumspect about the matter of drugs versus drink and tried to refocus on the main charges of rape and sexual assault. Still, drink spiking in this case did make sense if you assumed, as the prosecution claimed, that Marsalis had honed a bit of skill in the matter, and that he was a serial attacker with an almost made-for-television-like modus operandi.

But in trying to establish the *likelihood* of drugging, the press and the courts seemed at times, disturbingly, to rest their accusations of *assault* on it. It was a successful gambit for them, but risky. And it once again deferred the question of what right women had to bodily integrity when *voluntarily* intoxicated, as many of the women also were. So much emphasis was placed on the drugs that Marsalis' violence—his decision to rape and exploit—seemed like some mechanistically simple and inevitable outcome of his drugging scheme.

For instance, the courts belabored how he could have obtained drugs through his nursing and emergency medical technician (EMT) work. But by the time of the Marsalis allegations, in the early 2000s, obtaining drugs for such a purpose was hardly difficult. Benzodiazepines were everywhere. GHB was a popular club drug. Diphenhydramine (which was brought up as a possibility) is available over the counter. Basically, anyone who wanted to drug anyone else would not find many obstacles of a chemical sort. There basically are no barriers to means, nor have there been for a very long time.

What is more important here would be Marsalis presumed pharmaceutical skill, and the prosecution focused on his increasing medical credentials. Unlike the popular attribution of drugging in later cases, where high levels of alcohol consumption were also present, the differential between the number of drinks the women said they had had and the blackout behavior that followed was indeed extreme. Indeed, he would have had to put them in such a state as to blackout but not go unconscious—a gamble in a public place if there ever was one. They had to drink enough together—in public—to establish drinking as a pretext to what he claims were consensual sexual encounters at his apartment later. They had to travel together, at some point, from bar to apartment. The women who accused him of rape said they became aware of sexual contact with Marsalis either by reawakening during intercourse or with patchy memories of it the morning after.

Marsalis then had a pattern of turning on the care, charm, and persuasion. The idea was to convince them of the cover story—they they had drunk amiably together, returned home to have sex and then fallen asleep. "The women testified that because of some unknown drug Marsalis slipped them, they were knocked out, lost memories, were incredibly disoriented when they were conscious, and were confused about what had happened afterward because he treated them as if nothing was amiss," according to reporter Robert Moran, who covered the trial.[29]

Perhaps the idea was simply to enhance their confusion and doubts about what had happened long enough to prevent any decent gathering of evidence that could be used against him—a rape kit, toxicology tests, or even just a relatively quick recorded complaint to the police or crisis center, when details might be freshest. Or perhaps—and here the narrative imposed by the press seems appropriate—the postencounter charm offensive was just part of Marsalis' overall way of maneuvering and manipulating reality through everything he did.

The sheer number of complainants against Marsalis—in more than one place—was always in the prosecution's favor. The seven women who testified against him did not really have anything to gain by making up stories—Marsalis was, in reality, without financial means—except perhaps working through wounded pride at being fooled by his various VIP

---

[29] Robert Moran, "Impostor's Trial on Rape Charges Goes to Jury," *Philadelphia Inquirer*, June 8, 2007, B4.

identities. Even here, embarrassment usually reigns. The women involved tended to be professional and were described by the press as "smart." Sober minded, if not sober. Some, it appears, fronted money to him. The press was also very intrigued also by the case's online dating angle—Marsalis apparently met a number of victims via *Match.com* where he posted and boasted about being an astronaut or doctor. He had also been tried previously and found not guilty in January 2006 of raping three additional women under similar circumstances.[30]

The focus of Marsalis' defense was extreme sour grapes. Their client, they argued, was an inveterate liar and schemer, and a playboy, but nothing more. The women accusers, they said, were simply regretful after the fact when it became clear they had been fooled by him. Indeed, a number of the women had extensive further contact with him after the assaults, and did not report the assaults to police. (Police in fact contacted them after seizing evidence from Marsalis' computer. Yes, he kept a log.) Thus, it might have seemed like an easy defense, but it was unsuccessful. Marsalis was convicted in both places—a 21-year sentence on two counts of sexual assault in Philadelphia in 2007 (along with an acquittal on eight charges of rape) and a life sentence on one count in Idaho in 2009. "It wasn't clear why the jurors had determined that those women were sexually assaulted rather than raped, or why they believed those two but not the other women," said one article by Robert Moran of the *Philadelphia Inquirer* in the wake of the verdict.[31]

Moran had noted in an earlier article that the jury had asked for additional guidance on consent and intoxication, which suggested to the reporter that "at least some of the jurors do not believe the prosecution proved beyond a reasonable doubt that the women were drugged."[32] This conclusion was unwarranted; Moran himself notes that jurors did not speak to the press as they exited the courthouse. It may simply be that they had to work with only the evidence at hand, and to their credit, did not assume that Marsalis was innocent *of violence* simply because the

---

[30] Oliver Pritchard, "Man Acquitted of Three Rapes," *Philadelphia Inquirer*, January 18, 2006, B3.
[31] Robert Moran, "No rape on dates, hoaxer's jury says," *Philadelphia Inquirer*, Jun 14, 2007, A1.
[32] Robert Moran, "Still No Verdict in Marsalis Rape Trial," *Philadelphia Inquirer*, June 13, 2007, B3; "No Rape on Dates, Hoaxer's Jury Says," *Philadelphia Inquirer*, June 14, 2007, A1.

presence of drugs could not be proven. Given the two counts of sexual assault that they convicted him of, leading to a 21-year sentence, it is fairly likely they did not think of Marsalis as merely the playboy.

At the time, Marsalis did not testify on his own behalf or speak to the press; he did grant an interview in 2013 with reporter David Muir of *ABC News* in which he asserted his innocence and reiterated his countercharge that the accusers were bitter, and related an additional allegation of state manipulation of the women in question.[33]

Marsalis eventually appealed his Idaho conviction, and the appellate court's upholding of his conviction in 2011 provides a decent amount of detail to suggest to prosecutors that Marsalis was using his standard operating procedure.[34] The incident took place in Sun Valley. The victim and Marsalis went out for drinks after work. According to both the victim and the bartender, both consumed several beers and shots. The victim suspected that Marsalis dosed one of her shots; she claimed to be normally able to drink that much without memory problems. Despite observing some residue at the bottom of her shot glass, she drank more beers that he ordered. Already here we see him establishing her drinking behavior in a public place and making backhanded use of her insistence that she can hold her liquor; that she can nearly match him for drinks. After passing out in the cab, she awakes at his place feeling very sick and bruised. By the evening, she approaches the police, who take her for blood and urine tests. Her toxicology tests came back negative for drugs, as did some containers from Marsalis' apartment.

But at Marsalis' grand jury hearing, a police officer erroneously testified that the tests on the container were "inconclusive" as only a small amount of powdery substance was found; they were negative. During Marsalis' following petition to dismiss, the officer admitted his error, stating that he was mistaken, not intentionally misrepresenting the facts. Marsalis' defense team said this erroneous testimony insinuated a predatory drugging scenario. The district court denied Marsalis' petition for dismissal on these grounds, arguing that other nontoxicological evidence was

---

[33] David Muir, "Accused Serial Rapist Speaks Out," *ABC News*, August 29, 2013. http://abcnews.go.com/2020/video/accused-serial-rapist-speaks-8095440. Retrieved March 17, 2016.

[34] *State of Idaho V. Jeffrey Marsalis*, Court of Appeals, 151 Idaho 872, 264 P.3d 979; 2011 Ida. App. LEXIS 74.

sufficient for an indictment anyway. The higher courts let the district court's conviction stand, arguing that the error was not prejudicial. The charge in question, Judge Lansing said, was predicated simply on Marsalis assaulting the victim while she was too intoxicated to consent; in this respect, the public drinking observed by the bartender and the passing out in the cab, observed by the driver, worked against Marsalis rather than for him—just as the guidelines from the National Center for Women and Policing suggested. The victim mentioned the residue in the shot glass in her own testimony, the appellate court reasoned, but the jury did not actually need to believe she was drugged to find that she was incapacitated. There was a dissenting judge at the appellate level who thought the error was enough to support dismissal; Judge Gutierrez said that the "date rape drugging" scenario dominated the state's case for indictment, noting that they brought in a forensic drug expert to describe the effects of date rape drugs generally, how they might be administered, and how quickly GHB leaves the system—in effect, the state was bolstering its drugging theory and could not later argue that it was not.

Gutierrez' dissent, though the minority opinion in this instance, points out the dangers for prosecutors on relying on a drink spiking explanation once they had gone through the motions of toxicological testing without the desired incriminating results. This can be a double-edged sword for a prosecutor—so tempting because it negates the tendency toward victim blame in the case of "just alcohol" but triggering an additional burden if it comes out negative.

What Do Serial Cases Teach Us?

First, serial cases tell us that there are perils in the overreliance on drugging explanations in cases of sexual assault, even when—as in these cases—common sense would dictate that it is the most likely explanation. Would we feel good about a situation where a court held an assailant *less* accountable because the women might have consented to the drugs? Or might have consumed too much alcohol? Or might actually not be able to fully answer this question of how they came to be incapacitated? And if we limited reports to the police, indictments, and trials to cases in which drink spiking could be corroborated by other evidence, we would move forward with a small number of sexual assault cases.

Second, drugging rapists are probably not Lurking Any Man. A minor YouTube celebrity named Joey Salads decided to show us all in a video he recorded *how easy* it was to spike someone's drink in public without their knowledge, as if we somehow previously thought it was difficult to drop a Skittle into a drink. The video was treated with great seriousness by news outlets, including a CBS affiliate and *Vanity Fair*, although the latter thought the main problem might be Joey's funny name and that new spikers might copycat him.[35] But even in and around bars and parties, serial cases show us that other conditions have to be met.

The skill involved in drugging rape begins with fostering false trust. This is what enables the assailant to engage in the surreptitious drugging in the first place, to convince the victim to be in an isolated place with him—his comfort zone—to begin with, to sometimes believe his stories that "nothing happened" or that they were both intoxicated, and both engaged in consensual acts that she simply does not remember. A prior condition, of course, is the assailant's mindset: entitled, sexually gratified in situations that the victim cannot define or help create, some facility with gaslighting and moving between realities, and a possible delusion, in some cases, that he has some sort of relationship with the victim—whether it be rescuing or antagonistic. A number of the assailants attacked women they had ongoing romances or friendships with; in some cases, they were able to dissemble well enough that they maintained relationships afterward. Defense strategies often include the claim that the women wanted things from the men accused: a more intense relationship, a better voluntary drug experience, status, or money.

The acts of assault themselves somewhat match the sexually motivated, nonsadistic offender—indicated by the lack of excessive violence and the delusions or gaslighting about relationships. But on the other hand, there are fewer strangers as victims than we might expect. There is the drug-rapist's

---

[35] "Viral Video Warns How Easily Predators Can Drop Date Rape Drugs," *CBS News New York Local*, June 11, 2015, http://newyork.cbslocal.com/2015/06/11/date-rape-drug-social-experiment; "YouTube Digest: Why Did This Man Put His Disastrous McDonald's Marriage Proposal on YouTube?" *Vanity Fair*, June 5, 2015, http://www.vanityfair.com/culture/2015/06/youtube-digest-June-5. Both retrieved October 30, 2015.

6 Who and Where Are the Druggers?

distinctive lack of need for recognition during the rape, which might point to opportunism if there were not elaborate staging. There does seem to be some level of vindictiveness, some desire to humiliate and degrade, although the amnesia on the victims' part and the secretiveness on the offender's part deprives the offender of an audience for his attempt to vindicate his grievances against either his victims, or women in general.

Probably some small remainder of explanation, then, has to be chalked up to a predatory paraphilia, but the behavior does not fit completely. The obvious candidate would be somnophilia, a fetish where arousal and orgasm are tied to unconscious or sleeping targets.[36] Psychologists emphasize that this kind of fetish stems from thinking of lust as problematic, and therefore sex must be furtive or stolen.[37] Yet this tension often seems to be absent in serial cases: these offenders often have openly decadent, rather than guilt-ridden or conservative lifestyles. They typically try, once caught, to implicate the victims as simply ambivalent inhabitants of the same edgy demi-monde, or being as corrupt of motivation as they are. They also, in some cases, maintained conventional sex lives, marriages, or even steady girlfriends at the same time.

To ignore the paraphilia element would also be to ignore how many moving parts this mode of rape actually has. Far from being "the perfect crime in a pill" as legend would have it, it actually exposes the assailant to many risks that are easily avoided by the straightforward, malevolent opportunist.[38] This is a specialty crime, not a new chemical app that has widespread adoption potential.

Dawn Moore and Mariana Valverde suggest that the distorted thinking about the role of drugs in such assaults has the effect of shifting blame from perpetrators to chemicals, and also "degendering" sexual assault—as if rape stemmed from greater finesse in technique and not all of the

---

[36] Somnophilia need not be "predatory" if a willing partner engages in the fantasy; but I'm only concerned with the predatory version here where one party is forced into enacting the drama. See Anil Aggrawal, *Forensic and Medico-legal Aspects of Sexual Crimes and Unusual Sexual Practices*, Boca Raton, FL: CRC Press, 2009.

[37] Raymond Corsini, "Predatory Paraphilias," *Dictionary of Psychology*, London: Brunner-Routledge, 2002, 747.

[38] The phrase appears to come from the 1996 Congressional testimonies, but was probably popularized by an episode of *The Oprah Winfrey Show* on January 6, 1998 (cited in Jenkins 1998, p. 180).

other social, political, and psychological dimensions of the crime.[39] Additionally, it also undergirds the backhanded blame of the more typical rape victim, as it elevates drugs to the status of superweapons: now it can happen to "anyone" not just…well, you know, those drunk women. The specter of the Lurking Man, the victim as Anyone, and the venue as Anyplace together make fear of this crime inherently prone to overestimation of risk and an underestimation of barriers.

As such, there have been specific scares in some places, and what you might call "failed scares" in others. They appear to be interwoven with well-intentioned crime prevention campaigns.

Episodes and Local Scares

In this section, I first mean to differentiate between the general scare across countries about date rape drugs and the dynamics of local scares. Nearly all localized scares center on nightclubs, bars, and party venues rather than the lairs of private rooms, or the kitchen tables of companions. Yet certainly there are occasions in which drinks *are* tampered with in public. Just because it is difficult to commit a *further* crime against someone you have drugged in a public place does not mean you would not do it for some other reason. Such as: just because.

What of druggings that do not involve further victimization? Or ones that are perpetrated as malicious pranks? Unfortunately, the distortions created by the compulsive focus on a rape motive in spiking obscures the public health problem as a whole. Not all druggers are interested in robbing or raping their victims. Pranks have always ranked high in the annals of spiking, from Albert Hofmann's tales of coffee spiking in the Sandoz labs to the lunchroom antics of juveniles. John Trestrail's study of criminal poisoning cases found that among the juvenile offenders in his database (dating from 1838 to 2005), just over half targeted students or teachers. In a study of the drink spiking scare in Australia in the early 2000s, the Australian Institute of Criminology (AIC) found that most

---

[39] Dawn Moore and Mariana Valverde, "Maidens at Risk: 'date rape drugs' and the formation of hybrid risk knowledges," *Economy and Society*, Vol. 29, No. 4, November 2000, 514–531.

suspected druggings reported there were not related to sexual assault, and that 60–70% of suspected incidents were not followed by another victimization.[40]

Though some might claim that such suspected druggings were near-misses of rape or robbery, there is no evidence to support this, and spikings in public, crowded places obviously provide formidable barriers to further victimization unless some means of isolating the victim is enabled. Not surprisingly, then, those who *were* sexually assaulted were somewhat less likely to say they thought the drink spiking had happened in a public place—50%, as opposed to the two-thirds who reported no further victimizations after suspected bar spiking—and at the hands of a known person rather than a stranger. The AIC concluded, first, that many suspected druggings were likely to actually be underestimations of self-administered alcohol intake. Australia, like the USA and the UK, saw an uptick in binge drinking and related harms in the late 1990s and 2000s, particularly among young adults.[41]

Second, the AIC noted, confirmed drink spiking in public places may well be down to "where the intention is to see what happens or to have a joke"—that is, of the classic prank-spiking type. Reckless with the safety of others, and its own form of grandiose, controlling behavior, prank spiking is nonetheless distinct from the predatory sort which is a means to another end.

Australian Scares in the Early 2000s: The Canberra Scare as an Early Model

In Australia, the "protected narrative" managed to keep being debunked and rediscovered, sometimes at the same time—it was not linear, but incoherent. Canberra experienced a localized scare driven by a bit of word of mouth, followed by media advocacy, and then antispiking campaigns.

---

[40] Natalie Taylor, Jeremy Prichard and Kate Charlton, *National project on drink spiking: investigating the nature and extent of drink spiking in Australia*, Canberra: Australian Institute of Criminology, November 2004. AIC is a government agency.

[41] Australian Government, National Drug Research Institute, *Attachment A: Trends in alcohol use and harms across Australia*, June 2012, Retrieved November 14, 2015. http://www.nationaldrug-strategy.gov.au/internet/drugstrategy/publishing.nsf/Content/atiau.

The campaigns and publicity may have kept the scare alive much longer than it might have otherwise lasted.

The years 2001 and 2002 saw several dire warnings in the press about spiking that piggybacked on the Australian Capital Territory (ACT) Police's confusing claims about the dangers of increasing (voluntary) club drugs usage, particularly Ecstasy. Stories about club drug seizures undergirded the claims made that a handful of self-reports of suspected spiking represented a small portion of what was likely "hundreds" of drink spikings in the District.[42] It was clear that at that point, the police were convinced that there were vastly more cases out there. In 2001, there were 8 articles mentioning drink spiking in the *Canberra Times* and 19 in 2002; in the latter year, there were also 4 reports in Sydney papers that mentioned incidents in Canberra. I say "incidents" rather than cases because even in the five articles that were tied to specific events (such as people being found in alleys, disoriented), no follow-up was presented. One of those articles was about a female police officer from Canberra that had her drink spiked in Los Angeles. The four others were about a female netball player who tested positive for testosterone and said she was drink-spiked with the hormone near Canberra.[43] The remaining 14 articles made general reference to there being a problem in Canberra and passed on warnings to club goers and revelers.

By the end of 2002, ACT police had 92 reported incidents. There were no mentions of toxicological investigation or other confirmation. But by August 2002, national police authorities were trying to right-size concern about the matter in relation to alcohol, on the one hand, and sexual assault in general, on the other, in a guardedly diplomatic way. In an interview with the *Canberra Times*, [Australian Federal Police Superintendent Sweeny] said that "Although drink spiking was an issue in the ACT, he said the reported number of offences was quite low. 'We do know from

---

[42] Monika Boogs, "Police warn drink spiking rife in ACT," *Canberra Times*, August 14, 2001. p. A1. Via Lexis Nexis, retrieved November 13, 2015. It is possible that the term "liquid ecstasy" referred to by the reporter early in this article, followed by later references to "ecstasy," may have conflated MDMA (a stimulant) and GHB (a CNS depressant, sometimes called liquid ecstasy), though it appears that the alarm about *spiking* may have come from the ACT police anyway.

[43] Jacquelin Magnay, and Roy Masters, "Date-rape warning as netballer tests positive," *Sydney Morning Herald*, March 20, 2002, News 1.

our interaction with other agencies that there are people coming in and saying that they believe there had been drink spiking,'"[44] 2003's Canberra spiking story pattern was similar, with 17 articles.

But 2004 and 2005 were much sparser in coverage, with 7 and 11 articles, respectively. It does appear that the Canberra press lost interest once it was clear that the relationship between suspected spiking and actual spiking would probably remain nebulous at best, and although the tone of the coverage did not change in light of law enforcement's quietly changing views, perhaps enthusiasm did. 2004's coverage was, for most of the year, brief items related to policy; three were coverage of the release of the AIC report, which did not emerge until November 2004. Reporters pulled the most frightening number out—the estimate of "up to 4000" suspected spikings across Australia between July 2002 and June 2003. But even this maximal projection belied original projections in the Canberra press. In 2002, ACT politician Katy Gallagher had averred that Canberra alone experienced 30 spiking reports per weekend, though like most maximal estimators, she suggested it simply was not possible to know for sure.[45]

The AIC's cooling effect seems to have had a further chastening impact in Canberra as coverage in 2005 stayed low. Nationally, the press still kept the spiking dream alive. As law enforcement and victim advocates backed away with guarded statements—it is always important to be cautious, but that alcohol's the big story here—the press became a kind of independent moral entrepreneur for the salience and the invisible reality of the protected narrative. The AIC report observed that "anecdotal reports [in the media] outnumber formal complaints to the police by an estimated factor of 10." By 2006, the level of press distortion and hyperbole was of such concern that the New South Wales Police issued a corrective pamphlet.[46] Drawing on the AIC study and other data, the

---

[44] Monika Boogs, "Sex attacks often go unreported in ACT," *Canberra Times*, August 17, 2002. Via Lexis Nexis, Retrieved November 14, 2015.
[45] Danielle Cronin, "Hotline to help research drink-spiking for national report," *Canberra Times*, November 15, 2003, A9.
[46] NSW Police Public Affairs Branch, "Drink Spiking: Myths and Facts," December 2006, http://www.victimsservices.justice.nsw.gov.au/Documents/fact_sheet_drink_spiking_myths.pdf. Retrieved November 12, 2015. New South Wales includes Sydney.

guide emphasized that confirmed cases were very small in number, the continuing importance of alcohol and how high blood alcohol levels can be mistaken for drug effects, and reminded the reader that the "vast majority of the drink spiking incidents reported to police do not involve any other crime, i.e. assault, sexual assault or robbery. Further, the vast majority of reported sexual assaults do not involve the offender 'spiking' the victim." Finally, it emphasizes that the drug and rape connection is much more likely to be opportunistic—the assailant targets and assaults an individual who has voluntarily consumed drugs and/or alcohol.

Certainly, underreporting of drug rape incidents is a problem, but that problem is really inherent to sexual assault rather than drugs—the crime has a low reporting rate in general, for a variety of reasons. Echoing Moore's studies of the transformation of the term "date rape" in the UK and US press, Alexandra Neame, who has studied the problem closely, said that on the heels of a scare in Perth, Western Australia, "In these media reports, sexual assault is subsumed within the crime of drink spiking to such an extent that it literally cannot be spoken about without reference to a sedative or hypnotic substance, like Rohypnol, GHB, or ketamine."[47] She describes a media rollercoaster over the early 2000s that at first claimed a bar-spiking "epidemic" in Perth, and then, when this could not be corroborated by the police or hospitals in its conventional "protected narrative" form (someone surreptitiously puts drugs in a drink in a bar and then assaults the drinker), began to label it an "urban myth."

Looking back at this same time period, I found that this whiplash in attitudes in Canberra, at least, was due to the press simply not being able to sustain the inflated statistics that it had itself generated or repeated without scrutiny, such as the aforementioned 30 per weekend. As well, in March of 2002, the *Canberra Times* used two differently constructed databases to infer that 30% of reported rapes in the ACT were due to drink spiking.[48] There was simply no way that such a claim could be sustained, and while subsequent reports continued to push suspiciously

---

[47] Alexandra Neame, "Beyond 'drink spiking': drug and alcohol facilitated sexual assault," Briefing No. 2, Australian Institute of Family Studies, November 2003, https://www3.aifs.gov.au/acssa/pubs/briefing/b2.html. Retrieved November 12, 2015.
[48] Monika Boogs, "30pc of sex crime from 'spiking'," *Canberra Times*, March 23, 2002, A8. Via Lexis-Nexis Academic, retrieved November 13, 2015.

high numbers for drink spiking reports, and feature breathless "watch your drink!" headlines, they also mentioned that only in a handful of reported spiking cases did assault follow.[49] The press in Canberra also began to note that amphetamine was a common finding where drugs were actually present in tests. The press seemed easily to fold this finding into the date rape drugging scenario, reasoning that meth, like testosterone, can enhance sexual desire and stamina. Other motives were not considered. The police also cautioned that voluntarily taken illicit substances can create unexpected symptoms, as can alcohol.[50]

In some sense, the press was (eventually) correct that few such bar-spiking-rapist scenarios actually explain the connection between nightlife, intoxication, and sexual assault. But as Neame points out, since the suspicions of drugging were in many cases tied with complaints of sexual assault, the press also used the *absence of drugs* to question whether the assault complaints were in fact simply regretted behavior while intoxicated. In a fashion similar to the gambit represented by using unconfirmed drug allegations at court, the intertwining of drink spiking allegations with rape complaints seems to open up disbelief about *assault* if no drugs turn out to be present. Neame notes that our continued discomfort with the victims who has "just had alcohol" tends to foster this overly narrow view of the intoxicated rape problem: did he slip you drugs or not? Or did you just drink too much? There was a bit of a lull in the Australian scare in the mid-2000s as a number of officials and health workers attempted to bring the conversation about nightlife excess back to alcohol.

The pattern in Canberra coverage was similar to what Neame found after the Perth scare, although less dramatic. Mostly, it had to do with declining media enthusiasm, rather than apostasy, on the drink spiking question.[51] Some of the articles had to do with legislation and politics,

---

[49] Renee Cutrupi, "Device aims to put lid on drink spiking," *Canberra Times*, January 17, 2003, A9; Elicia Murray, "Drink-spiking cases double," *Canberra Times*, May 22, 2003, A11. Via Lexis-Nexis Academic, both retrieved November 13, 2015.

[50] Murray, 2003.

[51] Coverage declined in 2005 (11 articles, with only 1 being about a specific incident), and in 2006, there were 15 articles, mostly nonspecific, 1 specific incident, and 2 about cases elsewhere. The year 2007 saw only 4 articles about the scene in Canberra, and 12 articles in total. Search via Lexis-Nexis Academic, November 18, 2015, using search terms "Canberra" and "spiking," eliminating duplicates and topics unrelated.

as Canberra is the national capital. So while the articles that were published continued to push for greater attention to drink spiking, reporting seemed to decline once the story was brought back to alcohol. In 2006, for instance, a Canberra Sexual Health Centre nurse practitioner talked to a reporter about young women who are seen around the time of big formal dances and after-parties. Regarding the girls who are raped on such occasions, she explained, "'We encourage them to report it but I think a lot of it goes unreported to us and to the police, because the young people are just so embarrassed and can't believe it's happened,' she said. While she ruled out drink spiking as a potential cause, Ms. O'Keefe said young people didn't have the skills to get themselves out of a difficult situation, 'especially if they have been drinking.' "[52] It was a realistic assessment of the more ordinary dangers girls and young women face, but the fascination with drink spiking as a potential cause among the press lingered.

The Canberra scare, with a clear sort of incline and fading, also seemed to be very localized and focused on Anyman Rapist at Anybar. The screaming headlines were explicitly about the ubiquity of the threat—people getting spiked left and right—rather than the sensational themes available from national and international press coverage of serial offenders. Australia had its own rogues' march of serial spikers to reference to that point, even before Xydias and Barkas were caught. John Robertson, a Qantas flight attendant, was convicted in 1996 of dosing members of his cabin crew with Rohypnol in hot chocolate; his assaults took place in a number of locales in Australia and abroad.[53] Victoria man Mark Sutherland was convicted in 2006 of several 2002 drugging rapes that he carried out when he visited women's homes to give them furniture repair quotes.[54] Australian papers also covered the Luster case in the USA. But, again, none of these incidents conformed to the preferred setting for the drink spiking narrative; they were covered as serial rape cases with drugs involved.

---

[52] Karen Ingram, "Alcohol-filled Formals leads to unsafe sex, assault," *Canberra Times*, September 9, 2006, A1.

[53] Anita Chaudhuri, "The Sky's the Limit," *The Independent* (London), September 21, 2011. http://www.independent.co.uk/life-style/the-skys-the-limit-1197606.html.

[54] "Removalist sentenced for 3 rapes," *The Age* (Melbourne), May 22, 2004. Retrieved January 19, 2016. http://www.theage.com.au/articles/2004/05/21/1085120117124.html?from=storylhs.

In April 2005, the *Canberra Times* reported that the ACT had taken 76 reports of suspected spiking: "From March 2004 to February 2005, 76 cases were reported to police. No one was arrested or charged in any of the incidents."[55] The occasion was the announcement that area bar owners would stock protective lids and drink testing coasters. Ian Meldrum, the owner of a pub, The Holy Grail, told the paper he was unlikely to use the coasters as his bar did not really have a problem. "'If you have good security and surveillance, people know the odds of being caught.' Mr. Meldrum said he had bought 5000 bright orange drink covers several years ago but customers didn't use them so he put them in storage."

Either the problem itself, or fears of the problem, declined somewhat after the initial scare. Between March 2005 and February 2006, 65 reports were taken in the ACT, with 4 lab-confirmed cases. Specifically, "traces of ecstasy, ketamine … and methamphetamine (such as ice or base) in their bodies."[56] A total of 40 cases total were reported for the year 2006, and 28 for the January to August period in 2007.[57] Meanwhile, authorities had not lost sight of the binge drinking issue.

The newly marketed alcopops became a scapegoat for rising binge drinking levels among young people.[58] Australian politicians imposed a surcharge tax in 2008 on these "ready to drink" premixed bottles of alcohol and fruit juices, which ranged in strength. This move was aimed at curbing their appeal to underage drinkers and create tax parity with spirits, and managed to run up against the continuing spiking specter in the process. Critics countered that open drinks were physically easier to spike than bottled ones; fewer alcopop purchases would therefore mean more drink spiking.[59] Once again, the idea held fast that spiking was a

---

[55] Diana Streak, "Clever Coaster Helps Fight Drink Spiking," *Canberra Times*, April 19, 2005, A8. Via Lexis-Nexis.

[56] "In Brief," *Canberra Times*, March 16, 2006, A6.

[57] "Drinks are spiked all over ACT," *The Chronicle* (Toowoomba), August 14, 2007, p. A2. Via Lexis Nexis.

[58] Nick Harding "The demonised drink: How has youth drinking evolved 20 years since the launch of alcopops?" The Independent (London), June 28, 2013. http://www.independent.co.uk/lifestyle/food-and-drink/features/the-demonised-drink-how-has-youth-drinking-evolved-20-years-since-the-launch-of-alcopops-8675342.html. Retrieved November 13, 2015.

[59] Sharri Markson, "Youth call time on alcopop tax," *Sunday Telegraph* (Australia), State Edition, May 25, 2008, Local 40. Via Lexis-Nexis Academic, Retrieved November 13, 2015.

primarily public venue problem, and resulted from the technical ease of dosing a drink. The tax was repealed in 2009, on the more legitimate concern that self-mixed drinks might end up having more alcohol than the bottled ones.[60] It is not clear that alcopops have affected youth drinking levels in any direction.[61]

A 2009 Australian study of 97 Perth area ER cases of suspected surreptitious drugging found initially that nine cases were "plausible" given the described circumstances but not likely—and 4 were confirmed. Even the likely and confirmed cases differed in precisely the way one might expect—they happened in private settings, and not bars or parties. Polydrug use was common. One confirmed case involved unexplained methamphetamine in the system. The patient, a male, suspects his friends may have given him meth as a prank. Many patients had high BAC as well. Of those that were drinking, most had more than four drinks. Thirteen actually had no alcohol or drugs in their system at all. Around 35% continued to believe they were drugged despite the negative findings.[62]

In Australia, as in most places that have had any sizeable publicity directed toward drink spiking, the politics of spiking are bound up in strange ways with the politics of alcohol. Often times, screaming headlines about watching your drink were wrapped around admonitions about alcohol and other illicit drugs. A November 2003 article in the *Canberra Times* quoted an ACT Police spokesman reminding revelers to "remember that the most common drug used to spike drinks was alcohol. He also cautioned against using drink spiking as an excuse for deliberate overindulgence for which individuals themselves were entirely responsible. No arrests have yet been made or prosecutions brought for drink spiking, police blaming the clandestine nature of the crime for the difficulties in their investigations."[63] It well illustrates the dilemma to which Neave pointed.

---

[60] Gerard McManus, "Alcopops tax defeated in the Senate after second vote," *Herald Sun*, March 18, 2009. http://www.heraldsun.com.au/news/alcopops-price-to-drop-after-bill-defeat/story-e6fr-f7jo-1111119172860. Retrieved November 13, 2015.

[61] Harding, 2013.

[62] Paul Quigley, Dana Lynch, et al, "Prospective Study of 101 Patients with Suspected Drink Spiking," *Emergency Medicine Australasia*, 21, 222–228, 2009. Methods: subjects presented to ER within 12 hours, clinical, lab, and historical data taken. GHB above the usual endogenous level (10 g/L) was considered positive. Around 88 % female.

[63] "Party warnings;"'Tis the season to be wary of drink spiking," *Canberra Times*, November 16, 2003, A6.

Overcultivated Fear? Sort of

One cannot simply assume a moral panic or even a public scare from the distortions or preoccupations of the press, legislators, or other vocal claims-makers. These aforementioned groups tend to treat the problem as one that has not had adequate attention or "awareness," one that requires more administrative and law enforcement interest than it is getting. Yet the periodic resurgence of this problem in the press, often treated as a new threat, may actually stem from apparently tepid or somewhat conflicted interest from the public. As with the Canberra pub owner who ended up mothballing his drink spiking prevention devices after the scare, sometimes, there is a serious-not-serious paradox to be found in public concern about the problem. That is not to say that the problem is treated *skeptically* by the public—it is not, usually, and that is a problem—but rather that it seems to have become a background threat; something taken in stride among other threats. It may be a threat that one deploys—as a public outrage "out there" without being a big personal concern. Alternatively, it might be an available, but not necessarily taken up, potential account of an evening gone wrong.

Self-reports about Suspected Drugging

My sample of college student respondents first sensitized me to this. In 2006 and 2008, I surveyed students on one campus in the USA, while Adam Burgess and Sarah E.H. Moore surveyed and interviewed students at a campus in England. Our coauthored article in the *British Journal of Criminology* (2009) showed minimal first-person experience. "Only ten people in the UK sample (n = 236) claimed to have personally experienced drink-spiking, and none had been subject to sexual assault as a result. In the US survey, 17 (n = 334) believed they were the likely or possible victims of drugging, though, again, not all mentioned assault."[64] And in the US respondents, 7 of the 17 said they were not sure whether drugging explained what happened to them.

---

[64] Adam Burgess, Pamela Donovan, and Sarah E.H. Moore, "Embodying Uncertainty? Understanding Heightened Risk Perception of Drink 'Spiking.'" *British Journal of Criminology*. 49: 6, 848–862, 2009.

This low level of self-reported drug rape victimization, or even suspicion of it is, in the USA, and to some extent in Canada, also reflected in larger studies.[65] In particular, surveys about sexual assault among college women reveal that very few report surreptitious drugging related to sexual assaults they experienced. Krebs and associates (2007) define DFSA, or drug-facilitated sexual assault, more narrowly than subsequent studies, as being given drugs or alcohol before an assault without the respondent's knowledge. Most other studies use a broader definition for DFSA, which includes all cases of rape during intoxicated incapacitation, regardless of the voluntariness of the intoxication, though the Krebs' study also measures this using different terminology. Krebs' study finds that 11% of college sexual assault victims were incapacitated. Those who knew, or suspected, that they were given drugs or alcohol without their knowledge were 2.3% of the sexual assault/battery total (0.6% *since* entering college). Around 5.3% of the sample said they were given drugs or alcohol without their knowledge but not assaulted. In 2007, Kilpatrick, Resnick et al. published another major study on both women in general and college women specifically, intoxication, and sexual assault. Around 79% of those reporting intoxication involved alcohol only. DFSA is slightly broader in definition in this report (p. 7) but still narrower than those to follow. "The perpetrator deliberately gives the victim drugs without her permission or tries to get her drunk." Around 2.3% of the sample (which corresponds to an estimated 3 million women) said this had happened; 2.2% with alcohol and 0.5% with drugs.

A 2009 study in Ontario, Canada, at first appears to have a much higher percentage of women (20%) who self-report at least one symptom consistent with drugging, but the sample differs from the Krebs and Kilpatrick studies in several ways.[66] It is from victims of sexual assault who sought help at a hospital clinic, not a survey sample. It did not

---

[65] Christopher P. Krebs, Christine H. Lindquist, et al, *The Campus Sexual Assault (CSA) Study*, National Institute of Justice, Document No.: 221153, December 2007; Kilpatrick DG, Resnick HS, et al. *Drug-facilitated, incapacitated, and forcible rape: a national study*. Document No.: 219181, July 2007. Charleston, SC: Medical University of South Carolina, National Crime Victims Research and Treatment Center. Bernadette Butler and Jan Welch, "Drug-Facilitated Sexual Assault," *Canadian Medical Association Journal*, March 3, 2009, 493–494.

[66] Janice DuMont, Shiela Macdonald, et al, "Factors associated with suspected drug facilitated sexual assault," *Canadian Medical Association Journal* 180, March 3, 2009, 513–519.

involve toxicological study. While the screening tool used included questions about voluntary alcohol, drug use, and symptoms, no effort is made to differentiate opportunistic assaults on women versus covert drugging followed by assault, nor consider the role that voluntary alcohol or drug use may have played in the symptoms experienced. Yet in their finding summary section, they clearly stated: "Interpretation: Suspected drug-facilitated sexual assault is a common problem." This statement is a bit strong given the methodology used and the findings obtained. Yet careful reading of such studies by reporters is not impossible, or too much to ask.

A response in the same journal issue cautions against overinterpretation in the direction of covert drugging and pleads for sensitivity toward victims assaulted while voluntarily, as well as involuntarily, intoxicated.[67]

In the UK, the National Union of Students (NUS) survey in 2010 found a notably larger percentage (9%) of student victims of rape or attempted rape who linked the event to being "given alcohol or drugs against their will before the attack."[68] The ITV Crime Week 2014 poll asked a number of general questions about crime—mostly regarding attitudes toward policies but also some general perceptions.[69] Around 12% said they had had their drink spiked, another 8% said they were not sure, and 28% said they knew someone who had been. Around 76% of those who said they had been drugged said they did not report it to the police. To the extent that one assumed that the 12% really were drugged, you would have to come away with the perception that drink spiking is a huge, and largely unreported, problem in the UK. To some extent, these differences in the Anglophone world are to be expected, as the idea of being covertly drugged in order to explain vulnerability to assault is something that varies in its salience according to media, cultural, and peer norms. Why US women are less likely than UK women to attribute events to spiking is unclear, but worth considering.

---

[67] Bernardette Butler and Jan Welch, "Drug-Facilitated Sexual Assault," *Canadian Medical Association Journal*, March 3, 2009, 493–494.
[68] National Student Union, "Hidden Marks: A Study of Women Students' Experiences of Harassment, Stalking, Violence and Sexual Assault,"2010.
[69] ITV This Morning, "Crime Week poll survey results," January 27, 2014. http://www.itv.com/thismorning/hot-topics/crime-week-poll-survey-results; "Drink spiking: Are we too careless?" January 28, 2014. http://www.itv.com/thismorning/hot-topics/crime-week-drink-spiking. Retrieved November 12, 2015.

The student newspaper for Swansea University, in South Wales, UK, reported the results of its poll on the topic in November 2013. Fully a third of the student respondents said they had been spiked—and named nearby spots where they claimed it had happened. It was an online survey, and so bound to attract higher numbers than a telephone poll, but of interest was that 36% of women and 25% of men thought they had been spiked, which suggests an erosion of the assumption that all drink spiking is a precursor to rape. Some of the by-product of more saturated fear of spiking in certain locations, in other words, brings with it the understanding that it can happen for a variety of reasons. While university staffers responded with the obligatory "need to raise awareness" of the threat, accompanied by a reminder that you can use a "spikey" to cap your drink bottle, the local police simply said, "A spokesperson from South Wales Police said they were interested in raising awareness around spiking, but 'have not had any reported incidents of drinking spiking in either the university campus or Swansea city centre.' "[70]

"Spikey"-style stoppers have been around awhile, as have an array of test coasters, cards, swizzle sticks, and so forth. In North Wales in 2004, a drink spiking awareness campaign, termed a "Safe Drinking Campaign," orchestrated by the local Public Safety agency, including Wrexham, was launched after…well, nothing in particular, it appears. The spokesperson said that there were relatively few reports of suspected spiking, but that the stoppers might serve as a deterrent.[71] Local police were addressing what they called the potential problem of drinks tampering, not responding to any particular case and noted, "Fortunately, there are relatively few reported instances in Wrexham and these stoppers can act as a deterrent." Earlier in the year, the *Chester Chronicle* published news of the police running a "Spike Campaign" in Wrexham for two days with publicity, t-shirts, and tags on unattended drinks. Again, the police reiterated that

---

[70] Chris Flynn, "1 in 3 students say they've been spiked," *The Waterfront*, November 18, 2013, http://waterfrontonline.co.uk/news/1-in-3-students-say-theyve-been-spiked. Retrieved January 18, 2016.

[71] "Campaign to stop drinks spiking," *North Wales Daily Post*, December 2, 2004. Retrieved January 9, 2016. http://www.dailypost.co.uk/news/north-wales-news/campaign-to-stop-drinks-spiking-2918427.

it was a caution unrelated to an incident.[72] Although also aimed at warning against the dangers of excessive drink, the campaign was aided by a louche-looking cartoon hedgehog named Spike.[73] It is hard to know how much preexisting fear existed in the area before the campaign, but a well-cited research study shed some light about the context.

Toxicological Hints

In 2007, a research team at Wrexham Maelor Hospital (in North Wales) assessed 75 cases in which people presented to the ER there suspecting drink spiking. Eight of them tested positive for drugs of abuse; most had very high blood alcohol levels. Of the eight identified with drugs, four had amphetamine, one cocaine, two morphine, and one codeine; none said they had taken those drugs voluntarily. While self-reports about voluntary drug use tend to be unreliable, what is most interesting is the ease with which alcohol symptoms are mistaken for drugging, and when drugs are present, stimulants rather than CNS depressants are present. Even the opiates in question have been around awhile. Most came into the ER in a timely enough fashion to catch drugs in urine or blood samples; none tested positive for GHB or flunitrazepam. The researchers, led by Hywel Hughes, initiated the study because they had "noticed an increasing number of patients presenting, claiming that their drinks had been 'spiked.'" They began the observation in October 2004, not long before the Public Safety campaign—suggesting that inclining fear of spiking and potentially increasing incidence of spiking had heightened before the "Safe Drinking Campaign." In 2005, the local police told Hughes' team that only three cases were reported to them, although Hughes multiyear sample had low reporting-to-the-police rates (14%). The authors conclude by saying that their high BAC versus drugs suspicions were confirmed, and that more emphasis should be placed on warning people about the vulnerabilities produced by excess alcohol consumption.

---

[72] "Drink can be a prickly problem" Feb 24, 2004, *The Chester Chronicle*. Retrieved January 9, 2016. http://www.chesterchronicle.co.uk/news/local-news/drink-can-prickly-problem-5301554.
[73] Images of Spike the Hedgehog are available as of January 2016 at: http://www.pigstystudio.co.uk/spike.html.

What Do We Know about the Extent of Drugging?

By the mid-2000s, many scientific studies were more or less finding the same thing—a lack of evidence that spiking was widespread, and considerable evidence that fear of it was overcultivated.

Across studies, in various countries, it has been found that a consistently large portion of people who present with spiking fears are found instead to have high BAC—and not just 'tipsy' but in many cases, having ingested so much alcohol that they risked the most serious of medical consequences or accidental injury. Another significant portion has consumed drugs themselves, often several different ones. As for the small number of cases in which drugs are found that the person denies taking themselves, drugs *not* associated with "the Big Three" are usually found instead.

It also should be noted that in most cases, suspected drugging victims have not been the victim of another crime such as rape or robbery when they arrive at the hospital, though many might suspect a "near miss." Even though the toxicology literature is about drugging, and not about sexual assault, it is often misinterpreted in the press as being "about" drugged rape or attempted rape. Even if suspicions of drugging had been more widely validated, too much is assumed in regard to motive. As we have seen in the past, people are occasionally drugged for a number of reasons, and it is clear that the reason is some variation on: just because. Also, as we have seen, the substances themselves matter—it stretches logic overmuch to assume that any drug found in a test that the patient says they did not take—including stimulants and hormones—must be crammed awkwardly into the date rape drugging scenario.

7

What Do We Know (and Not Know) About Predatory Drugging?

Understanding Intoxication and Vulnerability

We have seen, from past decades, that it is possible to have real dangers and problems with predatory drugs and mythological problems with them at the same time. The date rape drugging *scare* is logically separate from the real problem of involuntary drugging, which, while being found in all eras, probably did accelerate with the onset of synthetic drugs in the 1800s. With recent improvements in toxicology and epidemiology, we actually know more about that small but real problem than we ever did before, although it seems that it took a big, overblown scare to make that happen. A review of the recent science on drugging is in order.

As is the case with measuring other social problems—even ones like this with a public health underpinning—an absence of reliable data tends to support an atmosphere of creative invention. On the one hand, some organizations label it an omnipresent threat, while skeptics in some law enforcement agencies, particularly in Britain, suggest that spiking is a rarity. While there are limits to our knowledge of the prevalence of the problem, mainly due to low reporting rates of sexual assault *generally*, it is simply not accurate to say we know nothing about it.

The first thing we know now, quite clearly, across many countries and settings, and after more than a decade of toxicological research, is that the vast majority of people who report to emergency rooms (ERs) fearing that they have been drugged, have not been. ER and clinic patient studies on their own would, of course, not be indicative of the underlying problem—though they do undergird claims that *fear* about the problem is probably exaggerated, and it constitutes an exaggeration with real-world consequences.

But surveys of victims of sexual assault also support the notion that surreptitious drugging is rarer than the media would have us believe, and that when drugs are found, they are not the "Big Three." What is rather consistently, and unfortunately common, is the opportunistic assault of people who are voluntarily intoxicated—particularly via alcohol but also less commonly street drugs.[1] The media in a number of countries has inflated, or conflated, the threat for a variety of reasons discussed in the pages to follow. Yet it is not always and everywhere the case that the public has followed along, at least with regard to enthusiastic interest or feelings of personal salience about the topic.

Not all of the blame can be put on the media, nor on drug warriors eager to redefine recreational drugs into predatory ones. The scientific and research community also bears some responsibility in this distortion, mainly due to a lack of clarity in measurement and in defining the problem. In a review of 389 studies on the topic of drug-facilitated sexual assault (DFSA), and a closer examination of 11 studies, Beynon et al. found only one that took any care in clearly distinguishing between voluntary and involuntary drugging. Beynon et al. note, "Scientific reports are drawing misleading conclusions about drug-facilitated sexual assault and are inflating concern regarding the magnitude of covert drug administration."[2] While a look at methods used by researchers in this

---

[1] The self-report studies to which I refer are mostly directed at young women, college students, or sexual assault victims. As the AIC report points out, self-report surveys of suspected drink spiking can be useful, but it is important to be clear about which population is the relevant one. Women? The general population? Those who go out at nights to pubs, bars, or nightclubs frequently?

[2] Caryl M. Beynon, Clare McVeigh, Jim McVeigh, Conan Leavey and Mark A. Bellis, "The Involvement of Drugs and Alcohol in Drug-Facilitated Sexual Assault: A Systematic Review of the Evidence." *Trauma, Violence, & Abuse*, Vol. 9, No. 3, July 2009. Other literature reviews and review articles based on samples from different countries reach the same conclusions, though differ in their

field confirms Beynon et al.'s concern about a vastly inflated threat, it is also the case that, even so, the numbers are remarkably small in comparison to some media-driven impressions.

By the mid-2000s, studies were more or less finding the same thing—a lack of evidence that spiking was widespread, along with mild pleas to consider the role of drinking in enhancing vulnerability to assault. Though headlines emphasized the drunk versus drugged angle, the studies also underscored the differences found between the *protected narrative* of drink spiking and the handful of actual apparent drugging cases that were found. In the 2009 Perth study, for instance, many patients had high BAC. Around 88% of the sample was female; the mean number of drinks consumed was 7.7, and three-quarters had had 4 or more drinks. Around 35 % continued to believe they were drugged despite the negative findings.[3]

In the UK in 2006, the Association of Chief Police Officers (ACPO) released the Operation Matisse Study.[4] Looking at 120 suspected drugging cases, no Rohypnol was found in any, and in two cases, GHB was found. Sedatives were found in ten others. Other drugs, both prescribed and street, were found, such as cannabis and cocaine. Only one victim reported not drinking at all, and about half had detectable levels of alcohol. In sum, the study suggested that most victims who suspected drugs were in fact intoxicated by alcohol at the time of the assault. However,

---

impression of what more sensitive toxicological and clinical data might potentially show. See Butler and Welch 2009; Michael Hurley, Helen Parker, David L. Wells, "The epidemiology of drug facilitated sexual assault," *Journal of Clinical Forensic Medicine* 13, 2006, 181–185. Hurley et al. found extremely high BAC levels in subjects, suggesting that they had consumed significantly more than they had realized, an estimated average BAC across the drinking sample of 0.22–0.33 % at the time of the assault. J.A. Hall and C.B.T. Moore, "Drug facilitated sexual assault—A review," *Journal of Forensic and Legal Medicine* 15, 2008, 291–297.

[3] Paul Quigley, Dana Lynch, et al, "Prospective Study of 101 Patients with Suspected Drink Spiking," *Emergency Medicine Australasia*, 21, 2009, 222–228. Drink spiking suspected within previous 12 hours or still displaying symptoms. GHB above the usual endogenous level (10 g/L) was considered positive. Four of these plausible nine cases denied taking the drug detected in sample. Median time from onset of symptoms (self-report) to lab sample collection was 4.5 hours. No samples had illegal drugs surreptitiously placed in a bar or pub. Around 28% were positive for illicit drugs. (Most common were cannabis and methamphetamine.)

[4] David Gee, Phil Owen, Iain Mclean, Kate Brentnall, and Cath Thundercloud, *Operation Matisse: Investigating Drug Facilitated Sexual Assault*, A Publication by the Association of Chief Police Officers, Association of Chief Police Officers, London, 2006.

the practice of drug spiking does appear to happen in a small number of cases. Other toxicology studies show similar results.

Across studies in various countries, it has been found that a consistently large portion of people who present with spiking fears are found instead to have high BAC levels—and not just "tipsy," but in many cases, having ingested so much alcohol that they risked the most serious of medical consequences.[5] Another significant portion has consumed drugs themselves, often several different ones over the course of the evening. As for drugs that the person denies taking themselves—providing reasonable suspicion, then, of spiking—drugs *not* associated with "the Big Three" are usually found instead. The only one of the Big Three found consistently across studies (though in not very high numbers) is GHB, and unfortunately, research design has not been attentive to the voluntary versus involuntary intoxication problem—complicated by the substitution problem in illicit sales—discussed in a previous chapter.

The work of Scott-Ham and Burton (2005) merits separate mention in that it developed a more rigorous means to investigate covert versus voluntary ingestion than most. The authors first identified the presence of any sedating drug (18.7 %) of their original sample of 1014. Then, they eliminated those where the drug was voluntarily consumed (97.9 % were either illicit use or prescribed use). Twenty-one samples remained and three were positive for Ecstasy/MDMA, which is not a sedative but which may have been intended to produce disinhibition in the victim. Nineteen out of 1014 remained, thus giving an estimate of 2 % for covert drugging.[6]

While toxicological sensitivity is enjoying improvement, it is unlikely that there are massive Type 2 errors (not detecting drugs when they are

---

[5] Beynon et al. 2008; Hall and Moore, 2008; Michael Scott-Ham and Fiona Burton, "Toxicological findings in alleged cases of drug facilitated sexual assault in the United Kingdom over a 3-year period," *Journal of Clinical Forensic Medicine* 12, 2005; 175–6; Cecilie T. Hagemann, Arne Helland, et al, "Ethanol and drug findings in women consulting a Sexual Assault Center—Associations with clinical characteristics and suspicions of drug-facilitated sexual assault," *Journal of Forensic and Legal Medicine* 20, 2013, 777–784; Nemeth et al 2010; Ian Hindmarch and Rüdiger Brinkmann, "Trends in the Use of Alcohol and Other Drugs in Cases of Sexual Assault," *Human Psychopharmacology* 14, 1999, 225–231.

[6] Scott-Ham and Burton, 2005; See also Matthew P. Juhascik, Adam Negrusz et al, "An Estimate of the Proportion of Drug-Facilitation of Sexual Assault in Four U.S. Localities," *Journal of Forensic Science*, November 2007, Vol. 52, No. 6, 1396–1400.

there). Realistically, quick metabolism only presents a problem in the case of GHB, and more common dosing with it would result in more widespread, dramatic ER presentations.

Are CNS Depressants Including Alcohol And Their Presence or Absence The Whole of the Story?

In thinking about the general prevalence problem of covert drugging, using modern scientific forms of inquiry, such as epidemiology and toxicology, one thing that is immediately obvious is that no one really knows what to do with positive drug results that do not involve the "Big Three." Florida's antipot warriors had a bit of fun with their marijuana-as-a-date-rape-drug, but we have known for a great while that all sorts of things show up in toxicology tests. Stimulants like cocaine, MDMA and methamphetamine, marijuana, traces of pharmaceuticals at levels that might or might not explain recent symptoms—all of these are commonly found, whether reported by the patients or not.

The Australian press in the early 2000s had no problem simply folding such findings into the drug rape scenario: stimulants or other non-CNS drugs were spiked into women's drinks, they implied, to enhance their libido: we might call this the birth of the "hypersexual variant" on the drink spiking scenario. The elision here between libidinal enhancement and the ability to consent—much more straightforward in the case of CNS depressants—is troubling in these category-challenging instances. It is assumed than an involuntary aphrodisiac effect can be induced, and thus a person is deprived of their ability to consent to sexual relations.[7]

For centuries, of course, the idea of slipping someone an aphrodisiac has melded, uneasily, with fantasies of sudden real desire on the part of the target, and rape. Oysters, sure. Spanish fly, no. None of these substances that enhance libido—in either reality or conjecture—make someone incapable of choice with regard to sexual engagement. But nearly anything unexpectedly *given with such intent* can do harm of other sorts, nonetheless. It makes sense for the courts, then, to focus on what such a tamperer

---

[7] Karl L.R. Jansen and Lynn Theron, "Ecstasy (MDMA), Methamphetamine, and Drug-Facilitated Sexual Assault: A Consideration of the Issues" *Journal of Psychoactive Drugs*, 38, March 2006, 1–12.

intended. It would be helpful, though, if the press did a better job of explicating the difference between possibly feeling more sexual and losing the ability to consent to sex, or for that matter, any other behavior.

Jezebel magazine reported on an herbal supplement purveyor who took out ads in the back of magazines with a largely male readership for "Sexciter for Women."[8] The formula's distributors claim that the liquid "can be taken by mouth or put in any liquid without detection, but you should get her permission. She will become wild, untamed, and desire to have sex with you." So be surreptitious, but get permission, of course. Sexciter is mostly yohimbe, which has a reputation as a sexual enhancement tool, and is used by some to treat erectile dysfunction. Strictly speaking, it is a stimulant and a vasodilator. By itself, its potency to change the intentions of a reluctant partner seems low. Nonetheless, the ad appeals to an entitled manipulator at best, and a sociopath at worst. The potential health side effects are numerous. Interactions with other stimulants, Selective serotonin reuptake inhibitors (SSRIs), and monoamine oxidase inhibitors (MAOIs) are dangerous, as is giving it to anyone with high blood pressure, heart problems, anxiety, or diabetes.

Of course, perpetrators of tampering can buy into the hype, too, as they did with chloroform in the past. There is no doubt that the occasional spiker thinks MDMA (often now called Molly rather than Ecstasy) might be just the ticket to gain a victim's compliance, and nearly any substance that a person does not expect to have *can* wreak havoc. In 2013, rapper Rick Ross was called out for a song lyric which seemed to insinuate precisely that. "U.O.E.N.O." featured the lines: "Put molly all in her champagne / She ain't even know it / I took her home and I enjoyed that / She ain't even know it."[9] Ross' initial awkward antiapology ("I'd never use the word 'rape' …") did not help matters. He quickly lost a Reebok sponsor contract. Ross later issued an "official" apology in which he said, "To the young men who listen to my music, please know that using a sub-

---

[8] Katie Baker, "Is Your Magazine Unknowingly Hawking Date-Rape Drugs?" *Jezebel.com*. April 9, 2012. http://jezebel.com/5899844/is-your-magazine-unknowingly-hawking-roofies. Retrieved June 2, 2014.
[9] RJ Cubarrubia, "Rick Ross Issues Official Apology for 'Rape' Lyrics," *Rolling Stone*, April 12, 2013. http://www.rollingstone.com/music/news/rick-ross-apologizes-for-pro-rape-lyrics-20130412#ixzz3wxUGVL6M. Retrieved January 11, 2016.

stance to rob a woman of her right to make a choice is not only a crime, it's wrong and I do not encourage it."

There have, in fact, been a few such notable cases of stimulant spiking with allegations of sexual conquest intent. In August 2015, a male model in the UK was cleared, after trial, of giving a young woman in a bar MDMA in a vodka and Red Bull drink after she refused his sexual propositions.[10] (Red Bull is also full of stimulants.) The Crown prosecutor in the case said, on the charges stemming from the incident a year earlier, "MDMA is traditionally a party drug and is not a traditional date rape drug. This is a different drug but whether it was to help her enjoy his company more it may well have had a seductive effect."[11] The woman was still with her friends at a pub and reported her strange feelings and blurred vision right away. A "seductive effect" was assumed because a CCTV camera captured a kiss between the woman and the accused, whose identity was tracked down by the woman on social media about two weeks after the incident in question.

From the beginning of the date rape drugs scare in the 1990s, antidrug constituencies have attempted to pull MDMA and meth into the emerging rubric, implying that if a victim of sexual assault had such substances in her system, they would be indications of incapacitation. While many experts on the effects of stimulants have tried to challenge this idea, the general slippage between *drugs people like to do* and *date rape drugs*, on the one hand, and *feeling more sexual or sensual* and *being more vulnerable to rape*, on the other, continues to develop on the edges.[12]

The unfortunate slippage between *love drug* and *date rape drug* seeped into popular consciousness, as well. In my campus research about students' awareness and impressions of date rape drugs, I asked, "If you have heard of them, which substance(s) do you think of as being date

---

[10] Sophia Sleigh, "Male model cleared of spiking girl's drink wants anonymity for sex suspects," *Evening Standard*, 20 August 2015, http://www.standard.co.uk/news/london/male-model-cleared-of-spiking-girl-s-drink-wants-anonymity-for-sex-suspects-a2917291. Retrieved March 18, 2016.

[11] Simon Carr, Bruce Thain, "Male model 'spiked woman's drink with MDMA after telling her they would have great sex'" *Daily Mirror UK*, August 11, 2015. http://www.mirror.co.uk/news/uk-news/model-drink-spike-charge-man-6228269. Retrieved March 18, 2016.

[12] Jansen and Theron, 2006; Julie Holland, *Ecstasy: The Complete Guide: A Comprehensive Look at the Risks and Benefits of MDMA*, New York: Park Street Press, 2001, 55–56.

rape drugs?"[13] Around 67 % gave specific responses. While I was not at all surprised to find that 184 out of 224 named Rohypnol, roofies, or some variant, the next most popular answer was Ecstasy or "E."

The hypersexual variant reprises an earlier set of claims about LSD in the 1960s—that it was being used to zombify vulnerable youth, even though it, too, is derived from stimulants. Simply because a drug is present in a victim's system at the time of an assault does not mean that it is the cause of it, and stimulants seem like precisely the kind of boundary-defining case that asks if the term "date rape drug"—rickety to begin with—is losing its meaning altogether. Conversely, are we so besotted with the drugging rape scenario that we are losing the ability to understand the variety of motivations for surreptitious drugging? And, in the numerous cases where sexual violence, alcohol, and drug use are found together, has the date rape drug formulation reduced our understanding of the accountable perpetrator?

Voluntary Drug Use

Voluntary use of drugs presented a data conundrum well before it presented one in the politics of blame, and researchers were aware of the problem early. Negrusz and Gaensslen's review of studies and their own data suggested that voluntary Rohypnol use was not uncommon, and that sexual assault risk was heightened among those that used it.[14] Nearly all ER studies suggest that those who seek help for predatory drugging are not a random sample of young revelers, as they are more likely to be

---

[13] Pamela Donovan, "The Role of Uncertainty in Knowledge of Suspected Drink Spiking Incidents," 78th Annual Meeting of the Eastern Sociological Society, New York, NY, February 2008. Beginning in 2006 and through 2008, I researched students' impressions of date rape drugs using a survey with both open- and closed-ended questions about knowledge, perceived risk, firsthand and other experiences, and drinking habits. I received Human Subjects Research one-year approval from the Institutional Review Board at Bloomsburg University, Pennsylvania, in July 2006 and again in September 2007, for data collected in the spring semesters of 2006 and 2008 from general education courses. Some of the other data in this and other chapters appears in the article: Adam Burgess, Pamela Donovan, and Sarah E.H. Moore, "Embodying Uncertainty? Understanding Heightened Risk Perception of Drink 'Spiking'." *British Journal of Criminology*, 49: 6, 848–862.

[14] Adam Negrusz and R.E. Gaensslen, "Analytical developments in toxicological investigation of drug-facilitated sexual assault," *Analytical and Bioanalytical Chemistry* 376, 2003: 1192–1197.

polydrug users. It is difficult, as a practical matter, to separate voluntary from involuntary drug use.

A different kind of data that inadvertently underscores this problem is available in the USA: poisoning reports from ERs, and here there is a different set of problems in interpretation. The DAWN report—which summarizes the work of the CDC's (Centers for Disease Control and Prevention) Drug Abuse Warning Network by polling ERs across the country about the kinds of problems that they are seeing—was issued in 2013 on intentional drug poisonings. The data was gathered in 2011 from over 15,000 cases of people who presented with symptoms consistent with drug intoxication but who reported not taking drugs themselves.[15]

Though the data appears soundly gathered, the interpretive problem begins immediately. For context, the authors cite Kilpatrick et al.'s 2007 study to note, "3 million American women have experienced drug-facilitated rape in their lifetime." But that study defines drug-facilitated rape as "[t]he perpetrator deliberately gives the victim drugs without her permission or tries to get her drunk, and then commits an unwanted sexual act against her." In other words, Kilpatrick et al. did not proffer that number as one of just druggings or poisonings; rather, the authors were looking at a broader definition, though still separate from Intoxicated Rape, which is voluntary use followed by assault. That study was trying to look at a wider context of assault and intoxication.

Like many reporters to follow, this government document mixes up the various definitions of drug-facilitated assault, and thus compounds the existing confusion. The clear intention of the DAWN report was to contextualize the organization's own data in relation to the drink spiking scenario; they advise, "Informational campaigns can educate people about the risks involved with leaving beverages unattended and accepting alcoholic beverages or drugs from others, either from strangers or from people they know."

---

[15] Substance Abuse and Mental Health Services Administration, *The DAWN Report: Update on Drug-Related Emergency Department Visits Attributed to Intentional Poisoning: 2011*. Rockville, MD. November 21, 2013. This was the second time that such a report was issued; DAWN did not publish intentional drug poisoning data from ERs until 2011. DAWN data before 2003 cannot be compared with data after, due to significant classification and sampling changes. "Malicious poisoning" is a new category which had not been separated out from "drug abuse—other" previously.

However, the case-based data that DAWN presents appears to be much broader. The nomination of an ER visit as an intentional poisoning case is based mainly on self-report and on other medical chart features, but not necessarily, they note, on toxicological results. They point to a genuine set of problems in drug screening: not only the usual problem of time between event and test, which might preclude a conclusive test result, but also that ER personnel are not necessarily screening routinely or for the right drugs. In 65 % of cases, the drug is unidentified. In 40 % of cases, unidentified drugging and voluntary alcohol were suspected.[16] While the report mentions the possibility of multiple motives for drugging someone, their study design does not include any information about motive or setting.

Furthermore, it was unclear if the DAWN data—similar to DuMont's Canadian study discussed earlier—was picking up on increased fear, as other studies around the world suggest, or increased drugging, or perhaps both.

Tests Too Late to Catch Drugs?

The large proportion of sexual assaults that go unreported or reported too late for forensic examination will, unfortunately, likely remain so.[17] To consider the true incidence and prevalence of drugging rape hidden in those unreported cases is not a straightforward task; we cannot assume

---

[16] In 17 % of cases, alcohol was combined with an illicit drug, and in 12 % of cases, pharmaceuticals were found. Another 19 % involved drugs alone. Across all of these situations, there are some cases where more than one drug was present. In 30 % of cases overall, some illicit drug was present, most commonly marijuana, cocaine and other stimulants, or ecstasy/MDMA. Neither GHB nor ketamine is mentioned specifically. Benzodiazepines account for 14 % of those attributed to pharmaceuticals.

[17] Reasons for this are suggested in the 2013 edition of the US Department of Justice's *National Protocol for Sexual Assault Medical Forensic Examinations, Adults/Adolescents, Second Edition*. These "SANE guidelines" (as they are known, which are model nursing protocols for working with victims of sexual violence) propose swift readiness to screen for drugs and alcohol where indicated, but do not recommend routine screening. Instead, the April 2013 edition emphasizes planning and training for response to voluntary drug and alcohol use, particularly reassurance to patients that drug and alcohol use is no excuse for someone to assault them, and reminders to guard against the intoxicated "victim disqualification" bias by either medical or law enforcement personnel.

7 What Do We Know (and Not Know) About Predatory Drugging? 225

that incidents that are reported and those that are not have the same characteristics.

Linda Ledray and Jan Kraft studied characteristics of women reporting sexual assault to an ER in Minnesota.[18] How did late/delayed reporters and nonreporters differ from those who reported straight off? Ledray considered age, activities at time of assault, drug and alcohol involvement or suspicion of it, including DFSA, timing of report, and relationship to the accused. She did not define DFSA, but did treat it separately from voluntary alcohol consumption. Delayed reporters were somewhat younger on average than the whole sample, while nonreporters were somewhat older. As for DFSA suspicion, this suspected circumstance was 7 % of the whole sample, none of the delayed sample, and 31 % of the nonreporters.

Delayed reporters were less likely to report alcohol use (25 %) than the whole sample (42 %), while nonreporters were somewhat more likely (55 %) to report alcohol use. Voluntary illicit drug use showed more dramatic differences. Around 8 % of the overall sample and 8 % of the nonreporters said they had used drugs, while 75 % of the delayed reporters did. Ledray suggests that the Sexual Assault Nurse Examiner (SANE) interview may have reassured the delayed reporters that they would not be charged with a drug crime. (Minnesota law guarantees this.) Both delayed and nonreporters were considerably more likely to have been the victims of a previous sexual assault (50 % and 75 %, respectively, as compared with 24 % of the whole sample). Possibly increased levels of self-blame contributed to this outcome. The authors note that the sample was small and came from one ER; nonetheless, the differences along the lines of reporting behavior were suggestive.[19]

People fail to report crimes against them, even violent crimes, for a variety of reasons. The US National Crime Victim Survey (NCVS) asks

---

[18] Linda Ledray and Jan Kraft, "Evidentiary examination without a police report: Should it be done? Are delayed reporters and nonreporters unique?" *Journal of Emergency Nursing* 27, 2001, 396–400.

[19] Implementation of the SANE protocols are not reimbursed for collection, testing, and storage costs of kits in some states if the crime is not reported to the police. SANE protocols specify testing with the complainant's consent even if she is not sure she will report, but funds to underwrite this expense are not always available. For practical reasons, kits might not be done in a timely enough manner or at all. See Ledray, 2001.

respondents to talk about violent incidents against them and what they did about it. Robbery and physical assaults do not have particularly high reporting rates, either, though they tend to be somewhat higher than rape.[20] People are more likely to report a violent crime if they are injured or if the assailant brandished a weapon. The crime is more likely to be reported if it is completed rather than just attempted, and if the perpetrator was a stranger. Situational and interpretive reasons come into play, as well. The most common reason to demur from contacting the police was that the victim sees it as a private or personal matter. Specifically, victims fear being blamed for the rape themselves, and fear that their families will find out or that they will be subject to publicity. Victims are also sometimes unaware how the law defines rape and sexual assault, and whether what they experienced is a crime. More recently, the Bureau of Justice data drawn from the NCVS underscores the reluctance of rape victims to report crimes to the police, with 65 % saying they did not report it. Around 28 % of the nonreporters said they feared reprisal or worried about getting the offender in trouble—a much higher figure than with other unreported crimes.[21]

So what can we learn from the data we do have about sexual assault victims in general, and another group of people who report to ERs with concerns about being drugged? How does this relate to the potential number of unreported drugging rapes? Does drugging make someone more or less likely to report an associated crime? Being drugged perhaps involves less self-blame, or fear of being blamed, than does vulnerability associated with too much alcohol or drugs taken voluntarily, which would argue in favor of suspected drug rapes being *more* likely to be reported. On the other hand, drugging—or even the suspicion of it—might be accompanied by a great deal more physical disorientation and cognitive uncertainty about the events, or a greater conviction that nothing could be done. The desire for privacy among victims or avoidance of embarrassment, regardless of intoxication status, though, appears to override any

---

[20] NCVS, 2010, as discussed by Karmen, 2013, 169–172. The NCVS asks respondents about specific incidents with screening questions and then uses legal definitions to determine whether the incident qualifies as a crime, regardless of how the respondent may label it so or not.
[21] Candace Krutschnitt et al, *Estimating the Incidence of Rape and Sexual Assault*, (Washington, DC, National Academy of Sciences), 2015, table 3.1, 37.

of these considerations. Most rapes go unreported and thus by inference, most drugging rapes do, too. But let us remember that in ER studies, most patients are *not* reporting another crime.

Definitional Problems Are Similar (But Not the Same) as with the Measure of Sexual Assault Overall

Journalists are a bit too fond of drink spiking allegations in the context of reporting on nightlife and campus life, relative to the more sensitivity-provoking questions regarding alcohol itself. In Australia, and to a lesser extent, the UK and USA, the media has played an independent role in lobbying for the widespread, yet unrecognized drink-spiking scourge. Sociologist Joel Best suggests that one method of statistical inflation in cases where a threat is nebulous is to engage in a bit of "numbers laundering."[22] Find essentially the wrong statistics, or several with admittedly similar terminology—for instance, the work of Krebs and Kilpatrick's teams that found that, generally, intoxication among sexual assault victims was significant—and substitute this large number for the smaller number that you desire to inflate—the number of involuntary intoxications in the data.

For instance, in promoting a drink-spiking detecting cup invention in September 2013, the New York CBS affiliate ran a story titled, "Seen at 11: Sipping Danger, Crafty Criminals Could Be Drugging Your Drinks: New Line of Products Aims To Protect Drinkers From Common Drugs."[23] It claimed that "[n]early half a million people are drugged annually at bars, clubs, and on college campuses, according to the Justice Department." This seems to be a number from nowhere. Of course, it is not clear which Justice numbers were misinterpreted—it does not match

---

[22] Joel Best, *Damned Lies and Statistics*, (Berkeley: University of California Press), 2001, 34–38. The term "numbers laundering" is attributed by Best to David Luckenbill.
[23] Alice Gainer, CBS New York Local, "Seen At 11: Sipping Danger, Crafty Criminals Could Be Drugging Your Drinks," http://newyork.cbslocal.com/2013/09/02/seen-at-11-sipping-danger-crafty-criminals-could-be-drugging-your-drinks/. Retrieved January 20, 2016.

Kilpatrick's broad *or* narrow definition numbers, nor that of Krebs et al., or the NCVS, for instance. In all likelihood, it came from the product's marketing team.

But blame cannot be placed on the media alone. Part of the reason that inflated statistics and coverage of drink spiking routinely make their way into the press is that researchers who release findings on the matter are often themselves less than consistent in categorizing and delimiting the problem. A handful of journalistic accounts of the problem do a much more careful job of looking at the right numbers than the vast number of others, and do prove that it is possible to make sense of this issue for the general reader of news.[24] There are two areas of definitional imprecision: first, the more widely known problem of how the term "sexual assault" is defined, and second, the cloudy definition of drugging often used. As if the estimating was not difficult enough, the scientific community is contributing to the problem by using wildly different definitions in the research. Terminology is not consistent; this has led to inflated press figures.

Sexual Assault Statistics: Wide Variation in Counting Methods

In the 2014–2015 academic year, there was a great deal of public concern raised about sexual assault on college campuses. A variety of factors contributed to this increased publicity, and subsequent controversy over both statistics and high-profile cases. The use of the term "epidemic" emerged; it is not entirely clear why. Campus rape has been a specific concern at least since the early 1990s, where the number 1-in-4 gained publicity. It has never been *studied* so intently and comprehensively as it has been in the first decade of the 2000s, when the prevailing number has been 1-in-5. The term *epidemic* has a specific meaning in public health—more cases than expected in a given population based on past patterns—that does not apply here, and it is unfortunate that this word is misused.

---

[24] In particular, good stories include: Susan Nielsen, "Sexual assault on Oregon campuses: Despite progress with rape reports, challenges remain," *The Oregonian*, February 23, 2012; Jessica Bliss, "Police, experts: Alcohol most common in sexual assaults," *USA Today*, October 28, 2013.

In December 2014, the Department of Justice published a report that noted that noncollege women are victimized at higher rates than college women of the same age, and that while campus rape rates are still unacceptably high, there is decidedly no epidemic.[25] There has been, however, a coalescing of awareness and attention to the problem of campus rape, and an associated media interest in the topic. Not all of the media attention was of high quality.

According to the NCVS: in 1993, when the current questions were first developed, the NCVS estimated that 900,000 rapes/sexual assaults took place each year. In 2011—again, using the same questions—this had dropped to less than 300,000.[26] The largest and most frequently updated survey, the NCVS tends to run somewhat lower than other estimates, since it does not prompt respondents about specific acts that were coercive. Police data (in the USA, *Uniform Crime Reports*) are not useful for examining how common sexual assault is as most incidents go unreported. The NCVS is not perfect, either, but it has been imperfect in a standardized way from year to year.

A great deal of wrangling has also occurred in recent years over the 1-in-5 statistic (which is not drawn from the NCVS) regarding college women and sexual assault. Some cite studies to show that it is greatly inflated; others cite studies to undergird the number. The devil is in the details, however, of what specific questions are asked, how they are asked, and what counts as a case. For instance, are we counting the percentage of the sample who has been sexually assaulted at some point (lifetime prevalence)? Or the number of incidents in a given recent time period, such as while in college, or the past year (incidence)? Are attempts at rape that are thwarted (attempted rape or sexual assault) counted toward the total? How close to the conventional legal definitions of rape and/or sexual assault do the questions asked stay? What if the

---

[25] No epidemic: Callie Marie Rennison, "Privilege, Among Rape Victims: Who Suffers Most from Rape and Sexual Assault in America?" *New York Times*, December 21, 2014. The study itself: Lynn Langton and Sofi Sinozich *Rape and Sexual Assault Among College-Age Females*, 1995–2013. Bureau of Justice Statistics, 2014. http://www.bjs.gov/index.cfm?ty=pbdetail&iid=5176. Retrieved September 18, 2015.

[26] Krutschnitt, Figure 4.1, 67.

respondent experiences an event that fits the legal definition but does not label it rape?[27]

Definitional Mischief Around Intoxication and Rape: What's in a Term?

Drug-Facilitated Sexual Assault. Intoxicated Sexual Assault. Drugging. All of these terms are currently in use by authors of government reports, researchers, and the press. However, there is a shocking lack of consistency in their definition across settings. Often times, people are not actually talking about what we think they are talking about. What government and scholarly researchers usually mean by DFSA is "assault upon a person who is intoxicated from drugs or alcohol, without reference to whether they ingested the substances voluntarily or not." In fact, the Krebs' report defines DFSA and suspected DFSA in the narrow way, while Kilpatrick's does the opposite. As you can imagine, this is a large number. But to many people, including journalists, what the term DFSA looks like is the more narrow circumstances of surreptitious drugging followed by assault. You will find this confusion occasionally in government documents, which does not help matters. Some reporters clearly understand the difference, but others just either pass on inflated statistics from third parties or misreport government statistics.

---

[27] The NCVS asks about sexual assault in two different ways. First, if the respondent has, in the last six months, experienced "any rape, attempted rape or other type of sexual attack" and then also, "have you been forced or coerced to engage in unwanted sexual activity by (a) someone you didn't know before, (b) a casual acquaintance? OR (c) someone you know well?" The strength here is that the categories are broad: unwanted sexual activity that is forced or coerced can potentially elicit a wide range of sexual violence without sweeping up noncriminal acts that were just "unwanted." The weakness may be that not everyone knows what rape is, nor the wide range of things that can be forceful or coercive. Incapacitation, for instance, is not prompted specifically, though it is not excluded either. The NCWSV (National College Women Sexual Victimization Study) was first conducted in 1997 and asked about specific coerced and forced sexual behaviors, finding 8.7 victimization incidents per 1000 college women. This is much higher than the 1997 NCVS rate of 1.4 per 1000 women in the general population. Since that time, it has been generally known among sexual assault researchers that more specific, explicit questions will yield higher numbers than general questions about sexual violence in the NCVS style. So the NCVS is reliable from year to year, but it may still be underestimating the overall number of assaults.

If you wanted to use the broader scenario, the more typical case would be as follows: a young woman who had been drinking and then attacked by a man already known to her and forced into sex, or whose ability to detect menacing behavior is dulled, or whose ability to fend off unwanted advances or convey her desire to stop was completely weakened, thus attracting an opportunistic rapist. The more narrow typical scenario is where an assailant administers some psychoactive substance and waits for his victim to become incapacitated before raping her.

If you're like most students, or most people unfamiliar with the research literature in this area, you would probably have chosen the latter as the definition of drug-facilitated sexual assault. By contrast, if you had done research in this area or developed public health messages or news articles about DFSA, however, you would be more familiar with the first definition, for that is how DFSA has come to be defined. In the last decade since roughly the year 2000, there has been a concerted effort to blend these two scenarios into one blanket term.

Some of the play in the data comes from the inclusion of alcohol in the term "drug-facilitated." In all studies using this or similar terms, alcohol accounts for most cases, and the alcohol is consumed by the victim voluntarily, after which the assault is carried out. There is also, in the research literature, the return of the idea of being "plied with alcohol." Kirkpatrick's 2007 study, for instance, asks if an assailant "tried to get you drunk" as an example of the sort of case that would fit. The term "drunk" too is a bit unspecific and imprecise (as is, in my view, the whole phrase and concept of someone "trying to get you drunk"). Some studies are careful enough to specify that they mean incapacitated levels of intoxication, others seem to imply that any drunken state, followed by assault, is a drug-facilitated rape. Part of the confusion here stems from the legal recognition that an incapacitated person cannot consent to sexual relations. In that sense, it indeed "doesn't matter" how voluntary intoxication is. But this is rarely where controversy emerges in any case.

The distinction between voluntary and involuntary intoxication matters on a number of levels. Distinguishing carefully—and fully—between voluntary and involuntary intoxication has important legal implications. For instance, in Illinois and other states, causing someone to ingest a substance without their knowledge constitutes aggravation of the connected felony, such as rape or robbery. Tampering is itself a freestanding offense regardless of what happens next in most places. Of course it matters, even if we are just talking about criminal justice intervention.

The distinction is also important from a public health and public safety standpoint. Health-care providers, rape crisis centers, and law enforcement agencies need to know what people are taking on their own, how they are taking it, and how offenders take advantage of impaired people. Accurate numbers—understanding the scope of a problem—are always important in resource planning, proper training, potential interventions, effective victim support, and clear communication to the general public. If intoxication takes place involuntarily, then that constitutes a no doubt smaller but important problem that must also be planned for.

We already know that alcohol plays a large presence in the incapacitation problems seen by toxicologists and ER personnel. But looking more closely, we can see some of the difficulty in presenting good statistics for reporters and others to quote. In Juhasik et al.'s study, for instance, 43 % of 144 subjects (selected from a population of women who had reported to a sexual assault clinic in a hospital) and 7 % of 859 complainants were characterized as DFSA.[28] Seven percent sounds high, until you find out that most, by far, involved alcohol, marijuana, or cocaine. If all readers understood that the term DFSA was being used to cover all cases of incapacitation, then there would be no problem. And of course, like all researchers, they did set out a definition. The study noted that subjects tended to notably underreport their use of drugs when self-reports were compared with the toxicological screens. Only five samples tested positive for benzodiapenes, but given the low level of drug self-administration reporting, it is unclear how they got there. In at least one of these cases, the benzodiazepine was prescribed and taken voluntarily:

> In Case 1, the complainant stated she suspected she was given a drug. She had a prescription for and was taking clonazepam, which was found in the presenting visit urine specimen. She further stated that she was drinking alcohol. No drugs other than clonazepam were found. The combination of the benzodiazepine and alcohol could have rendered her incompetent to

---

[28] Juhascik and Negrusz et al., 2007.

7 What Do We Know (and Not Know) About Predatory Drugging?   233

consent to sex. It was unclear if she knew about the potential effects of alcohol and the prescription drug. This case was classified DFSA. The findings comport with the history, except that the complainant believed she had been drugged.

The researchers clearly state,

> We originally thought that it might be possible to estimate the proportion of involuntary drugging versus voluntary drug ingestion cases, but these estimates necessarily depend on history and self-reporting by subjects. Limitations on the ability to detect certain drugs within the time window, and the demonstrable under-reporting of actual drug use, make self-reporting an unreliable criterion.

So while the loose, expanded definition of DFSA may make sense to answer certain questions in public health, the researchers here clearly say they were interested in measuring involuntary drugging, even though they could not develop reliable data on the matter.

Researchers and governmental statistics keepers have been remiss in the area of consistent terminology and distinguishing between involuntary and voluntary intoxication before assault. DFSA as a broad term links to criminal law concerns, especially in the USA, where no heavily intoxicated consent is thought to be valid. (Not that this has been much of a boon for increased sexual assault conviction.) In England and Wales, the accused must instead have a reasonable basis for perceiving consent.[29] For this reason, the eliding of distinctions between voluntary and involuntary consumption is understandable, for consent is either present or not. The UK Advisory Council on the Misuse of Drugs in 2007, for instance, created a combined category, drug-facilitated sexual assault, which combines the predatory and the opportunistic scenarios. In Europe in general, Deborah Olszeweki notes, the combined category is preferred, as the legal distinction between the two types is not vastly different, hinging on the fact that in neither case can a person consent to

---

[29] Jo Lovett and Miranda A.H. Horvath, "Alcohol and Drugs in Sexual Assault," in Miranda Horvath and Jennifer Brown, eds., *Rape: Challenging Contemporary Thinking*, (London: Routledge), 2013, 129.

sexual relations.[30] In contrast, in the USA, predatory drugging may carry with it separate charges or a penalty enhancement, so the distinction is somewhat more crucial.

Hall and Moore, in reviewing studies about intoxication and rape, note that after the ACPO and other reports in the UK, a key distinction in terminology was suggested by the ACPO: proactive versus opportunistic DFSA. Hall and Moore endorse this distinction as key to public health understanding and also toward the aim of producing effective health education. Unfortunately, there was little uptake of the idea.

The broad definition of DFSA appears in many places, including epidemiological, social science, public health, and toxicological literature. Researchers Miranda Horvath and Jennifer Brown, who have worked to develop increased clarity about the matter, note, "There is still a good deal of confusion over what exactly constitutes DAR [drug assisted rape]. There are significant differences between the definitions suggested by researchers, complainant support groups and the law."[31]

Given that so few sexual assault allegations end up being settled in legal settings, it seems like an unwarranted confusion. Olszewski is correct when she says that a combined construct "opens up the discourse about sexual assault and begins to challenge public attitudes about the attribution of blame" and may in turn encourage higher rates of victim reporting. Certainly, pushing the public, victims, and key professional sectors to drop its disqualifying bias against voluntarily intoxicated victims is a goal worth pursuing. And while it is also a laudable goal to hold greater numbers of perpetrators responsible for their acts more of the time, the greatest impact that researchers can have at this time will take place outside courtrooms in most cases. For this reason, precision in definition is not only desirable but ethically demanded. The public and the press have demonstrated confusion about the DFSA term instead: rather than expanding their thinking, it seems, they have constricted it to the narrow scenario and inflated that scenario's prevalence.

---

[30] Deborah Olszewski, "Sexual assaults facilitated by drugs or alcohol," *Drugs: Education, Prevention, and Policy*, Vol. 16, No. 1, 2009, 39–52.

[31] Horvath and Brown, "Drug-Assisted Rape and Sexual Assault: Definitional, Conceptual and Methodological Developments," *Journal of Investigative Psychology and Offender Profiling*, 2, 2005, 203–210.

Beynon et al. note that such definitional collapsing cannot help but be misunderstood in a media environment already primed to be interested in the drink spiking scenario at the expense of the more common opportunistic assault. But it is not all the fault of press misinterpretation. Beynon et al.'s review found that 11 studies "discussed DFSA in terms of covert drug administration, but 10 then failed to remove voluntary consumption of alcohol and drugs in their interpretation of results."

Alcohol in the Alcohol

Yet this very broad definition of DFSA is not the only way to develop maximal, but questionable, estimates of the problem. The "extra alcohol" variant on the drink spiking scare sometimes appears. Rather than accepting that most people who become incapacitated or black out after ingesting alcohol have voluntarily, albeit sometimes unknowingly, consumed too much alcohol, the "alcohol spiking" advocates seem to aver that predators are "spiking" people's drinks with alcohol and the victim cannot tell. An advocate in Ireland, for instance, tells the *Irish Independent* newspaper that "drink-spiking includes giving a person a double or a triple shot, when they think they've got a single ... the culture of permissiveness around alcohol—as well as a belief by some victims that they may subsequently not get a sympathetic hearing—cannot be ignored."[32]

Certainly, the fair hearing problem is real; that is true in all alcohol cases. But is hard to know what to do with claims of surreptitious double and triple shots in drinks as "spiking" given that mixed drinks tend to vary widely in their strength anyway. This came up in Australia during the scares in Canberra and Perth, too. Beer and wine can of course also be spiked with extra alcohol, but not without noticeable taste differences. In other words, the entire problem of avoiding victim blaming of intoxicated victims seems embedded in the alternative endorsement of a surreptitious-dosing scenario. In what world are all drinks expected to be the same strength in any case, unless they come premixed from a factory?

---

[32] Mark O'Regan, "Alcohol is the number one 'date rape' drug in Ireland—experts," 28 April 2015, http://www.independent.ie/life/health-wellbeing/safe-4-women/alcohol-is-the-number-one-date-rape-drug-in-ireland-experts-31176688.html. Retrieved June 10, 2015.

The simple freedom to drink, or take drugs, even to excess, without fear of assault, or blame if assault happens, appears to be a proposition that many people wish to avoid—a problem to which I return later. Suffice for now to say that there is *something* about the increased vulnerability when exercising such freedoms that must be reflexively denied, and a rarer scenario substituted as an explanation.

The Use and Abuse of Drugging Statistics

The fact of the matter is: all rapes are, at their basis, perpetrator-facilitated. I mean this not glibly, but rather as an attempt to step back for a moment from the current preoccupation with intoxication as a precursor to sexual assault. Intoxication is often a risk factor for sexual assault, and if involuntary (such as in a drugging), then it is a means of subduing a victim, but it is not itself a cause of sexual assault. And intoxication is something we typically do to ourselves—because it is pleasurable and because it is our right to do so unmolested. But given alcohol's prominence in the problem of sexual assault, there appears to be a cultural drift underway in which alcohol intoxication, too, is seen as involuntary and as a devious means to an end.

Since the early 1990s when anecdotal reports of drugging rape—particularly involving a new generation of synthetic drugs—were received by advocacy organizations and researchers, the date rape drugs problem has been subject to a vociferous debate about its incidence and prevalence. How many cases have there been? Is the number growing? Compared with other kinds of predatory behavior, how common is it? And how do we know what we know about how common it is?

All methodologies in natural and social science have their limitations, but the debate over the date rape drugs numbers also gets into the area of definitional mischief and motivated estimates. Andrew Karmen in his book *Crime Victims* notes that many "new" crime victimization problems are often, at first, given to wildly various estimates between the poles of "minimalism" and "maximalism."[33] Maximalists use specific data sources

---

[33] Andrew Karmen, *Crime Victims: An Introduction to Victimology*, Eighth Edition, (Belmont, CA: Wadsworth), 2013.

7 What Do We Know (and Not Know) About Predatory Drugging?

to urge that the problem is widespread, growing or increasing in severity or both, and that it is an omnipresent-enough fear to require both individual precaution and social intervention. Minimalists, on the other hand, tend to use different data sources, or the same ones in a different way, to suggest that the problem has been overestimated either in prevalence or in severity.

Karmen notes that political and governmental actors, particularly at the national level, along with college health organizations, have tended to assume that maximal estimates of the date rape drugs problem are correct and thus acted accordingly. (My own review suggests this was only true in the early period, roughly between 1998 and 2006 or so, after which the official pattern was more mixed.) Law enforcement agencies tend to see the crime as rare but frustrating when it occurs because evidence is difficult to obtain since the complainant's memory is either hazy or "black box" nonexistent, and she may not report the crime for days—well beyond the point when even a quick-acting investigator can get her to a clinic for toxicological screening.[34] Like other rape reports, late reporting in cases where a victim was intoxicated, either voluntarily or not, is far from unusual.

That said, this remains a set of quibbles and might unnecessarily take us into the realm of outsize skepticism. It would be surprising if it *never* happened. Yet it remains clear that even if all of the cases of involuntarily drug ingestion were validated, the problem remains much smaller than we have been led to believe. And in the vast majority of cases, the motivation for the drugging is unclear as it is not accompanied by another criminal complaint such as sexual assault—just suspicion that this might have been the motivation. The Australian studies' quick notice of the stimulant–pranking nexus reminds us that drinks tampering is a multi-motive affair.

---

[34] I use the term "she" and "her" to refer to victims and complainants, respectively, but it should of course be noted that males can be and have been victims of both drugging and of sexual assault.

8

Drugs, Drinking, College, and Warding off Blame

It was really in the aftermath of the rise of Ecstasy that we found the origins of today's concern with date rape drugs, even though it never did get fully pulled into the date rape drugs construct, at least officially. It is unclear whether its stimulant qualities explain this fully. The many decades of drug scaremongering, often led by the USA and its enormous appetite for drugs, have led to a kind of governance formula or script: simply keep up with new and emerging drug use, tally the adverse effects, find some very bad cases and incidents, add to the list of prohibited substances, rinse, and repeat. While the War on Drugs imposed draconian penalties for illicit sales, the script of the drug scourge had more or less been already written. Thus, the Big Three *probably* could have been prohibited and regulated severely even without the rape angle. There was something else deep in the realm of sexual assault politics that has been going on to shape and develop this threat.

Given decades now of pharma-ubiquity, a reasonable question is why predatory drugging is not more of a problem? As we have seen from previous eras, there is nothing socially, technologically, or criminologically new about predatory drugging, despite what the press sometimes implies

© The Editor(s) (if applicable) and The Author(s) 2016
P. Donovan, *Drink Spiking and Predatory Drugging*,
DOI 10.1057/978-1-137-57517-3_8

about "nowadays." The barriers remain mainly social and logistical, rather than moral or technical. Chloral hydrate, the most storied of all knockout drops, was at many points in history easier to get than the illicit ones are today. A surprising number of over-the-counter and widely prescribed pills can do the trick if a perpetrator was so inclined.

The answer is not, as we have seen from scientific reports, that there is a vast hidden cache of GHB drugging we have not detected yet due to relatively fast metabolization. The symptoms of heavy alcohol intoxication, voluntary drug use—both street drugs and prescribed, and involuntary use are easily confused, and in some cases, difficult to disaggregate. But self-report studies also suggest an upper cap, and undergird the role of alcohol in producing incapacitation. While previous chapters addressed the state of knowledge regarding the prevalence of drugging, this chapter will discuss the context of intoxication, generally, by looking at college campuses in particular.

The tendency to exaggerate a drug's dangers—particularly the likelihood of its predatory use as opposed to being an object of voluntary drug-seeking—is also tied up in the always-suspect political hyperbole that precedes, or attempts to ward off challenges to, drug and alcohol prohibition. Yet antidrug campaigns alone cannot explain the current scare fully: there is also the "date rape" part. Within the following consideration of "date rape drugs" is the way in which a crime itself—sexual assault—is being reshaped in relation to drugs and alcohol. In my view, this scare is eroding progress made in recent decades regarding our understanding of the ordinary dynamics of sexual assault. We saw this in the evolving career of the term "date rape" in the press. We saw it in the strange inability of researchers to settle on a common definition of drug-facilitated assault. And we will see—once again—how tied up the drink *spiking* problem is with drinking itself. Scratch the surface of any date rape drugs discussion, in other words, and you find a subterranean realm of claims and discomforts around alcohol consumption and sexual assault.

Exit the Social Drinker, Enter the Era of Teetotalers and Binge Drinkers

Given that a significant reservoir for concern about drink spiking appears to be among college students, it is worth looking at how the lives of college students have changed. Binge drinking is not some kind of newcomer to the college campus, but since the 1990s, there has been an upward trend in the number of drinkers who binge drink and who do so frequently. This pattern of alcohol consumption appears to be at the expense of drinking patterns that were in most cases light or moderate, punctuated by occasional "big nights." Episodes became more frequent, and adverse effects also increased. Aaron White and colleagues have studied acute physical effects of this trend, noting that increasing alcohol overdoses (up by 25% between 1999 and 2008 among 18–24 year olds) took place alongside "stable or declining" drinking levels in that age group overall. It also appears to be contributing to a dramatic increase in combination drug-and-alcohol overdoses (up 76%). Those who drink a lot, in other words, are drinking more and doing so more frequently.[1] Colleges also like to point to increases in the number of students who do not drink at all, but step back and what you see is a polarized pattern that is reshaping drinking norms.

This change has been measured not just in the USA, but in Canada, Australia and New Zealand, and the UK.[2] The Harvard School of Public Health College Alcohol Study (CAS) was administered yearly between 1993 and 2001. A national sample of college students answered questions

---

[1] Aaron M. White, Ralph W. Hingson, I-Jen Pan, Hsiao-Ye Yi, Hospitalizations for Alcohol and Drug Overdoses in Young Adults Ages 18–24 in the United States, 1999–2008: Results from the Nationwide Inpatient Sample. *Journal of Studies on Alcohol and Drugs*, 72, 774–786, 2011. The data comes from ER admissions. White and colleagues consider the possibility that some of the increase is due to a greater likelihood of seeking medical help.

[2] Martin Plant and Moira Plant, *Binge Britain: Alcohol and the National Response*, Oxford: Oxford University Press, 2006; Thomas Vander Ven, "Getting Wasted: Why College Students Drink Too Much and Party So Hard", New York: New York University Press, 2011; Australian Government, National Drug Research Institute, *Attachment A: Trends in alcohol use and harms across Australia*; Health Canada, *Canadian Addiction Survey (CAS): A national survey of Canadians' use of alcohol and other drugs: Prevalence of use and related harms: Detailed report by E.M. Adlaf, P., Begin, & E. Sawka*, eds. Ottawa: Canadian Centre on Substance Abuse, 2005.

about drinking frequency and intensity. This survey was one of the major reasons why concern about binge drinking among college students increased during this time. Researchers Wechsler and Nelson at CAS defined binge drinking as five drinks in a single episode for men and four drinks in a single episode for women.[3] Grucza et al. tracked an increase for women in the USA at college age that was steeper than for men, although men still do drink more. Interestingly, there has not been any dramatic increase, and in some categories some decrease, in binge drinking among those of the same age *not* attending college.[4]

There is how much young people drink, and there is how much they think they drink. It is as simple as this: young people tend to wildly underestimate the amount they drink.[5] At no age are we particularly good at it, actually. Barron Lerner, in his book *One for the Road* about driving under the influence (DUI) as a social problem, underscores the problematic tendency for health communications to use overly subjective judgments of alcohol intake. By and large, people do not like to be told how much to drink; rather, we are implored to "know our limits" and "drink responsibly."[6] In fact, public health measures and standards may vary slightly, but researchers have been able to identify consumption levels at which both personal and aggregate risks of adverse effects rise

---

[3] Henry Wechsler and Toben F. Nelson, "What We Have Learned from the Harvard School of Public Health College Alcohol Study: Focusing Attention on College Student Alcohol Consumption and the Environmental Conditions That Promote It," *Journal of Studies on Alcohol and Drugs*, July 2008, 1–10. The definition, already in use by the CDC and other surveys, was criticized by some as prone to overestimate adverse effects of social drinking. Though the definition did not take into account body weight or other individual-level factors, the researchers defended the use of the definition on both substantive and methodological grounds: the definition was a widely known, already existing threshold amount at which adverse events began to spike in nearly any sample population. It made CAS data comparable to other alcohol use data that had been gathered using the same definition, including that of the Core Institute Survey and the definition used by the World Health Organization. Trends derived from those sets are corroborative of trend.

[4] Richard A. Grucza, Karen E. Norberg, Laura J. Bierut, "Binge Drinking Among Youths and Young Adults in the United States: 1979–2006." *Journal of the American Academy of Child and Adolescent Psychiatry*, 48:7, 2009.

[5] Aaron M. White, Courtney L. Kraus, Julie D. Flom et al., "College Students Lack Knowledge of Standard Drink Volumes: Implications for Definitions of Risky Drinking Based on Survey Data," *Alcoholism: Clinical & Experimental Research*, 2005. For comparison purposes, for instance, year-to-year differences, this matters little—the tendency to underestimate seems steady. But when using self-report questionnaires to estimate the *overall* prevalence of problem-level drinking, this fact—shown in many studies—must be kept in mind.

[6] Lerner, 2011.

sharply. That is, we know how much, roughly, will be too much. These risks are among moderately high episodic drinkers, not people who are alcohol dependent and drink at the heaviest levels.

Aggregate risk, though, is a hard sell in an individualistic culture; and of course individual tolerance does vary. But overconfidence is common, and norms are shared, and this is where the trouble begins: keeping up. Thomas Vander Ven's book, *Getting Wasted*, describes the ways in which drinking among college students, as well as interpreting and framing of both exhilarating and destructive outcomes, are collective endeavors. Peer culture not only develops the social events in which excessive drinking is encouraged, but also helps strengthen norms around drinking.[7]

My own campus research suggests students are somewhat defensive about their own and their peers' drinking in cases of suspected drugging, as in: *she only had a few drinks*.[8] There appears to be a disconnect for some between consuming three to five drinks at a rapid pace and experiencing a heavy, drug-like effect or a blackout. And in terms of predicting how servings will affect us, generally people (and not just young people) rely too heavily on past intoxication experiences, often forgetting circumstantial factors (drink portion size, distance from meals, medications, dehydration, weight and height, body composition). Three to five drinks on one day will not necessarily be the same as three to five on another. It should be cautioned that my research was focused on knowledge of date rape drugs, and was not a general survey of substance use. Both men and women reported unexpected effects of drinking, and none of the responses directly linked the incident to sexual assault. Defensiveness was accomplished either by identifying symptoms with a specific drink ($n = 21$) rather than "drinking" or by including information about how little alcohol the victim had consumed ($n = 12$), such as:

> "They were given a drink and woke up in a guys room."
> "I accepted a drink from someone I didn't know & woke up a day later w/ no clothes in someone's car."

---

[7] Vander Ven, 2011.
[8] Pamela Donovan, "The Role of Uncertainty in Knowledge of Suspected Drink Spiking Incidents," 78th Annual Meeting of the Eastern Sociological Society, New York, NY, February 2008; Burgess, Donovan, and Moore, 2009.

"She was given drinks, only a couple, but came back acting severely intoxicated."

"On my 2nd beer, extreme dizzy feeling, had to immediately sit down, once sitting couldn't keep my eye open, began vomiting & soon passed out."

"Girl I know had one drink at a party and then blacked out and woke up sitting on a curb."

Respondents were somewhat more likely, then, to exonerate alcohol rather than blame it.[9]

The local party drink for college students, besides beer, is something called "Jungle Juice." Typically concocted in a plastic bin, it combines beer, fruit juices and fruit, liqueurs, vodka, and grain alcohol. My students and I surmised together that each red plastic cup (16 ounces volume) of it, even with ice, would contain no less than four, and as many as six or seven servings of alcohol. But they tend to think of these cups as a serving, or perhaps two.

We also cannot assume that failure to understand binge drinking's effects stems from sheer ignorance; in fact, students are bombarded with specific messages about the dangers. Our local campus has had its share of alcohol-related tragedies, well-publicized: fatal fires, car accidents, and alcohol poisonings in particular. The level of student drinking has created enormous strains on the small town it is in, and exacerbated town-and-university tensions. The problem is compounded by the fact that the campus itself—where the vast majority of the students-in-residence live—is officially a dry campus and has a "zero-tolerance" policy. From the point of view of the insurers and lawyers, this policy simply defines the problem out of existence. It removes any regulation, oversight, or limitation that would be enabled on a wet campus, through a tavern or permit system. Thus, there exists here a remarkable bifurcation: a very alcohol-positive culture among students and an alcohol-negative view from campus leaders and administration—a recipe for prolonged adolescent dependency and associated boundary-testing if there ever was one.

It is clear in my survey research that few students endorse the widely cautioned idea that "alcohol is the number one date rape drug."

---

[9] From the subsample of respondents ($n = 116$) who wrote about specific events in an open-ended portion of the survey.

(Hereafter, AITNODRD.) In short, they do not buy it. Of the 224 responses I got to the question about which substances they associated with date rape drugs, 37 mentioned alcohol. Clearly, a subset of students had heard that message. Some students' defensiveness about their peers' drinking may explain it in part, but the fact is that the AITNODRD construct is inherently weird. It may have been well-meaning, but it seems to imply an element of involuntary intoxication by alcohol that most people find difficult to relate to their own and their peers' drinking experiences.

Unlike some media "worries of the week," the claim that the excess alcohol problem has worsened in recent years is well-grounded in research. The adverse effects of excess alcohol consumption need not be reiterated here in too much depth, but for young people, it is a leading risk factor, in the top three causes of death: injury, suicide, and homicide. In sexual assault, it is a prominent risk factor.[10] What it is not, typically, is unknowingly consumed.

A Note about Inclining Adverse Effects of Drugs

By the 1990s, concern had been raised regarding the rise in binge drinking. Less attention has been paid to the rise in prescriptions for antianxiety and anti-insomnia drugs among a generation of young adults raised on "Just Say No" and then "zero tolerance." The marketing and distribution of benzodiazepines, as we have seen, expanded, nearly unabated, right before and during the incline of the "date rape drugs" scare when logic would dictate greater scrutiny of their use and omnipresence. For instance, critical-minded, broad cultural questions were raised about attention deficit hyperactivity disorder (ADHD) drug marketing, adoption, and diversion. White and Hingson's overdose studies showed that between 1999 and 2008, drug overdose visits among 18–24 year olds increased by 55%.[11] Their study further notes that women are less likely

---

[10] Antonia Abbey, "Alcohol-related sexual assault: A common problem among college students," *Journal of Studies in Alcohol*, Supplement No. 14, 118–128, 2002; Meichun Mohler-Kuo, George W. Dowdall, Mary P. Koss, and Henry Wechsler, "Correlates of Rape while Intoxicated in a National Sample of College Women, Journal of Studies on Alcohol," January 2004, 65, 37–45.

[11] White and Hingson, 2011.

than men to use diverted prescription opioids or benzodiazepines recreationally, but those who do are more likely to ingest high doses. Of course, many of those who overdose are not college students, but college offers little protection.

Several decades now have seen a notable easing of ready access to any number of psychoactive pills, and the increased norm, particularly among young people, of using drugs of psychological support for depression, anxiety, and attention deficit disorders. The anxiety around potential predatory use of drugs cannot help but be linked to our deferred conversation about this wave of legitimated pharmaceutical presence in young people's lives.

Year of the College Rape Controversy

Emerging Themes in Campus Antirape Activism

Almost simultaneously during the academic year 2014–2015, a number of high-profile sexual assault cases on college campuses appeared. Some included allegations of suspected predatory drugging, and others did not. These cases were followed by high levels of publicity, and the documentary film, "The Hunting Ground" covered some of them, though two of the ones covered by the film, including a Florida State case, are still highly contested.[12] In September 2015, Lady Gaga released a song and video public service announcement (PSA) about campus rape that also points viewers and fans to the "Hunting Ground" film. The video has been criticized for not specifically suggesting that victims report the crime to the police or campus security, while offering help hotline numbers and other resources.[13]

---

[12] Emily Yoffe, "The Hunting Ground: The failures of a new documentary about rape on college campuses," *Slate*, February 27, 2015. Retrieved September 18, 2015. http://www.slate.com/articles/double_x/doublex/2015/02/the_hunting_ground_a_campus_rape_documentary_that_fails_to_provide_a_full.single.html.

[13] Emily Shire, "What Lady Gaga's Rape Awareness Video Should Have Said," *Daily Beast*, September 18, 2015. http://www.thedailybeast.com/articles/2015/09/18/what-lady-gaga-s-rape-awareness-video-should-have-said.html. Retrieved September 18, 2015.

8 Drugs, Drinking, College, and Warding off Blame 247

But I think the problem runs deeper. Artists are, of course, under no obligation to produce social commentary that only references the typical, but the three vignettes have been billed as a PSA about campus rape. Yet the video fails to even mention the typical campus rape at all. In one, some friendly banter in a dorm room leads to a strong arm assault. In another, a woman (who may be trans) is blitz-attacked in a bathroom by a man; it is not clear whether he is known to the victim or not. In the third, two women are roofied at a party and then assaulted while unconscious. In the video's favor, the devastating psychological and psychosocial aftermath is well-depicted, as is the healing power of social support and solidarity.

More typically, sexual assault takes place when the assailant exploits the social trust in existing relationships (e.g., acquaintance, workmates, friendship, dating, or simply socializing); this is only suggested in the strong arm assault vignette. Alcohol itself is never mentioned: neither to depict the assailant's aggression and violence, nor to illustrate the enhanced vulnerabilities of victims who have been drinking a lot. And thus, a golden opportunity is missed: to show how rape is a violent crime, and that alcohol—very commonly present—does not erase the perpetrator's responsibility for the event, and does not make it not a crime. As with the current taboo generally about discussing alcohol and rape, we also miss the opportunity to make the case that intoxicated victims deserve every bit of freedom from violence as sober victims, and to acknowledge that rapists are opportunists who think otherwise.

Emily Bazelon, who reviewed recent developments in campus rape activism, notes a marked suppression of conversations about alcohol for fear of victim blaming. In its place seems to be a plea for men to behave better, and an insistence that alcohol consumption is completely irrelevant and admitting it as a risk factor reinforces victim's (as opposed to perpetrator's) responsibility to stop rape.[14] The whole formulation essentially confuses justice for safety, and oddly depends on men to do

---

[14] Emily Bazelon, "The Return of the Sex Wars," *New York Times Magazine*, September 10, 2015. Retrieved January 16, 2016. http://mobile.nytimes.com/2015/09/13/magazine/the-return-of-the-sex-wars.html.

the right thing. Actually, it depends on precisely the wrong men to do the right thing.

Meanwhile, campus antirape politics have developed an *in extremis* problem. The big problems—the fact that sexual assault is common (albeit not "epidemic" as some claim) on college campuses, that it remains vastly underreported, and that campuses have generally done a poor job in responding to it—has been overshadowed by campaigns organized around specific incidents. Situations in which drugging explanations are insisted upon when both tests and circumstances suggest otherwise has the dual negative effect of sidelining claims about the sexual assault itself, and contributing to a basically melodramatic view of the problem. Left out in the cold, then, are all the more mundane experiences that most assaulted women recognize as their own.

To be fair, assaults with more dramatic features (weapons, threats, collateral injuries, blitz attacks) are more likely to be reported to police or campus authorities in the first place, so the media cannot bear the entire blame for covering the "newsier" rapes rather than the searing-but-ordinary ones. Consider, though, how *Rolling Stone*'s 2014 University of Virginia (UVA) rape-reporting fiasco was put into motion in the first place: part of the reason that the reporter was led down the primrose path was because she sought a really sensational, over-the-top story. She had apparently rejected a number of other campus cases—at UVA and elsewhere—as not dramatic enough as that of the pseudonymous (and, interestingly, sober) "Jackie" for the signal event in a magazine article that she says aimed to explicate the larger situation on college campuses.[15] As *Slate* critics Allison Benedikt and Hanna Rosin put it, the reporter had picked a story that "even by the standards of horrific, despicable frat behavior…

---

[15] The story in question (now retracted) was by Sabrina Rubin Erdely, "A Rape on Campus," *Rolling Stone*, no. 1223, November 19, 2014. In it, Erdely related the story of the pseudonymous "Jackie" who was brutally gang-raped and injured at a fraternity party when she was tricked into going on a date. Her friends (also pseudonymous) were described as callous, and the UVA administration unresponsive. The story quickly fell apart under scrutiny, and Erdely admitted failure to properly vet claims made to her by Jackie. *Rolling Stone* then asked the Columbia University School of Journalism to review the incident and report on what went wrong. The resultant investigative report is: Sheila Coronel, Steve Coll, Derek Kravitz, "The CJR Report: *Rolling Stone*'s investigation: 'A failure that was avoidable'," *Columbia Journalism Review*, April 5, 2015. Retrieved January 16, 2016. http://www.rollingstone.com/culture/features/a-rape-on-campus-what-went-wrong-20150405.

stands out" for its brutality, collateral violence, and bystander indifference.[16] After the story was retracted by *Rolling Stone*, the victim advocate that had first brought attention to the problem of sexual violence at UVA was interviewed by Ravi Somaiya at the *New York Times*. The advocate, Emily Renda, "offered another reason that she felt the *Rolling Stone* article was flawed: The magazine was drawn toward the most extreme story of a campus rape it could find. The more nuanced accounts, she suggested, seemed somehow 'not real enough to stand for rape culture. And that is part of the problem.'"[17]

Fraternities and Drink Spiking Suspicion

The incident at UVA did not involve drug or alcohol issues, but it did catalyze increased concern about fraternity parties. In this section, I want to take a closer look at three incidents involving allegations of predatory drugging on college campuses: at the University of California at Berkeley (UCB), the University of Wisconsin at Milwaukee (UWM), and Brown University. One illustrates the frequent elusiveness of any clarity about drugging allegations which nonetheless builds an overall atmosphere of fear. Another illustrates the dubious social justice benefit of insisting on a drugging explanation for events when evidence suggests otherwise. The third illustrates an emerging civil liberties problem of authorities using the mere suspicion of drugging as a pretext for a search warrant, and enacting free-ranging drugs raid on that basis. Together, these three incidents ended up producing a consolidated national claim about fraternity parties that was built on rather rickety factual foundations.

In October 2014, Berkeley campus police received reports of students getting sick at a fraternity party. The specific allegations were against DKE, an unaffiliated frat that had been removed from campus for hazing

---

[16] Allison Benedikt and Hanna Rosin, "Double X: The Missing Men," *Slate.com*, December 2, 2014. http://www.slate.com/articles/double_x/doublex/2014/12/sabrina_rubin_erdely_uva_why_didn_t_a_rolling_stone_writer_talk_to_the_alleged.2.html. Retrieved March 19, 2016.
[17] Ravi Somaiya, "Rolling Stone Article on Rape at University of Virginia Failed All Basics, Report Says," *New York Times*, April 5, 2015, http://www.nytimes.com/2015/04/06/business/media/rolling-stone-retracts-article-on-rape-at-university-of-virginia.html. Retrieved March 19, 2016.

in 2009.[18] Eric Tejada of campus police said that they did not have any other evidence and turned the case over to the City of Berkeley Police Department. The same day these allegations were reported, a student who had been accused of drugging and sexually assaulting a woman had his charges dismissed, accompanied by a rare factual finding of innocence.[19] Allegations also surfaced of sexual assaults at other fraternities around Berkeley the same week, not related to drugs. Then, in early November, the campus police received an anonymous letter claiming that a drug-related assault took place at an unnamed fraternity on Halloween.[20] Campus police are obligated by federal law (the Clery Act) to publicize these potential public safety threats, but the effect is that the allegations just hang there, forever unresolved. October 2014 seemed to be did-they-or-didn't they, roofies-or-no-roofies month in Berkeley, without any eventual clarity. No complainants ever came forward, and it appears that the press lost interest, except to tally it positively in a nationwide roll call of shame.[21] In the overlapping late part of October, Brown University in Providence, Rhode Island, reported an alleged drugging of two partygoers at a frat house, Phi Kappa Psi (PKP), followed by a sexual assault of one at another location. Brown's administration immediately suspected PKP's activities, pending further investigation. In early November, Brown notified the campus that one of the two

---

[18] It was not clear whether the initial report came from complainants or a third party. *NBC Bay Area*, "5 People Allegedly Sexually Assaulted at Frat House Near UC Berkeley," October 17, 2014. http://www.nbcbayarea.com/news/local/279598702.html. Somewhat confusing matters in the same report were two other allegations of sexual assault the same weekend, unrelated to the DKE incident. Reuters, "Five report sexual assaults at University of California Berkeley fraternity," October 17, 2014. http://www.reuters.com/article/us-usa-berkeley-sexassaults-idUSKCN0I700920141018. Retrieved January 16, 2016.

[19] Emilie Raguso, "Update: UC Berkeley student exonerated of rape charge," *Berkeleyside.com*, October 17, 2014. http://www.berkeleyside.com/2014/10/17/breaking-case-dismissed-against-uc-berkeley-student-charged-with-rape/. Retrieved January 16, 2016.

[20] Alan Wang, "Cal Police Receive Anonymous Letter Documenting Sexual Assault at Frat House," *ABC 7 News San Francisco*. http://abc7news.com/education/cal-police-receive-anonymous-letter-documenting-sexual-assault-/384606/. Retrieved January 17, 2016.

[21] Allie Jones, "Every Rape Reported at Fraternities This Year," *Gawker.com*, December 22, 2014. http://gawker.com/every-rape-reported-at-fraternities-this-year-1671299377. Retrieved January 17, 2016.

8 Drugs, Drinking, College, and Warding off Blame   251

women who had the "alcoholic punch" tested positive for GHB.[22] As with previous press releases on the incident, Brown reiterated that the students' symptoms were rapid intoxication and memory loss, out of sync with how much they had to drink. The campus' Task Force on Sexual Assault convened a meeting on the heels of the announcement. One student reported that she had been told in freshman year that "spaces where date rape occurs are well known by some students on campus, adding that her friends were told which fraternity houses use date-rape drugs."[23] The concern about the fraternity–drugging link was already established, at least at Brown.

In mid-January 2015, Brown announced that PKP would be suspended for four years as a result of the incident, for facilitating sexual misconduct. The sexual misconduct charge was not against a member of that fraternity, and it was not alleged that he was the one that spiked the punch drinks with GHB. The alleged misconduct took place elsewhere, after the complainant left the party.[24] The sanction thus implied that either the PKP hosts had drugged the drinks themselves, or were lax in their surveillance and allowed it to happen. PKP denied it, and questioned the toxicological evidence early on. It did admit that it had not obtained the proper permits to have the party in the first place.

And then, in February, newer toxicology tests came back with a different result. As in the Hillory Farias case, the initial tests had failed to control for natural levels of GHB in the body. Further, it had never been explained why the second partygoer, who drank from the same serving, did not test positive. As a result of the new test, which used both urinalysis and hair samples, Brown reduced PKP's suspension to two and

---

[22] Lynn Arditi, "Brown University: Student tested positive for date-rape drug," *Providence Journal*, November 8, 2014. http://www.providencejournal.com/breaking-news/content/20141108-brown-university-student-tested-positive-for-date-rape-drug.ece. Retrieved January 17, 2016.
[23] Camilla Brandfield-Harvey, "Undergrad sexual assault forum draws few attendees," *Brown Daily Herald*, November 12, 2014. http://www.browndailyherald.com/2014/11/12/undergrad-sexual-assault-forum-draws-attendees/. Retrieved January 17, 2016.
[24] Associated Press, "Brown University: Two Fraternities 'Facilitated' Sexual Misconduct," *NBC News*, http://www.nbcnews.com/news/us-news/brown-university-two-fraternities-facilitated-sexual-misconduct-n289296. Retrieved January 17, 2016.

a half years. It also, PKP pointed out, allowed the man accused of sexual misconduct to remain on campus.[25]

If you expected that attention at Brown would then turn to the allegation of sexual misconduct, specifically the alleged actions of an individual who opportunistically exploited the ill-feeling and disorientation of another student, or perhaps to explore the general problem of sexual assault on campus—well, you would be wrong. Instead, student activists simply failed to accept the new toxicology results. On March 7, about 30 students led a silent protest at a women's academic leadership panel that included Brown's President, Christina Paxson. They handed out slips of paper that said, "We are protesting the mishandling of cases of sexual violence on college campuses. We especially hope to draw attention to the way influence and money obstructed justice for the two women who were given date rape drugs at Brown. #MoneyTalksAtBrown." The protest concerned the matter of drugs-or-not-drugs instead. A disciplinary hearing had been dropped for a PKP member initially suspected of drugging the punch when the new lab results came in; the student in question had big-donor family ties to the Brown Corporation (the foundation that manages Brown's endowment and finance).[26]

Meanwhile, the hearing for the man actually accused of sexual misconduct was just concluding. Brown upheld a finding by the Student Conduct Board that the accused and accuser could not agree on whether the sexual contact had been consensual, nor whether the accuser's intoxication level was so obvious that the accused should have known she was incapable of consent. (The parties had differing accounts of how alert

---

[25] Lynn Arditi, "Fraternity criticizes Brown University's actions in alleged 'date-rape' drug case," Providence Journal, February 24, 2015. http://www.providencejournal.com/article/20150223/News/150229705.; "Dear Members of the Brown Community," Phi Kappa Psi Rhode Island, https://www.documentcloud.org/documents/1674358-phi-kappa-psi-ri-alpha-public-statement.html. Both retrieved January 17, 2016. Brown also obtained a third set of lab results that could not confirm GHB's presence in either sample above endogenous threshold levels.

[26] Susannah Howe, "Students protest at women leaders panel," *Brown Daily Herald*, March 6, 2015. http://www.browndailyherald.com/2015/03/06/students-protest-women-leaders-panel/. Retrieved January 17, 2016; Kaitlin Mulhere, "Questions on Money, Influence and Competence," *Inside Higher Ed*, March 16, 2015. https://www.insidehighered.com/news/2015/03/16/brown-u-sexual-assault-investigation-draws-criticism-accused-and-accusers. Retrieved January 17, 2016.

8 Drugs, Drinking, College, and Warding off Blame

and responsive the complainant was.)[27] There was the ominous matter of the complainant's testimony of her patchy memory; it was precisely what tipped the scales toward giving the accused the benefit of the doubt. Certainly, due process protections in any forum demand this; still, the horror realized here, if he did actually assault her, is doubled by fragmented memory undermining her complaint. And at the edges, one cannot help but wonder whether the likely mistaken allegations of drugging did not somehow influence the sexual misconduct finding; if then, the default of alcohol pops back up and subtly disqualifies the victim? Ideally, the question of the accuser's ability to consent should stand alone, particularly in this case where the accused is not suspected of providing either drugs or alcohol to her. Still, did the negative and inconclusive toxicological findings creep in, taking the assault charges with it?

Certainly, national press interest faded in the case not long after. Things remained weird on campus. In April 2015, Emma Sulkowicz, a Columbia University student known for carrying a mattress around campus as part art project and part protest after Columbia failed to remove a student she accused of sexual assault from campus, spoke at Brown. Her remarks were disappointing to the student activists that attended. She argued that often there is no definitive scientific evidence of sexual assault; the only available evidence may be the victim's testimony that she did not consent, which is something the accused may deny. This did not sit well with students still holding onto the GHB scenario in the recent on-campus case. The Editorial Board of the *Brown Daily Herald* insisted that "date-rape drugs such as GHB, when accurately determined to be in someone's system, indicate lack of consent or the lack of the ability to give consent in a sexual encounter." This, of course, excludes the more common scenario of someone taking a drug and either consenting to sex, or then being assaulted, and completely weds the crime to the means of intoxication. The Board called Sulkowicz's cautions about scientific corroboration "troubling for survivors" and insisted, "It is essential that we assure students that sexual assault cases can be objectively investigated

---

[27] Caroline Kelly, "Student found not responsible for sexual assault; Due to complainant's incomplete memory of incident, initial ruling upheld upon appeal," *Brown Daily Herald*, March 6, 2015. http://www.browndailyherald.com/2015/03/06/student-found-not-responsible-sexual-assault/. Retrieved January 17, 2016.

through rape kits and accurate laboratory testing."[28] The fact that very few rape cases, precisely because they center around differential claims of consent, will be able to make use of these methods reveals a very dated, ill-informed understanding of the majority of sexual assaults.

For her part, admittedly, Sulkowicz did drift off into an odd diversion about whether GHB could be part of a role-playing fantasy, which may have been especially off-putting to this audience.

Articles covering the Brown case also cited the reports at Berkeley and Milwaukee, implying a national pattern of fraternity drink spiking.[29] Berkeley, as we know, simply failed to materialize. Milwaukee would not pan out, either. None of the national news sources to report on the Brown case updated their posts on the case; only the Providence-based papers did. And so we are left with another case in which allegations of drugging first pull all the attention away from the alleged assailant (he was barely mentioned again) and then, failing to be scientifically validated, are simply assumed into a key role in sexual assault response anyway.

At the UWM campus, also in the fall of 2014, TKE fraternity president Thomas Kreinbring faced several drug charges resulting from a search of the fraternity house. Police had obtained a warrant on a Tuesday to search the premises after three women and one man attending a party there went to the hospital on the previous Friday with symptoms of acute intoxication. The search warrant was granted, in part, because the police at the time stated that they suspected multiple victims of drink spiking. Some of the partygoers had X marked on their hands, including some of the students who fell sick and were described by witnesses as stumbling around.[30] Kreinbring alone was arrested for drugs he possessed, found by

---

[28] Editorial Page Board, "Editorial: Response to Emma Sulkowicz's talk," *Brown Daily Herald*, April 19, 2015. http://www.browndailyherald.com/2015/04/19/editorial-response-to-emma-sulkowiczs-talk/. Retrieved January 17, 2016.

[29] Camilla Brandfield-Harvey, "Students report spiked drinks at Phi Psi party, alleged sexual assault later in the night also to be investigated by University officials," *Brown Daily Herald*, October 25, 2014. http://www.browndailyherald.com/2014/10/25/students-report-spiked-drinks-phi-psi-party/. Retrieved January 16, 2016.

[30] Jesse Garza and Ashley Luthern, "Police probe whether UWM fraternity members put drugs in party drinks," *Milwaukee Journal-Sentinel*, September 19, 2014. http://www.jsonline.com/news/education/national-fraternity-suspends-uw-milwaukee-tau-kappa-epsilon-chapter-b99355105z1-275806711.html. Retrieved January 17, 2016.

police pursuant to the warrant: methamphetamine, Adderall, and marijuana. Among the charges he faces are intent to distribute (marijuana) and a related charge of "keeping a drug house" (he admitted selling small amounts to other house residents) and illegal possession for the stimulants.[31] By the time of Kreinbring's indictment, neither the police nor the courts believed that a drugging scheme or mass drugging had taken place that night at TKE or anywhere else on or near campus.

The fruits of the search did not turn up any CNS depressant drugs that might explain the distress reported by the students. The first call that the police received that night was to a dormitory, where they administered a field alcohol test of one of the women, showing a BAC level at 0.20, which is quite high and more than two times the legal limit. She was taken to the hospital. They were called back to the dorm and saw a number of other students who had been to the party and appeared to be very intoxicated, many with an X on their hands. Upon arriving at TKE, they found a number of empty containers, 42 underage drinkers (whom they cited), and much vomit. Another woman who attended had a BAC of 0.225 and reported having blacked out earlier. There were rumors of a Facebook accusation about roofies, and some cloudy-looking vodka.[32] It was clearly a mess, but what kind? Ordinary or predatory?

The "X on the hand" theory of targeted drug spiking did not pan out, either, and it appears that campus police knew this fairly quickly, as well.[33] As such, the UWM case has raised concern about drink spiking suspicion being used to improperly obtain a search warrant.[34] Kreinbring's attorney

---

[31] Kreinbring's case, as of March 2016, awaits sentence. In January 2016, Kreinbring pled guilty to the drug charges. See Case Details, *State of Wisconsin v. Thomas L. Kreinbring*, Milwaukee County Circuit Court, Case #2014-CF-4185 at Wisconsin Circuit Court Access: https://wcca.wicourts.gov.

[32] Ashley Luthern and Karen Herzog, "Police probe whether UWM fraternity members put drugs in party drinks," *Milwaukee Journal-Sentinel*, September 18, 2014. http://www.jsonline.com/news/crime/uw-milwaukee-fraternity-probed-over-drugs-slipped-into-party-drinks-b99354529z1-275664681.html. Retrieved January 17, 2016.

[33] Graham Kilmer, "UWM Official Found a Key Allegation into TKE Fraternity Appeared False, Motion Says," *Media Milwaukee* (Department of Journalism Student News, UWM), Retrieved March 20, 2016. http://mediamilwaukee.com/news/tke-fraternity-allegations.

[34] Bruce Vielmetti, "Ex-frat leader argues UWM police botched search warrants in date-rape drug investigation," *Milwaukee Journal-Sentinel*, February 19, 2015. http://www.jsonline.com/blogs/news/292492731.html. Kreinbring's motion to exclude the drug evidence seized can be found at:

filed three court motions to suppress the discovered drug evidence. The first issue was whether campus police had the right to search TKE, which was off campus and under the jurisdiction of the City of Milwaukee police force.[35] The second issue was how police decided that there might have been drugging rather than heavy intoxication due to alcohol consumption. The suspicion of drink spiking was based on hearsay and speculation; the police observed firsthand evidence that alcohol might be a more likely explanation. Worse yet for the prosecution, the emergency room doctor who received the five students for care that night told the police officers that she thought them to be suffering from acute alcohol intoxication rather than drugs. The fact that the police failed to mention the doctor's assessment in the search warrant petition while including the speculation, the defense alleged, constitutes a violation of Kreinbring's Fourth Amendment rights—as it represented the totality of the circumstances dishonestly in order to obtain the search warrant. "UWMPD invented a sinister theory that the fraternity members were mass-drugging guests," the motion argued.[36]

Strangely, only the intoxicated women who had gone back to the dorms were the basis for the drug theory; the women who remained drinking at TKE were *not* suspected as likely drugged persons, and were not treated as such upon the police's arrival. One student from the dorms was tested at the hospital within the 12-hour time frame for drugs and the results were negative; again, this information was made available to police, as with the others brought to the hospital.

Although it appears that the police and courts had dropped the spiked drink theory, as late as August 2015, when Kreinbring was still fighting his charges, *CBS Milwaukee* kept the drugging scenario, which has received national notoriety, alive. "The TKE house first came under scrutiny last fall when it was alleged that members were putting drugs in women's drinks at a massive 'recruiting party'"—ignoring

---

http://defensewisconsin.com/wp-content/uploads/2015/02/Kreinbring-MTS-2-final-version.pdf. Both retrieved January 17, 2016.

[35] In the USA, generally, only *arrests with probable cause* may be made out of jurisdiction, pertaining to crimes within, imminent danger being the only exception. This warrant was served more than 72 hours later.

[36] Kreinbring's Motion, 8. Kreinbring's Motion to Suppress was not ultimately successful.

the information developed in the interim, such as the fact that neither Kreinbring nor TKE was still suspected of providing such drugs, and the *actual lack of a mass drugging*. There were also no associated allegations of sexual assault related to the incident.[37]

Stories involving fraternities drugging the punch seem just too good to not be true, it seems. Much like not wanting to confront the nexus between intoxication and sexual assault on its own terms, not wanting to confront objectionable fraternity behavior on its own terms clearly animates the current frat drug scare. It is not as if American fraternities have not provided enough real material in the last year to warrant scrutiny. Brown, UCB, and UWM serve different student populations, social class wise, but animus toward fraternities seems to tie them together. There is a countrywide sense that freshmen women are being "plied" with drink by predatory men; that may, in fact, be the intent of certain fraternity members. But vaulting over the issue of choice about whether to drink too much or not does not serve anyone well—not female partygoers, and not victims of sexual assault.

The Return of Plying

In pursuing criminal charges in a case of rape, a proven drugging is like the brass ring—prima facie evidence of intent, with no possible defense of consensuality. There is nonetheless a reason why victim and health advocates on campuses are more concerned with reinforcing the counsel that "alcohol is the biggest date rape drug," which does seem to admit a desire to reorient the conversation back to a more ubiquitous threat.

Plying is a dainty and old-fashioned concept, and its revival seems to have been borne of two strands. The first is the peculiar and fraught incarnation of the long-overdue concerns about campus rape. On the one hand, student spokespersons have made it clear that they do not want their drinking habits questioned. But there are also worried parents out there who seem to have a difficult time seeing excess alcohol as voluntary.

---

[37] Christie Green, "Former President of a UWM fraternity fights date rape drug allegations," *CBS News 58 Milwaukee*, August 27, 2015. http://www.cbs58.com/story/29895314/former-president-of-a-uwm-fraternity-fights-date-rape-drug-allegations/. Retrieved January 17, 2016.

A lack of agency, then, is assumed about young women being offered alcohol in social settings. But there is a second strand as well, and that is the framing quality of the problem that the date rape drugs scare has brought to the table. Intoxicants in this scenario are administered, not taken. The phrase "Alcohol is the number-one date rape drug" is an aphorism that attempts to be all things to all people. It rightly points to the relative rarity of surreptitious drugging in sexual assault situations, but on the other hand, it reformulates alcohol as a foreign substance introduced into an otherwise neutral and symmetrical situation.

But for now we consider "just" alcohol. Certainly, a person should be able to regret drinking too much but still not blame herself, or accept blame from others, if she is sexually assaulted? The fact that a minority of male respondents to surveys express interest in using alcohol on women to enhance the likelihood of sexual compliance again does not tell us much about either surreptitious-dosing or sexual assault. And "tried to get you drunk" or "gave you alcohol" at least conventionally does not qualify, either. That is not to say such situational information regarding a sexual assault is not interesting, but qualifying it—and quantifying it—as "drug-facilitated" stretches the category overmuch and paints the recipient of this pressure to drink as completely devoid of agency. While we can reasonably assume that she had no desire to be assaulted, we actually do not know how she felt about drinking or getting high, and how intoxicated she intended to be. This is another example of failing to distinguish between coercion in drug and alcohol use, on the one hand, and the inherent violence and exploitation of sexual assault under *any* circumstance, on the other.

Given that some male respondents will tend to say they use alcohol (presumably giving a woman alcohol) to score, the temptation is to see drink plying as a strategy for sexual aggression. But again, here, in a number of studies, we find some imprecision: sexual acquiescence and rape are often conflated in these same studies. For instance, in Carr and Van Deusen's study (2004), they report:

> Alcohol-related sexual coercion was reported, with 12% men using alcohol to obtain sex, and 15% men being sexually forceful or aggressive when drinking. (Table I) Thirty-five percent of the sample said their friends approve of getting a woman drunk to have sex with her, and 20%

reported having friends who have gotten a woman drunk or high to have sex with her.

The 15% seems to be considerably more relevant than the 12% here, if you are interested in sexual assault. "Obtaining sex" is of course not the same as rape, even if it uncovers an interesting-on-its-own attitude of sex as conquest. Getting "a woman drunk or high" even strategically as a means to have sex is not either, unless of course her intoxication is involuntary or affects her ability to consent. This information in no way sheds light on what the women in question intended. Certainly, this kind of manipulative or exploitative outcome is included in these questions, but so are a lot of other ordinary sexual encounters.

Plying also erroneously assumes that we who drink alcohol always "know our limits" accurately and that we react to alcohol at all times in a uniform way. This is, of course, not even true of experienced light or moderate drinkers, let alone young people learning to self-manage their alcohol consumption. *New York Times* columnist Nicholas Kristof describes research by David Lisak, who studies rapists, in a column improbably titled, "When the Rapist Doesn't See It as Rape." One of Lisak's interviewees was a young man named Frank who bragged that he and his friends encourage freshmen girls to get chugging, noting that it was easy because their nervousness made them drink more than they otherwise might have. Kristof introduces the violence that follows in one case by saying that Frank "plied" a young woman with "alcohol-spiked punch" and "led her to bed." But what follows, according to this assailant's own description, is hardly the stuff of misunderstanding. He describes holding and pushing her down, pulling her clothes off, ignoring her verbal wishes to slow down, and her incapacitation as so obvious that he knows she cannot effectively get away from him. Despite the obvious use of force, Kristof uses this event to launch his claim that most rapists "proffer a plastic cup of booze" rather than brandishing a gun.

It is clear to me—and disturbing—that Kristof regards alcohol as a weapon, not something that is voluntarily consumed. Somehow, Frank's victim cannot really be a true victim in Kristof's eyes unless she was somehow bamboozled into drinking. Kristof describes Frank's means of assaulting the victim, only to ignore it. I actually doubt he really thinks this, but the amount of attention he gives to the "ambiguity" of drunk-and-in-bed situations suggests that there is something about confusion surrounding consent here that needs preservation in a world of great big punchbowls. Honestly, where is the ambiguity in this scenario? Frank is a rapist. He does not "use alcohol" as a weapon—he assaults women who drink.

At some point, we have to assume that ultimately the best person to decide when, where, and how much to drink is the person themselves, and that would include female freshmen, underage drinking laws notwithstanding. "Plying" someone with alcohol implies that they cannot say no to it, nor are they in charge of how much alcohol they should consume. Should someone else decide this besides the drinker herself? The return of the dainty "plying" concept, however, is consistent with a new cycle of seeing alcohol consumption as unfairly mandatory and coercive, simply because there is heavy peer pressure to engage in it.

In 2014, legislators in Maryland sought to ban grain alcohol (150 proof and above) as a means to curb the adverse effects of heavy and binge drinking, particularly among young people. The date rape drug concept managed to wedge its way in. "Sen. Karen S. Montgomery (D-Montgomery), in a scolding tone, said the time for joking about excess drinking was over. 'This is a date rape drug,' Montgomery said. 'This is a take-somebody's-clothes-off-and-take-pictures-of-them. This is a dangerous alcohol.... This is the kind of alcohol that leads to that sort of thing.'"[38]

Drink Spiking and "Real Rape"

Victim blamers seem to use drink spiking to demarcate a new kind of "real rape" from "date rape" in Estrich's formulation. It is perhaps expected from those quarters, but it is disheartening to see it among campus activists. It is counterproductive from a feminist standpoint, or from any standpoint which defends the right of persons to their sexual autonomy as against coercion or exploitation, to insist on the weapons metaphor

---

[38] Fredrick Kunkle, "Maryland Senate backs ban on sale of grain alcohol in bid to curb binge drinking," *Washington Post*, February 5, 2014. https://www.washingtonpost.com/local/md-politics/maryland-senate-backs-ban-on-sale-of-grain-alcohol-to-curb-binge-drinking/2014/02/05/717f72aa-8e88-11e3-b46a-5a3d0d2130da_story.html.

in understanding the intersection between intoxication and rape, if only because the vast majority of victims will not locate themselves in this formulation.

People who become victims of sexual assault often are drinkers. Sometimes, they use drugs. Sexual assailants look for such opportunities, and they may facilitate them. But only rarely do they secretly cause people to ingest drugs or alcohol. To expect a person who has been assaulted while drunk or high to take on the additional burden of pretending they were "plied" with drugs or alcohol as the only route to the legitimacy of their experience of violence is doubly burdensome. It denies the larger reality of drug and alcohol use across the world as a route to pleasure-seeking and sociability. It favors only the sober victim, the old-school innocent victim against whom all the rest are measured.

Some of the intensity of focus on drink spiking on college campuses might actually be attributed to what criminologists call the "safety paradox." The idea behind a safety paradox is that both historically and from place to place, we can often see excess fear in the safer times and places. Expectations for safety are higher in such places—that is a good thing, usually. Colleges are among the safer places for young adults to be (including women), but they are not completely safe. Campus sexual assault rates are not low enough to see the college years as a refuge. But they are lower, apparently, than for noncollege women.[39] This recent reminder from a Department of Justice report was met with disbelief by some campus antirape activists. It is regrettable that at the current time, the issue of rape in the media is heavily focused just on campus rape, and that much of the detailed research comes from college data.

Elaboration of the "Smart Girl" Meme in Drugging Talk

Perhaps, the focus on campus drink spiking is linked to the *smart girl* meme. I think it is fair to say that the *smart girl* has replaced the *proper girl* as the aspired-to norm among women socializing. This came up in the

---

[39] Sinozich and Langton, 2014.

Marsalis case, and it is also characteristic of drugging talk in general: Alcohol is no match for the Smart Girl—of course, she knows how to handle her drink or fend off an aggressive male singlehandedly; no admittance of ordinary vulnerability. But drink spiking is her downfall; the one thing that ruins her superpowers. Popular culture helps reinforce this link between drink spiking, smart girls, and sexual assault. No better illustration of this tendency can be found than on the acclaimed TV series *Veronica Mars*, featuring a troubled teen sleuth.[40] The series affixes a drink spiking rape as its origin story. In the pilot episode of September 2004, Veronica, the high school–aged protagonist is "roofied" at a party that she was reluctant to go to in the first place.

A later episode, "M.A.D.," reveals that the drink was actually meant for another girl, Madison, and that that it was spiked with GHB, not Rohypnol. Veronica is trying to help another girl who was drink-spiked and videotaped at a party. GHB fits very well into this series, where much is unexplained or misexplained, the facts are often contested, and memory and meaning are often rewritten over time.

In the initial drink spiking scene, Veronica (in a flashback voiceover) says that she does not remember how the drink got into her hands in the first place. She drinks it, and fading into unconsciousness, she lies down on a pool chaise. Later, she awakes in a bedroom and it is obvious that she has been raped. Although her dad is a private detective, she does not tell him what happened, though she does go to his rival, the standing sheriff, to report it, and he does not believe her. So far, we observe only that all-too-common callousness and injustice served up to rape victims, which in this case may have the more immediate cause of the sheriff not liking her father.

In a later episode, "A Trip to the Dentist," Veronica tries to piece together what happened to her that night. Up until now, she has assumed she was unconscious. Reconnecting with old friends and acquaintances that were there that night, she finds out that she was seen flirting and making out with some other party attendees, and later having sex with a former boyfriend. It seems clear that a number of witnesses did not know she had been drugged, and assumed that her encounters were desired.

---

[40] "Veronica Mars," Television series. UPN network, 2004–2006, CW network 2006–2007.

8 Drugs, Drinking, College, and Warding off Blame

There is also some intimation that the former boyfriend, Duncan, had also been drugged—not just that time, but on other occasions by people in this same group of peers. Critics noted this scripted diffusion or diminishment of responsibility for Veronica's rape; which seemed to imply that Duncan and Veronica accidently had sex, as opposed to Duncan (and possibly others) raping her.

This same subsequent episode, "A Trip to the Dentist," has also been criticized for its depiction of rape and rape victims. It is notable that Veronica thinks she would not (could not?) have been raped were it not for the fact that one character had purchased some GHB and passed it around. It is as if there were in fact no other means by which our intrepid protagonist (smart, plucky, resourceful) could have been attacked at a party. Critics seemed to miss this element of the distortion, taking the GHB depiction at face value.

But on the edges, people did see other troubling things about it. Though it is troubling enough for the narrative to play with the "confusion" separating intoxicated coupling with rape, it is also strange that GHB in the bodies of both Duncan and Veronica transform a psychologically searing, violent event into one that was…not quite as bad? Simply a bit of an aphrodisiac for them both? At least that was how Veronica saw it. Of course, it is not at all uncommon for rape victims to rewrite the trauma they have experienced to lessen its toll; the trouble many viewers and critics had was that the script itself seems to collaborate in this revision. Almost seeming to know this, or perhaps responding to criticism, the second season features an episode, "Not Pictured," in which Veronica now learns that in fact another character assaulted her that night, one that turned out to be an all-around violent and scheming sociopath.

Sarah Whitney's analysis of the role rape plays in the series takes note of the various ways in which responsibility for Veronica's rape shifts from a morally accountable, specific actor to a distributed indictment of her jaded and privileged classmates at Neptune High.[41] GHB as the facilitator partially enables this displacement, and corresponds with what

---

[41] Sarah Whitney, "No Longer that Girl: Rape Narrative and Meaning in Veronica Mars," in Rhonda Wilcox and Sue Turnbull, eds., *Investigating Veronica Mars: Essays on the Teen Detective Series*, (Jefferson, NC: McFarland & Company), 2010.

sociologist Sarah E.H. Moore has called the "any man" as villain in drink spiking scenarios, contrasting with specific typifications of other types of rape lore.

The first two seasons of the show take place in high school, and the writers did seem to understand that young people mainly sought out GHB for recreational use. The third season takes place in college—where drink spiking plays a bizarrely different role on shaping a world of fear and violence for young women. This time, the predatory drugging rapist is a serial offender stalking campus, mysterious in identity until the end of the season—and not among the obvious suspects. Furthermore, his crimes manage to spawn a fake rape crisis launched by scheming and angry antirape activists, aimed at politicizing the boorish behavior of the campus fraternities. Again, nothing is what it appears.

If young women are overestimating the likelihood of being drink-spiked when in fact the symptoms they experience during a night out are much more likely to be the result of too much alcohol, does this mean that they are making "excuses" for themselves? Only if you believe that "excuses" for women enjoying a night out are required at all. Would this misestimation mean that rapes that occur during a woman's incapacitation as the result of drinking are any less violent or criminal than ones that occur when sober, or when involuntary drugged? In no way from the viewpoint of law or morality or ethics would this be the case—unless you somehow believe that rape is a kind of seduction gone bad, and that victims are at least partially to blame for their own plight to begin with.

Conversely, is questioning the emphasis on drink spiking, in light of scientific evidence that suggests its prevalence is low, a form of victim blaming and antifeminism? Skill in drugging stems from social trust in a robust party atmosphere. Power in risk-taking is asymmetrical in any violent crime: victims engage in behavior that ranges from more or less normal, basically functional levels of social trust ("I ordered a drink") to somewhat foolhardy by their own standards ("he seemed nice, but I was alone with him before I knew what was happening"), in order to be sociable. Offenders engage in elevated levels of risk-taking in order to engage in predatory and amoral behavior, exploiting the social trust of victims.

Those who consider themselves, and their daughters, too "smart" to be vulnerable in more ordinary ways will have to recognize that social trust in many convivial settings can only be avoided at extremely high personal and collective cost, and is especially unrealistic for young people. Heightened levels of risk-taking during adolescence and young adulthood may also be developmentally positive in most situations. If people who believe they are defending victims against blame insist that victims were engaged in no real risk-taking, they are not only ignoring the circumstances in a large percentage of cases, but also backhandedly endorsing and even undergirding the notion that only those who act in accordance within narrow bands of prudent behavior deserve our empathy and support. It also paints violent offenders (such as rapists) as people who seek out difficult targets rather than ones who are, or who are perceived to be, vulnerable. Smart girls are vulnerable, too, not because they are smart, but because they are human.

9

Conclusion

Drugging is a mighty social force beyond its incidence. It curbs our conviviality even if we are ambivalent in our belief about its potential to reach us personally. Who does not watch their drink? Amanda Hess, like me, also hoping to eventually see the defeat of "the date rape drugs industrial complex," watches her drink too.[1] Carries it around. Asks people to babysit it. Drink spiking manages to shape our antidrug politics and consistently manages to reshape our understanding of alcohol consumption. Partiers want to hold it harmless, knowing from a billion brochures that they should not. Scolds, in an attempt to not offend, are once again claiming that evildoers are *plying* us with drink.

Drink spiking symbolizes both our hopes and fears about new pharma technology; it universally provokes our fear of high-tech zombification at the hands of strangers. Or perhaps at the hands of people we know. It helps us evade contentious conversations about alcohol, coercion, drugs, and sexual violence. I hope this varied history I have presented has made it clear that this confusion has always been the case, ever since the rise of synthetic anesthesia. The problem has rarely been easily separable from

---

[1] Hess, 2009.

alcohol, not for sailors, recovering alcoholics, tavern patrons, night clubbers, or college students.

But noninstrumental spiking continues to be ignored; given past episodes of tampering, adulteration, pranking, and "skuldruggery," this is surprising. The majority of reports of "feeling drugged" are not accompanied by claims of sexual assault or robbery. Thus, even if all such reports were, in fact, drugging, we do not always know what motivation exists. There have been plenty of male victims historically and today, but the issue tends not to be framed that way. In this way, the current drink spiking concern really can be thought of as two public health threats: one, the predatory, means-to-an end for robbery or rape that sometimes occurs, and also the apparent just-because of public venue spiking. There is no reason to think that this form of tampering is limited to Australia—but elsewhere no one has really conceptualized it this way.

I hope that I have done more in this book beyond simply saying, *everything you know about date rape drugs is wrong*. I do think the rich history belies the construct, and the construct has a corrosive effect on our understanding of both drugs—in both their healing and their dangers—and sexual violence. I also suspect that the timing and shape of the current scare has to do with excessive pressure to get everything right; to reduce a broad and diffuse problem to one amenable to advice lists and little test strips.

Sporadically Successful Moral Panic, Cautionary Tale, or Drug Scare?

So far, throughout this history, I have purposely used the terms *drug scare* or *drugging fear* rather than the sociological term *moral panic* because I am genuinely uncertain whether the fear of predatory drugging really is one, at least in full. Moral panic is a match for the situation in some ways. Consider Stanley Cohen's original formulation:

> Societies appear to be subject, every now and then, to periods of moral panic. A condition, episode, person or group of persons emerges to become defined as a threat to societal values and interests; its nature is presented in

a stylised and stereotypical fashion by the mass media; the moral barricades are manned by editors, bishops, politicians and other right-thinking people; socially accredited experts pronounce their diagnoses and solutions; ways of coping are evolved or (more often) resorted to; the condition then disappears, submerges or deteriorates and becomes more visible.[2]

First, it is important to notice that despite our common association of moral panic with disproportionality and exaggeration, Cohen's definition does not require this, though his original example of the outsize reaction to unruly mobs of Mods and Rockers at seaside resorts in the early 1960s fits the bill, and led us to assume that this gap between scope and scare is a necessary feature.

It might be possible for a moral panic to emerge simply as a misspecification of a problem. A problem might be real and significant, yet dominant opinion-shaping forces attribute it to improbable prior causes, or predict from it ripple effects which are unlikely. Consider, for instance, the very real problem of crimpers, who did systematically drug and abduct men for physical labor in the 1800s. It certainly would be possible for there to be panic and a genuine problem at the same time. Of course, it was not entirely clear that sailors blamed the drugs so much as the industry itself; it was legislators who wrote laws about "stupefying substances" which served as models for other felony law formulations of this sort.

The first issue is whether "panic" is really the right term for the enactment of predatory drugging fears. While histrionic reactions to this threat have developed at times, particularly with the onset of synthetic drugs, I am not sure the problem was so much that it has been understood as a threat to social values and interests, so much as a rich symbol for those who already thought society had morally degraded. Perhaps one version of a threat to social values, as we shall see, is among those who like to frequent parties and nightclubs today; the roofied drink bears the burden of spoiler, as alcohol is held harmless. In an age of pharma-ubiquity, too, the scare might also represent a submerged discomfort of how readily we have come to reach for

---

[2] Stanley Cohen, *Folk Devils and Moral Panics: the Creation of Mods and Rockers*, (New York: Routledge), 2011 [1972].

medicine. But as a general societal threat, it seems limited. And using these criteria, it is harder to explain earlier spiking scares: knockout drops, the Mickey Finn, chloroform scoundrels, and LSD in your drink.

Part of the problem has already been addressed by Sarah E.H. Moore, and I think correctly: drink spiking and date rape drugs often lack a folk devil. The perpetrators in these stories are often presented as shadowy or even as unknowable. Even where the press covered serial offenders like Andrew Luster or John Xydias, the link they made to the *general* problem of predatory drugs was weak. By and large, in terms of typification, the press has preferred the shadowy Lurking Spiker at Any Bar to the skilled serial drugger pulling women into his lair; relying on the tacit, unspoken impression that the practice is so common in drinking situations that it need not even be investigated—just worked into peer conversations about the perils of partying in the contemporary age. The devil today, though, is so much in the details of the perils of partying that he is often forgotten altogether. Moore suggests that the date rape drugs scare operates more like a "cautionary tale," as do Weiss and Colyer, demanding eternal, personal vigilance.[3]

One commonality that fits with moral panic is the manning of moral barricades. There is a little paternalism here, or a disjointedness between the enthusiasm of the press, legislators, and campus activists and the often tepid response of young people themselves to the threat, particularly in the USA. In other words, the American press was happy to organize a panic, and try again year after year, with little interest. That said, there were real consequences. Real-world legislation was affected as a result, though it is not clear that it has aided prosecution of spikers so much as made legislators look up with the times and suitably outraged at the "new" problem. The scare, however, as we saw in the wrangling over Proposition 47 in California and in the Kreinbring case in Milwaukee, may be evolving to leverage the threat of spiking in the ordinary business of drug busts. It appears that in the UK, the fear that is synergistic with press advocacy has made heavier inroads into consciousness, but it is not at all clear that self-protective behaviors have been adopted as a result.

---

[3] Sarah E.H. Moore, "Cautionary Tales: Drug-Facilitated Sexual Assault in the British Media," *Crime, Media, Culture*, vol. 5, no. 3, 2009; Weiss and Colyer, 2010.

As for Cohen's "socially accredited experts," they tend as a whole to be debunkers or gentle redirectors, so that the sector of authoritative influence is either missing or actively contested. This sector includes public health and victim advocates, social scientists, toxicologists, and law enforcement agencies. Thus, where moral entrepreneurialism on the subject emerges, it tends to be from individuals who believe they have been, or actually have been, drugged; these voices tend to emerge as first-person narratives. Organized activism on the subject tends to be marginal and lack expert endorsement.

Weiss and Colyer suggest that by and large the press also prefers the *protected narrative* over the more likely drugging scenario among social companions and in private settings, and this, I think makes the panic element somewhat limited in scope to the nightclub or party. Evidence of coping is thin: repeatedly, people have tried to market any manner of coasters, test strip, lids, and so forth in service of detecting the spiked drink without much public interest beyond "gee whiz, clever!" plaudits from the media. In my own research, most students felt they were cautious enough, and those that did engage in specific behavior change as a result of "the threat of date rape drugs" (37%, $n = 100$) were likely either to physically watch their drinks ($n = 62$) or to restrict their social environments and interactions to trusted ones ($n = 29$).[4] Oona Brooks' interviews with British women about their safety in public nightspots suggest that they both embrace safety advice ("watch your drink!") and reject it as too impractical, particularly as the night progresses.[5] Such solutions, whether individualized or shared among women going out, are also resented as burdensome and unfair to women. Coping and solutions, then, seem to be weakly adopted, if at all, as further evidence that the moral panic rubric is not a great fit here.

Auburn University (AU) in Alabama in 2015 had an employee plead guilty to manufacturing and dealing in GHB (actually a common precursor chemical that converts to GHB). He had been caught when he, according to a local media source, "sold an undercover agent 20 ounces

---

[4] Pamela Donovan, "The Role of Uncertainty in Knowledge of Suspected Drink Spiking Incidents," 2008.
[5] Oona Brooks, "'Guys! Stop Doing It!': Young Women's Adoption and Rejection of Safety Advice when Socializing in Bars, Pubs and Clubs," *British Journal of Criminology* 51, 2011, 635–651.

of a liquid substance used to incapacitate women."[6] Another article connected to the arrest notes ominously that back in 2013, six "incidents" involving reports of GHB spiking emerged.[7] Yet AU security noted that it had not investigated any GHB drugging reports, and an October 2013 report by the local ABC affiliate, WTVM-TV, said that while AU security had cautioned students, it had no active investigations of such cases, and the news report did not mention any others in the area.[8] The suspect, Stephen Howard, did brag unwittingly to an undercover agent recording the transaction that he used it on "3 or 4 girls," but there were no associated sexual assault allegations.[9] Howard was sentenced to eight and a half years in prison.[10]

The AU security press release and local media coverage accompanying the wholesaler's arrest in 2015 ran through the litany of things you can do to avoid having your drink spiked. At no time does the article address any potential health problems or other adverse effects associated with voluntary use—certainly more widely applicable public health knowledge, particularly in a university environment. The AU students interviewed for the article seemed nonplussed, feeling that they were cautious enough already.[11] Once again, official discomfort with discussions of voluntary intoxicant use, including GHB, on the one hand, and squeamishness about sexual assault involving intoxicated victims, on the other, forcefully divert the media back into the drink spiking scenario, and deprives the

---

[6] Erin Edgemon, "Auburn University lab tech charged with selling date rape drug," *AL.com*, May 26, 2015. http://www.al.com/news/montgomery/index.ssf/2015/05/auburn_university_lab_tech_cha.html. Retrieved November 2, 2015.

[7] Amber Sutton, "After date rape drug arrest, Auburn students cautious, not scared," *AL.com*, May 28, 2015. http://www.al.com/news/montgomery/index.ssf/2015/05/auburn_students_reaction.html. Retrieved November 2, 2015.

[8] Courtney Smith, "AU safety experts urge community to watch out for date rape drugs," *9 ABC TV*, WTVM.com. October 28, 2013. http://www.wtvm.com/story/23810014/au-safety-experts-urge-community-to-watch-out-for-date-rape-drugs. Retrieved November 2, 2015.

[9] Erin Edgemon, "Former Auburn University lab tech pleads guilty to selling date rape drug," *AL.com*, October 28, 2015. Retrieved November 2, 2015. http://www.al.com/news/montgomery/index.ssf/2015/10/former_auburn_university_lab_t.html.

[10] Maria McIlwain, "Stephen Howard sentenced to 8 years in prison," *Auburn Plainsman*, February 24, 2016, http://www.theplainsman.com/article/2016/02/stephen-howard-sentenced-to-eight-years-in-prison. Retrieved March 20, 2016.

[11] Sutton, 2015.

audience about responsible information about GHB and other drugs, which are most often voluntarily consumed.

The roofie threat may be felt as a salient threat to a select group, and experienced as tacit fear without precaution for the rest. In some sense, young people may feel that the roofie problem, to the extent it concerns them, is par for the course if you're going out drinking. Because of the zero-tolerance attitude of the older generation now in university and public health leadership positions, and because young women have increased their rate of binge drinking more rapidly than young men, binge drinking has become a kind of rebellion and a badge of freedom. Drink spiking may actually work better as an *explanation* or *account* after the fact than an avoidant fear, whether one's estimate of risk is right-sized, low, or high.

At the same time, it is time to face pharma-ubiquity and its implications. Several generations now of antidrug campaigning have apparently also manifested themselves in ignorance about how most people use the Big Three. We forget the effects of pharmaceutical psychoactive drugs because they are prescribed. Halo effects were similarly insisted upon by the medical men in the dawn of the anesthesia era, and this "problem, what problem?" attitude reemerged with every new and better class of psychotropics. It's true that such drugs are often safer than their predecessors, but that itself begs the question of our ability, collectively, to enjoy their benefits while managing their risks effectively. Current toxicological studies reinforce two things: it is hard to separate alcohol from drug effects, and hard to separate drugs we intended to take from those we didn't. One of the ironic benefits of the press always "discovering" new "date rape drugs" is that perhaps at some point we will realize the ongoing, omnipresence of a potential threat has always been there, and the moniker may lose its special and distorting effect.

As for Moore's missing folk devils: what if drawing attention away from an accountable perpetrator of assault is by design? It is fairly convincing to me that, as Moore suggests, we still have yet to fully absorb the message of the embeddedness of sexual assault that came with the original formulation of "date rape" in the 1980s: "What it more obviously signals is a refusal or inability, at the level of the culture, to cede to the idea that rape can be an extension of normal heterosexual relations." We still long for the threat to be the monster in the alley, or the aberrant encounter.

Part of the reason we seek intoxicants in the first place in social settings is to feel more connected to those around us, not less. Drugs we did not want play the role of spoiler.

Ironically, it is specific cases of suspected drugging in which this is most visible, even more so than in conjecture about it. The most egregious example was found in the Brown University case, where by the spring of 2015, the sexual assailant was an afterthought. But there have been subtler examples, like the evaporating scares in the early 2000s in Australia, or the two rapes treated as an afterthought in the case of the Nickel Rose pub in Marin, California. We just do not like the old meaning of date rape: it makes us confront sexual assault as an outcome of normal social trust and conviviality, and accept that our work to reduce or end it must start from this understanding.

The Gendered Drinking Double Standard: A Clarification about Its Historical Dynamics

There has been a common double standard with regard to gender and drink, manifesting itself in a series of complicated ways in the industrialized Western world. It should be clarified that these particular patriarchal views tend not to be absolutist. The loosening of inhibition associated with mild-to-moderate intoxication, as well as the incapacitation associated with heavy drinking, is viewed differently in men and women. But the normative underlying excuse-making for rape under such circumstances is not actually "anything goes with a drunk girl—she deserves it," but more typically, a rapacious view of *male* sexuality without effective resistance. It reflects a dim view of men and drink. Ladies, know the lads are "natural" demons when they drink and so keep your head about you.

In decades past, this is what a respectable woman did. In the current era, this is what a "responsible" woman does. It is not my intent to dismiss the role of alcohol in enhancing the risk of rape, as some campus activists seem to, but rather to endorse the continued frustration that young women feel in being responsible not only for themselves but for others.

It is fundamentally different to breach the boundary of the responsible than the respectable. Mores have definitely changed regarding respectability, but less so responsibility, and the latter is more inchoate and cannot always be derived by simply adopting a set of limits and practices, however constrictive, as respectability was. The work done to renovate victims in the early cases was naturally all about family propriety and supervision of young women. The fact that victims like Mabel Scofield, Jennie Bosschieter, and Mamie Paige did not conform to these middle-class norms, nor did their families, created no barrier to sympathy: the papers just revised the stories as needed. It is fairly noticeable that in the early stories, more attention was given to the assailants' opportunism, callousness, and entitlement.

Happily, modern victims are not so worried about a script of propriety. Instead, in the burgeoning genre of the first-person narrative, and in talking to a variety of different researchers and medical first-responders, they *insist* they did not drink enough to cause symptoms. In a handful of cases, they may be right. The new script centers around their reasserting their mastery; their individualized self-control and situational self-definition as competent partiers—smart girls.

Between Responsibilism and Drunktopia

Responsibility, as opposed to conformity, must be to some extent self-authored. Think again about how different Hines-Davenport's mid-twentieth-century *being yourself* is from *being able* and *being good*. Self-authorship is demanded; all responsibilities are yours, even over things which you could not possibly control. We hear this like a mantra. And the things for which we are now *individually* responsible are increasing and formidable.

Drugging as an explanation for a night gone wrong (not just sexual assault, but acute health risks, car accidents, physical assaults, or blackouts) has always acted as a bit of a problem solver. It is the ultimate pharma technology of neutralization. A predator neutralizes resistance from a victim (for rape or robbery); a victim neutralizes self-blame and wards off victim blame from others. Emphasis on drugging makes intoxication more involuntary than it tends to be, and often actively denies the role of excess alcohol in producing vulnerability and dulling judgment about someone who is potentially dangerous. Make no mistake: this is a form of victim blame, much more so than acknowledging the enhanced vulnerability of intoxicated victims ever could be.

The threat may be used as a spoiler which can be *universally* be understood as unfair—that is, not playing fair—while preserving the propriety of the excess. Who could see that coming? Is it the case that binge drinking does not seem, on its own, an appropriate context to explain the victim's vulnerability? Have young women essentially rejected the message about sobriety as an enhancement to personal safety, or worse yet, do they blame themselves and each other if they are "merely" drunk when assaulted?

Of course, we could imagine a scenario in which the risks of excess drink were understood, accepted, and undertaken anyway. However, there are more leisure and pleasure politics here than just that of rape representation. My own study, at least provisionally, suggests a sort of defense of alcohol inebriation without enhanced vulnerability. There seems to be a partial, but strident rejection of the idea that alcohol alone might make someone vulnerable to assault. It is utopian, in a way, and I do not mean that pejoratively.

The exquisite tension between having possession of your senses and choosing to let them go characterizes perhaps an innate characteristic of, if not individuals, then cultures as a whole. To the extent that sexual assault rates have not really changed, and by some measures even declined, despite increased binge drinking (an important and interesting caveat), you have to turn to the problem of expectations. Maybe it is simply that girls expect more from boys now, and in turn, women expect more from men. If so, a problem might seem like a "crisis" but it is rather just the cusp of a positive social and cultural step forward.

Drunktopia: An Amazing Thought

I borrowed the term "drunktopia" from Gabrielle Moss, who wrote about the new stars of girl power party-pop of the 2000s.[12] She notes that among other things, the appeal of the genre works by "conjuring the fantasy of

---

[12] Gabrielle Moss, "Party out of Bounds," *Bitch Magazine*, Summer 2011, 43–47.

a nonjudgmental safe space where its listeners are free to party however they choose, and by engaging with, and subsequently deflating, the idea of the 'drunk girl.'" Later in Moss' essay, she explores what it means to demand this "dance floor drunktopia" in a world that still demands that women be responsible, and therefore to blame, for anything that goes wrong. Sweeping freedoms, amidst faltering social trust.

The Sacramento State University *Hornet* student paper, in September 2013, ran a column about the invention and marketing of yet another drink spiking prevention product, the DrinkSavvy cup, which gained widespread media coverage that fall[13]:

> Imagine feeling safer at every bar you walk into, knowing some pervert can't slip you an undetected date rape drug.
>
> Soon a seemingly simple plastic cup and straw design will revolutionize the bar scene and hopefully help reduce the number of sexual assaults involving alcohol. The Center for Women and Families' statistics show 90 percent of rapes on college campuses involve alcohol.
>
> Knowing one day I will go out to a bar with some friends and not have to spend my entire night with my eyes glued to the rim of my glass is an amazing thought.

Forget for a moment the confusion about the particular kind of magical powers attributed to the cup, and notice how much *watching your drink* feels like the only thing holding you back from friendship and a better, safer bar scene. Our author, you should know, is a smart girl: "I know how to be careful—I was raised by the king of protective dads. This doesn't change the fact that I'm not perfect and some people are just bigger, stronger and smarter." Ah, the spoiler. "Dropping date-rape drugs into drinks is not an act targeted at a specific group of people, anyone can be susceptible to this where no one can really tell when an odorless, colorless and tasteless drug is dissolved into their drink." The cup: it could solve the problem. It is framed as all pretty random—who could see it coming?

---

[13] Natalie Gray, "New cup and straw design detects invisible date-rape drugs in drinks," *State Hornet* (Sacramento, CA), September 17, 2013. http://www.statehornet.com/opinion/new-cup-and-straw-design-detects-invisible-date-rape-drugs/article_50479b1a-1fea-11e3-88a8-0019bb30f31a.html. Retrieved January 18, 2016.

And then, the other shoe drops, heavily. The remainder of the article, for want of a better expression, sobers up greatly. Quoting a local violence and sexual assault advocate for Student Health and Counseling Services, the author is brought back to reality: "'We have to remember that most sexual assaults are facilitated by alcohol alone, and this product won't do anything to help with that.'" The advocate also talks about the large number of drugs that could be used (including ecstasy!) to drug a drink, not just the ones covered by the cup technology, and the fact that most people are assaulted by someone they know.

Taking this in, the author suddenly goes to a very dark place: "Going to a party and saying you feel safe because you 'know everyone there' is about as foolproof as a cement lifejacket." Ouch. I genuinely felt sad when I found this column in the course of gathering articles about spiking. The author walked in holding fast to the promise of drunktopia (or at least, buzzed-topia), and it all went so bad with just the slightest correction. Sort of the opposite of an amazing thought. A terrified, isolated, almost paranoid thought. That is the bleak world that the younger partier associates with the reality that social trust plus alcohol or drugs can sometimes equal a breach of safety. A real revelation to her? Probably not—remember, she knew how to be careful. I simply have not seen a clearer distillation of the emotional costs of facing the big risks, which are the ordinary ones.

Where Drunktopia Meets Responsibilism: Sober-Minded, if Not Sober

While victim blaming of intoxicated crime victims is not unique to rape, it is more intense in the case of rape, and remains tied to an intractable gendered double standard. Stalled progress on perpetrator accountability exacerbates the problem. Women gained enormous advances in personal freedom as the result of second-wave feminism (along with some shifts in the economy and technology). But overlapping global changes by the 1980s began to unravel a kind of postwar consensus, and these big changes are often gathered under the term "neoliberalism." This fundamentally changed, some scholars argue, how individuals come to parse out their own autonomous responsibilities versus the various communities and collectivities of which they are a part.

Individuals are expected to bear their own risks more so than before, and so young women have been coming up in a world that granted them freedom but offered little solidarity, and it remains a dangerous one for women regardless of changed, less judgmental attitudes toward gender roles, casual sex, drinking, and even drugs. Criminologists and sociologists have referred to this nexus as the era of ascendant "prudentialism" or "responsibilism."[14]

Pat O'Malley, in a 1992 article, launched this discussion on the responsibilism thesis, making mention of the preexisting tendency to make women feel responsible for preventing the violence against them, and suggesting, I think correctly, that in Western societies, this expectation is becoming generalized, owing to structural economic changes and the political responses to it. Elizabeth Stanko and others further elaborated the argument in a gender-conscious way; there is a fetishization of "personal responsibility" in discussions of intoxication and rape that was only possible with the decline of traditional patriarchy. There is no longer any faith in *propriety* of female behavior being an adequate protective force, nor chivalry. It is reasonable to assume that, to some extent, the double standard has narrowed and rape victims, while still facing a host of reputational problems, are no longer expected to prove impeccable conventional behavior. Rather, it seems that "personal responsibility" is the new propriety. We have the complication of postchivalrous, postpatriarchal protection environments, all to the good—and yet no safety mechanism to replace it.

The provision of public safety generally has been pushed back onto individuals in recent decades and away from collective provision of safety; this is better described as a tendency rather than a full unraveling. Suddenly, our media and government sources dispense a myriad of

---

[14] Pat O'Malley, "Risk, Power, and Crime Prevention," *Economy and Society* 1, vol. 21, no. 3, 252–275; Valverde and Moore 2000; Elizabeth Stanko, "Safety Talk: Conceptualizing Women's Risk Assessment as a 'Technology of the Soul'" *Theoretical Criminology*, vol. 1, no. 4, 479–99; Jim McGuigan, "The Neoliberal Self," *Culture Unbound*, Vol. 6, 2014, 223–240. Eileen Berrington and Helen Jones, "Reality vs. Myth: Constructions of Women's Insecurity," *Feminist Media Studies*, vol. 2, no. 3, 307–323.

advice that basically no one will follow, or can follow, without egregiously restricting their own freedom of movement and enjoyment—from constantly watching your drink to not leaving your windows open when it is nice outside. From an actuarial standpoint, it is accurate to point to increased risk, but the costs of the behavior often prevent people from following it.

No Room for Error

Yet even when people reject or neglect safety advice, they may still, on some level, feel like they should all be prudent calculators of risk and "personally responsible" subjects. If anyone does anything voluntary within the chain of events leading to their violation or exploitation, then they are treated as if they are not a "real" victim. Traditionally, we have worried about this problem in terms of how hard-hearted people and denialists stigmatize victims this way. Certainly, that social strain is still with us, and plenty has already been said about this troubling tendency to unrealistically expect that victims are completely without error in advance of a victimization.

But throughout this book, I have attempted to explore another way in which this same disqualifying task is often inadvertently accomplished by those *caring* people and cultural strains that instead intend to advocate for, support, avenge, speak on behalf of, or simply defend victims. For instance, I discussed the risks and problems inherent in linking sexual assault allegations too closely to involuntary drugging explanations in legal and quasi-legal settings. There is a tendency to vacate interest and inject doubt about the rather serious matter of sexual assault if drug evidence is not really available. In legal cases, as we saw in previous chapters, doubling down on a drugging explanation in the absence of evidence produces the risk that judges, juries, peers, and the media will make "drugs" the theory of the crime rather than the perpetrator and his actions. If then the drug evidence is weak, the entire case is placed in doubt. This seems to be true even when drugging is, in fact, by common-sense standards (as in a number of the serial offender cases) the most likely explanation.

The recent incarnation of the *drugging narrative of ruin* has emerged at the nexus of drunktopian longings and the harsh emergence of what Jim McGuigan calls the neoliberal self:

> Now that the old collective supports and scripts no longer apply, everyone is abandoned to their fate like an angst-ridden French philosopher. Individualisation is a contradictory phenomenon, however, both exhilarating and terrifying. It really does feel like freedom, especially for women liberated from patriarchal control. But, when things go wrong there is no excuse for anyone. That would be *mauvais foi*. The individual is penalised harshly not only for personal failure but also for sheer bad luck in a highly competitive and relentlessly harsh social environment.[15]

Alcohol and drugs have always afforded us permission enough for ambiguity, denial, and deflection for both victims and villains. What may be different now is how we interpret, manage, and accept the vulnerabilities and risks they can produce for individuals and collectivities. There is nothing wrong with managing them smartly, but that is no substitute for doing so humanely, and in a sober-minded way. Accepting vulnerability of all sorts, in ourselves and others, and acting on that basis, might be the best piece of advice.

---

[15] McGuigan, 234.

Suggested Reading

American Temperance Movement, *Permanent Temperance Documents of the American Temperance Society* (Seth Bliss, Boston, 1835). Available at: http://archive.org. Harvard University collection.

P. Andreas, K.M. Greenhill (eds.), *Sex, Drugs, and Body Counts: The Politics of Numbers in Global Crime and Conflict* (Cornell University Press, Ithaca, 2010)

H. Benedict, *The Virgin and the Vamp: How the Press Covers Sex Crimes* (Oxford University Press, New York, 1992)

R. Davenport-Hines, *The Pursuit of Oblivion: A Global History of Narcotics* (Norton, New York, 2001)

S. Estrich, *Real Rape: How the Legal System Victimizes Women Who Say No* (Harvard University Press, Cambridge, 1988)

J. Gusfield, *Symbolic Crusade: Status Politics and the American Temperance Movement* (University of Illinois Press, Urbana, 1986)

P. Jenkins, *Synthetic Panics: The Symbolic Politics of Designer Drugs* (New York University Press, New York, 1999)

R. Kunzel, *Fallen Women, Problem Girls: Unmarried Women and the Professionalization of Social Work, 1890–1945* (Yale University Press, New Haven, 1993)

M. Lee, B. Schlain, *Acid Dreams: The Complete Social History of LSD; the CIA, the Sixties, and Beyond* (Grove/Atlantic, New York, 1985)

B. Lerner, *One for the Road: Drunk Driving Since 1900* (Johns Hopkins Press, Baltimore, 2011)

J. McGuigan, The neoliberal self. Cult. Unbound. **6**, 223–240 (2014)

P. O'Malley, Risk, power, and crime prevention. Econ. Soc. **21**(3), 252–275 (1992)

E.F. Parsons, *Manhood Lost: Fallen Drunkards and Redeeming Women in the Nineteenth Century United States* (Johns Hopkins University Press, Baltimore, 2009)

L. Rotskoff, *Love on the Rocks: Men, Women and Alcohol in Post-World War II America* (University of North Carolina Press, Chapel Hill, 2002)

S. Snelders, C. Kaplan, T. Pieters, On cannabis, chloral hydrate, and career cycles of psychotropic drugs in medicine. Bull. Hist. Med. **80**(1), 95–114 (2006)

C. Spohn, J. Horney, *Rape Law Reform: A Grassroots Revolution and Its Impact* (Springer, New York, 1992)

E. Stanko, Safety talk: conceptualizing women's risk assessment as a 'technology of the soul'. Theor. Criminol. **1**(4), 479–499 (1997)

L. Stratmann, *Chloroform: The Quest for Oblivion* (Sutton, Gloucestershire, 2003)

A. Tone, *The Age of Anxiety: A History of America's Turbulent Affair with Tranquilizers* (Basic Books, New York, 2009)

T. Vander Ven, *Getting Wasted: Why College Students Drink Too Much and Party So Hard* (New York University Press, New York, 2011)

B. Wilson, *Swindled: The Dark History of Food Fraud, from Poisoned Candy to Counterfeit Coffee* (Princeton University Press, Princeton, 2008)

Index

A

Abbey, Antonia, 245n10
Abbott, George and family (Brooklyn), 74–78, 74n42
Absinthe, 61, 63, 67, 67n26, 71
"acid fascism" (Dalton), 112. *See also* Lysergic acid diethylamide (LSD)
Adams, Cecil, 45, 45n52
Adams, Senator Brock, 126–127
Addiction, 2, 4, 6, 18, 24, 27, 47, 92, 97, 108, 115–116, 120
Advisory Council on the Misuse of Drugs (UK), 233
Alcohol
    acute intoxication, 130, 241, 254–256, 276
    adulteration of, 21–22, 22n11, 22n14
    alcoholism, 6, 25, 98, 101, 242n5

"alcohol is the number one date rape drug", 5, 10, 147, 235, 244–245, 258
alcopops, 207, 207n58, 208, 208n60
bathtub gin, 86, 89
binge drinking, 88, 143, 150n56, 201, 207, 241, 242, 242n4, 244, 245, 260, 260n38, 273, 276
blood alcohol content (BAC) level, 11, 130, 151, 204, 208, 213, 214, 217, 218, 255, 256
cocktails, 1920s and, 65, 88, 92
College Alcohol Study (CAS), 241
"drink responsibly", 242–243
forced consumption of, 18, 50
grain/high-proof, 1, 63, 64n19, 67, 130, 244, 260, 260n38
methanol (industry use), 84

© The Editor(s) (if applicable) and The Author(s) 2016 **285**
P. Donovan, *Drink Spiking and Predatory Drugging*,
DOI 10.1057/978-1-137-57517-3

Alcohol (*cont.*)
  plying with, 25, 73, 257, 258, 260, 267
  rapid consumption of, 68, 273
  servings and strength of, 6, 24, 40, 63, 88, 105, 151, 163, 235, 243, 244
  spirits *vs.* fermented, 19, 21
  synergistic effects with drugs, 9, 65
  used to spike drinks, 208
Alpert, Richard, 95, 101–103
Alprazolam (Xanax), 145
Amnesia, anterograde, 4, 125, 145
  See also Blackout, alcohol/drug induced
Amphetamine, 9, 109, 111, 205, 207, 208, 162, 213, 217n3, 219, 255
Anesthesia
  development of modern, 1800s, 2, 9, 35
  early use in obstetrics and midwifery, 30, 30n26, 32
  hallucinations during, 35, 160, 160n78
  See also Chloral hydrate, chloroform, ether, ketamine
Anti-Alcohol movements and Temperance
  anti-saloon movements, 80
  early Temperance, 19, 24
  religious aspects, 19, 31, 32
  scientific and medical Temperance, 21
  See also Social Purity movements, Prohibition
Anxiety and agitation, 2, 90, 90n13, 91, 95, 99n27, 109, 152, 220, 246

Aphrodisia and aphrodisiacs, 2, 152, 219, 263
AquaDots, 132
Asbury, Herbert, 44, 45n50, 45n51
Association of Chief Police Officers (ACPO-UK), 217, 217n4
"Attempted Abduction" tale (Brunvand), 8, 118
Attention deficit hyperactivity disorder (ADHD), drugs for, 245
Auburn University (AU), 271, 272n6, 272n9
Auden, W.H., 90, 90n13
Australian Institute of Criminology (AIC), 200, 201n40, 203

B

"Baby, It's Cold Outside" (song), 89, 89n12
Barbary Coast (San Francisco). *See* Shanghaied
Barkas, Harry, 190–191
Barlay, Stephan, 118, 118n63
Bars, taverns, and saloons. *See* Setting/venue
Bartol, Curt and Anne, 175n2
Bazelon, Emily, 247, 247n14
Beale, Stephen T., 34–36, 35n36, 44
Benadryl. *See* Diphenhydramine
Benedict, Helen, 81, 81n60
Benzodiazepines, 9, 18, 35, 92, 95, 120, 144, 158, 159, 163, 193, 245, 246
Bevacqua, Maria, 137n31
Beynon, Caryl, M., 216–217, 216n2
Binge drinking. *See* Alcohol

Blackout, alcohol/drug induced, 4, 42, 119, 125, 150, 181, 182, 194, 243
"Blue Star Tattoo" legend, 115–116
Bohannon, Danny, 183
Bosschieter, Jennie, 53, 56, 57, 61, 61n12, 64n17, 65n22, 72, 74, 275
Boyd, Patti, 104, 104n37
Bronte, Charlotte, 15–16
Brooks, Oona, 271, 271n5
Brown, Jennifer, 233n30, 234
Brown, Jerry, 169, 169n93
Brownmiller, Susan, 137, 137n30
Brown University, 249, 250, 251n22, 251n24, 252n25, 274
Brunvand, Jan Harold, 8n3, 118, 118n62
Burgess, Adam, 209, 209n64, 222n14
Burking, 16
Burton, Fiona, 218n5
Butterworth, Robert, 146, 146n43

C

Campbell, Andrew, 61
Canadian Addiction Survey, 241n2
Canadian Alliance, 128, 147
Chloral hydrate
    chloralism and chloral addiction, 27, 37, 97
    patent medicines and elixirs, 16, 37, 38
    therapeutic use, 26, 33, 149
Chloroform, 4, 12, 18, 27–38, 50, 59, 65, 166, 220, 270
Clarissa (novel), 16

cocaine, 9, 65, 96, 109, 128, 167, 213, 217, 219, 224n17, 232
Cocculus indicus, 22n14, 40
Cohen, Stanley, 268, 269, 269n2, 271
College antirape activism, 246–249
Columbia University, 63, 248n15, 253
Colyer, Corey, 7, 124, 134, 270, 271
Connell, Noreen, 137n29
Controlled Substances Act, 111, 126, 153, 156, 162
Cosby, Bill, 119, 120n67, 120n68
Criminal Codes and Laws, 9, 10, 31, 34n35, 166n88, 169
Cyanide, 174, 178

D

Dalton, David, 112, 112n55
Date rape drugs, as new category. *See also* Media, influence of, categorization of drugs
Date Rape Drugs Act (US), 145
Date rape, various meanings of, 141n35, 274
Davenport-Hines, Richard, 91, 91n14
DAWN Report (CDC-US), 223, 223n16
Death, William, 61
DeLeon, Daniel, 69, 69n31
Delysid, 98, 101, 105
De Quincey, Thomas, 15
Diphenhydramine, 9, 119, 119n66, 193
"double cruelty" (memory loss and violence), 36
Drug Enforcement Administration (US), 148, 149n54, 156n69, 157–158

Drug-facilitated sexual assault (DFSA), definition of, 163n84, 180n9, 210, 210n65, 211, 211n67, 216, 216n2, 218n5, 219n8, 222n15, 230, 231, 233, 270n3

"drugging narrative of ruin", 23, 26, 281

Drug legislation, scheduling, and regulation, 111, 120, 121, 145, 146, 149, 150, 151n60, 156, 162, 165–166

Drugs
illicit or nonmedical use, 17, 105, 124, 149, 151, 218
leaders' use to manipulate followers, 177
political use, 237, 240, 279
as psycho weapons in government experiments, 3, 12, 26, 100, 100n29

Drug scares and anti-drug movements, 17, 86, 94, 123, 124, 135, 144, 239

"Drunktopia" (Moss), 275–281

DuMont, Janice, 210n66, 224

Dyck, Erica, 98n24, 101, 101n33

E

Ecstacy, 117–121, 128, 150, 152, 153, 159, 184, 202, 202n42, 218, 219n8, 220

Edgewood Arsenal experiments, 99

Edholm, Charlton, 48, 49n57

Ellsberg, Daniel, 109
ElSohly, Mahmoud, 163, 164
Elster, Dr. J.B., 46, 72
Epidemiology, 215, 217n2, 219
Esposito, Richard, 161
Essig, Mark, 55, 55n2
Estrich, Susan, 48n55, 165
Ether, 18, 28, 30, 30n26, 32, 32n31, 33, 34, 35n36, 37, 65, 150, 166n87
Excedrin tampering case, 178, 179

F

Farias, Hillory and family, 154, 162, 251
Fitzgerald, Nora, 132n17, 134, 134n24, 134n25, 135
Flunitrazepam (Rohypnol), 7, 46, 125, 144–162. *See also* Hoffman-LaRoche Pharmaceutical
Fraternities, allegations against, 249–257, 264. *See also* names of individual campuses

G

Gaensaellen, R.E., 163
Gamma hydroxybutyric acid (GHB) and its precursor chemicals, 7, 132, 132n16, 154n64, 156, 157n71, 162, 163, 167, 183–185, 186–190, 208n62, 217, 218–219, 240, 251, 253–254, 262–264, 271–273

Gaslighting, 99, 180–181, 192, 198
Go Ask Alice (Book), 95, 108, 108n47
Gough, John B., 20, 20n8, 24
Grucza, Richard A., 242, 242n4
Gusfield, Joseph, 20, 20n6

H

Hagemann, Steven, 183
Hall, J.A., 217n2
Hangover (movie), 150
Henry, Donald, 107
Heroin, 16, 108, 149, 167. *See also* Opiates, natural
Hess, Amanda, 142, 142n38, 267
Hobart, Dr. Gideon, 75
Hoffman-LaRoche Pharmaceutical, 124, 144, 145, 147, 149, 163, 164
Hofmann, Albert, 97, 98n23, 109, 109n48, 200
Hollingshead, Michael, 104, 104n38
Horvath, Miranda, 233n30, 234
Hughes, Hywel, 213
Hurley, Michael, 217n2
Huxley, Aldous, 94, 94n18
"hypersexual variant" *See* Aphrodisia

I

Immigration, 2, 17, 20, 45, 68, 96
Inciardi, James, 45
Individualization, 91, 243, 271, 275, 281
Industrial capitalism and industrial labor, 17
"*in extremis*" reshaping of social problems, 23, 126, 143, 181, 206, 240, 248, 270
Insomnia, 3, 33, 91, 97, 125, 144, 148, 180, 245
Intentional poisoning, 5, 10, 47, 55, 58, 60, 67, 84, 109, 166, 174, 178–179, 186, 200, 223–224, 223n16
Intoxication, acute alcohol. *See* Alcohol

J

Jenkins, Philip, 131, 131n14, 162
Juhasik, Matthew P., 218n7

K

Karmen, Andrew, 236, 236n34
Katcher, B.S., 89n10
Kerr, George, 61
Ketamine, 7, 125, 126, 144–162, 167, 204, 207, 224
Khachadourian, Raffi, 99, 99n27
Kilpatrick, Dean, 210, 210n65, 223, 227, 228, 230
Knockout drops. *See* Chloral hydrate
Kobler, John, 102
Koss, Mary, 138
Kraft, Jan, 225, 225n19
Krebs, Christopher P., 210n65
Kristof, Nicholas, 259
Kunzel, Regina, 47n54

L

Lady Gaga, 89n12, 246, 246n13
Leary, Timothy, 95, 101–103, 106n42, 109, 112

Ledray, Linda, 225, 225n19
Lee, Martin, 104n37
Lemons, Stephen, 188, 188n19
Lerner, Barron, 242
Levine, Harry, 17n3, 86, 88
Librium, 92
Liddy, G. Gordon, 109, 109n49
Lieberman, E. James, 100
Lindquist, Christine H., 210n65
Liquid X, 121, 153, 186, 202, 202n42
Lisak, David, 259
Loesser, Frank, 89
Luster, Andrew, 168, 186–190, 270
Lysergic acid diethylamide (LSD), 95–107
   folklore and, 109
   and schizophrenia, 113, 114
   See also "acid fascism" (Dalton)

M

Macdonald, Sheila, 210n66
Maiden Tribute to Modern Babylon (W.T. Stead), 23
Mandrax. *See* Methaqualone
Manson, Charles and associates, 110, 113
Marijuana, 9, 96, 98, 109, 121n70, 123, 124, 128, 158, 160n76, 170, 219, 224n17, 232, 255
Marsalis, Jeffrey, 192, 196n34
Master identity of drugs, 10, 13, 46, 46n53, 121 166–167, 271–273. *See also* Media, influence of, categorization of drugs
McAlister, Walter, 61, 61n12, 70

McDowell, David, 121n70, 160
Media, influence of
   categorization of drugs, 127
   follow-up on cases, lack of, 9, 142
   Rolling Stone "Jackie" story, 248n15
   symbolization and typification, 57, 169, 267
   understanding of statistics, 45, 133, 141–143, 162, 204, 227, 227n23, 228–230, 232, 233, 236–237
Medical journals, early skepticism about drug misuse, 30, 32, 43, 47, 101
Medical jurisprudence, 4, 55, 64n17, 64n18, 65
Medical model of psychological problems, 95
Men as targets of drugging, 5, 12, 38–43, 46–47, 208, 212, 268
Meprobamate (Miltown and Equanil), 91, 92, 94
Methaqualone (Quaalude and Mandrax), 119, 120, 120n69
3,4-Methylenedioxymethamphetamine (MDMA). *See* Ecstacy
Mickey Finn, 18, 39, 45, 45n52, 51, 127, 270. *See also* Chloral hydrate
Miltown. *See* Meprobamate
MK-Ultra scandal, 99, 99n25
Molly. *See* Ecstacy
Moore, C.B.T., 217n2
Moore, Dawn, 199, 200n39
Moore, Sarah E.H., 141, 141n35, 180n9, 209, 209n64, 222n14, 264, 270, 270n3

Moral panic (Cohen), 209, 268–274
Morin, Edgar, 8, 8n3, 118
Moss, Gabrielle, 276, 276n12
Motivation for spiking and tampering
　burglary, 4, 33
　coercive, 6, 12, 17, 18, 25, 117, 121, 229, 230n28, 260
　discrediting reputation, 24, 110
　involuntary conscription of labor, 2, 4, 38–43
　malicious/prank, 1, 3, 5, 6, 8, 73, 97, 108, 114, 116, 200, 223n16 (*see also* Intentional poisoning)
　rape/sexual assault (*see* Drug-facilitated sexual assault (DFSA), definition of)
　robbery, 2, 9, 39, 46–47, 72, 124, 133, 170, 201, 214, 226, 232, 268

N

National Center for Women and Policing (US), 164, 164n85, 197
National Drug Research Institute (Australia), 201n41, 241n2
National Union of Students (UK), 211
Neame, Alexandra, 139n33, 204, 204n47
Negrusz, Adam, 149n55, 218n7, 222n15
Neoliberalism, 278
Nickell, Stella, 178–179
Niesink, Raymond J. M., 154n64
Nietszche, Friedrich, 27

Noctec (Bristol Meyers Squibb), 127. *See also* Chloral hydrate
"No on 2" campaign (Florida), 170
Northup, Solomon, 43, 43n45
"numbers laundering" (Best, Luckenbill), 227, 227n23

O

Odyssey (Homer), 15, 15n1, 108
Offenders
　Massachusetts Treatment Center Rapist Typology (MTC-R3), 175
　psychology of, 173, 175
　repeat and serial, 177, 178
Oldenburg, Ray, 51n62
Olszewski, Deborah, 234n31
Operation Matisse, 217n4. *See also* Association of Chief Police Officers (ACPO-UK)
Opiates, natural, 3
Ortiz, Lauren, 130
Osbourne, Ozzy, 10–11, 10n5
Owsley (Augustus Stanley), 105

P

Parsons, Elaine Frantz, 24, 24n17, 284
"peace pills". *See* meprobamate
Peiss, Kathy, 50, 50n60
"Pharma-Ubiquity", 5, 83–121, 180, 239, 269, 273
Plant, Martin and Moira, 241n2
Poisoning
　drug tampering cases of 1980s, 108, 109, 124

Poisoning (*cont.*)
  forensic science and, 4, 123n1, 132n16, 157n71, 179n7, 218n7
  laws against (*see* Criminal Codes)
  legal aspects (*see* Criminal Codes and Laws)
  popular interest in, 20
Porton Down scandal, 101, 101n32
Prevention of Offences Act (UK), 30
Prohibition, United States, 1920-1933
  repeal of, 88, 89
  Volstead Act, 1920, 20, 87
Proposition 47 (California), 165–168, 168n89, 170, 270
"Protected narrative" (Weiss and Colyer), 7, 8, 84, 85, 201, 203, 204, 217, 271
Protection, decline of, 85, 137, 279
Protestantism, influence of on anti-alcohol movements, 83
psilocybin, 100, 101, 160n78

Q

Quaaludes. *See* Methaqualone
Quigley, Paul, 208n62, 217n3

R

Reid, Samantha, 125, 125n3, 126n4, 154, 154n65, 156, 162, 162n83
Reinarman, Craig, 17n3, 86, 87n8
Renard, Jean-Bruno, 116, 116n59
Rennison, Callie Marie, 229n26
Resnick, Patricia, 210, 210n65

"Responsibilism" (O'Malley), 275–281
Richardson, Benjamin Ward, 27, 27n20, 37n40
Richardson, Samuel, 16
Riley, K. Jack, 132n17, 134, 134n24, 134n25, 135
Risk, calculation of, 13, 115, 178, 236, 243, 273, 280
Robbery. *See* Motivation
Rohypnol. *See* Flunitrazepam (Rohypnol)
Rolling Stone (magazine), 112, 220n10, 248, 248n15, 249, 249n16, 249n17
Roofie, as generalized term for CNS drug in a drink, 7, 7n1, 8n2, 15, 124n2, 125, 143–162, 181–182, 220, 222, 247, 255, 262, 269, 273. *See also* Flunitrazepam (Rohypnol)
Rossetti, Dante Gabriel, 27
Ross, Rick, 220, 220n10
Rush, Benjamin, 19

S

Salads, Joey, 198
Salamone, S.J., 163, 164
Sandoz Pharmaceuticals, 97–98, 102, 105
Schlain, Bruce, 104n37, 105n40, 109n49, 110n51, 284
Scofield, Mabel, 54, 56–60, 59n6, 275
Scott-Ham, Michael, 218n5
Sculthorpe, August, 62–63, 66
"Seige cycle" (Snelders et al.), 26

Index

Setting/venue
  bars, pubs, taverns, nightclubs, 5, 12, 45, 120, 190, 200, 216n1, 269
  fraternity houses (*see* Fraternities, allegations against)
  homes and workplaces, 47, 177
  private *vs.* public, 5, 7, 52, 55, 86, 177, 191, 200, 208, 226, 271
Sexual Assault Nurse Examiner (SANE), 224n18, 225, 225n20
Shanghaied, 12, 39, 40, 42
  crimpers, 41, 42, 269
  See also Motivation for spiking and tampering
Siegel, Ronald, 161
Siff, Steven, 106n43
Simpson, James Young, 28, 30, 30n26, 32, 32n31
Sinclair, Upton, 85, 85n4
Sindone, Melanie, 154, 154n66
"smart girl meme", 11, 195, 261–265, 275, 277
Snow, John, 30n25, 31, 33
Social Purity movements, 8, 23–26, 50, 80, 84, 86
Somnophilia, 7, 199, 199n36
Spike the Hedgehog character, 213, 213n73
Spiking methods, lack of barriers to, 186, 200, 201, 240
Spitzer twins, George and Stefan, 147, 181–183
Stables, Gordon, 27, 27n22
Stanko, Elizabeth, 279, 279n14
Stead, W.T. *See Maiden Tribute to Modern Babylon* (W.T. Stead)

Stratmann, Linda, 28n23, 31
Strychnine, 109

T

Techno-utopianism, 12, 18, 90, 93–94, 95, 97, 143
Temperance. *See* Anti-alcohol movements
Tennyson, Alfred Lord, 16
Tetrahydrozoline, 123n1
"third place" (Oldenburg), 51, 51n62
Thomas, Charles, 58–60, 80
Thompson, Hunter S., 112, 112n54
Tiffany, Rose, 73–74, 73n40
Tone, Andrea, 92, 95, 97, 117, 284
Toxicology, clinical and forensic, 4, 8, 9, 55, 64n17, 65, 66, 108, 127, 144, 149, 151, 157n71, 163, 196, 214, 215, 218, 219, 251, 252
Trestrail, John, 200
Trust
  in authorities, 7, 18, 27, 100
  guardian/guild, 102
  interpersonal, 10, 29, 106, 155, 188, 191, 198, 271
  social (basic), 7, 80, 174, 177, 192, 247, 264, 274, 277–278
Tylenol tampering case (Chicago), 174, 174n1, 178n6

U

University of California at Berkeley, 249–250, 254
University of Virginia (UVA), 248–249, 249n17

University of Wisconsin at Milwaukee (UWM), 249, 254–257
"U.O.E.N.O" (song), 220–221
Uys, Joachim D. K., 154n64

V

Valium, 92, 92n15, 93, 104, 145, 182
Valverde, Mariana, 199, 199n39
Vandenburg, Dr. Horace, 63–64, 64n18
Vander Ven, Thomas, 241n2, 243
Vaughan, Dr. Victor, 64
Veronica Mars (television show), 262, 262n40, 263n41
Victims, male. *See* Men as targets of drugging
Victims of rape and sexual assault
    blame of, 10, 54, 81, 197, 200, 211, 258, 260–261, 264, 265, 275–276
    disqualification, informal, 136, 224, 234
    justice and legal aspects, 229, 230
    likelihood and timing of reporting, 228, 240
    "real rape" (Estrich), 165, 260–261
    SANE guidelines, 224n18, 225, 225n20
    statistics and measurement, 227–230
    "whitewash(ing)" (Benedict) or sanitizing cases, 54, 81

Vulnerability
    difficulty accepting, 236, 262, 264–265, 281
    enhanced, 226, 247, 276

W

War on Drugs, 94, 124, 131, 135, 144, 239
Weiss, Karen, 7, 124, 134, 178, 270, 271
Welner, Michael, 177, 177n5
White, Aaron M., 241n1, 242n5
"White slavery" claims and legends, 8, 17, 24, 45, 48, 49, 51, 85, 117–119, 124
Whitney, Sarah, 263, 263n41
Witthaus, Rudolph, 63, 64n17, 72, 73
Wohl, Anthony S., 35n38
Women
    changes in social and personal freedom, 86, 89–90, 278
    drinking norms, 85, 241
    respectable *vs.* responsible, 274, 275
    second-wave feminism, 93, 136, 137n31, 278

X

Xydias, John, 190–191, 190n25, 270
Xyrem, 151, 151n60. *See also* Gamma hydroxybutyric acid (GHB)

Y

Yohimbe, 220

HALIFAX

PO BOX 548

LEEDS

LS1 1WU

1,5062